13442

D1274895

THE PROXIMATE AIM OF EDUCATION

THE
PROXIMATE AIM
OF
EDUCATION

A Study of the Proper and Immediate End of Education

by

KEVIN J. O'BRIEN, C.SS.R., M.A.

THE BRUCE PUBLISHING COMPANY
MILWAUKEE

NIHIL OBSTAT:
A. REGAN, C.SS.R.
Censor Deputatus

IMPRIMI POTEST:
R. O'CONNELL, C.SS.R.
Provincial

IMPRIMATUR:
✠ JAMES P. O'COLLINS
Bishop of Ballarat
January 17, 1957

To

MY FATHER AND MOTHER

ACKNOWLEDGMENTS

THIS study of the aim of education was undertaken in the department of education at the Catholic University of America, Washington, D. C. It is a pleasure and a duty to express sincere thanks to the Very Rev. R. O'Connell, C.SS.R., Provincial of the Australasian province of the Redemptorists, for the invaluable opportunity of studying at the Catholic University, and to the Redemptorists of the Baltimore province for their fraternal hospitality during those years.

To the faculty of the education department at the Catholic University I owe a great debt. A special word of thanks is due on several titles and is warmly offered to the Rev. B. P. Rattigan, Ph.D., my major professor. Without him this book would never have seen publication.

I am indebted also to the charity of many friends — clerical, religious, and lay — for guidance and help, particularly to the Reverend A. Regan, C.SS.R., professor of theology at St. Mary's College, Wendouree; to the Reverend O. Austin, C.SS.R., professor of philosophy at the same college; to the Reverend J. Colleran, C.SS.R., professor of philosophy at Mt. St. Alphonsus, Esopus; to the Reverend Aldo Tos, New York; to Sister Marie Therese of Aquin Teachers' College, Ballarat East; to the editors and staff of The Bruce Publishing Company; to the personnel of St. Mary's College, Wendouree; and also to Mrs. A. Brent and Mrs. J. Daly, both of Virginia, for generous help in the preparation of the manuscript.

I wish to acknowledge the kindness of several publishers and authors for permission to use extracts from their publications: the Most Rev. Fulton J. Sheen; the Rt. Rev. Msgr. John Tracy Ellis; Dr. Theodore Brameld; Mrs. F. S. Breed; Dr. W. C. Bagley, Jr.; The Bruce Publishing Company; the National Catholic Welfare Conference; the National Catholic Educational Association; the Newman Press; the B. Herder Book Company; the Macmillan Company; the Education Department, Victoria; the Confraternity of the Precious Blood; Burns, Oates & Washbourne, Ltd.; St. Xavier College, Chicago; Harper & Bros.; St. Dunstan's University Press; Sheed & Ward; the McGraw-Hill Book Company, Inc.; the editors of *Catholic Action;* the editors of *The Pope Speaks;* the editors of *Thought;* the editors of *The Educational Forum;* the Catholic University of America Press; the American Catholic Philosophy Association.

CONTENTS

THE PROXIMATE AIM OF EDUCATION

CHAPTER I

INTRODUCTION

THE major problem in education is the clarification of goals, writes G. Lester Anderson,[1] and his pungent comments make vivid both the importance of the problem and the prevailing chaos. Though not all might agree in making this the supreme educational issue, no responsible educator minimizes its significance. Hence we have lists and then more lists of goals, both general and particular; but the more the words change, the more one realizes that it is the same unsatisfactory list.

Purpose

The purpose of this book is to examine the proper and immediate end of education. Many writers are puzzled about the ultimate end of education; indeed there is considerable variance about the mere notion of an ultimate end. Catholic educators, at any rate, are in no quandary about the ultimate end of education. But in regard to the more immediate ends there is some vagueness; the condition is malignant and manifests itself in divergent thinking and varying school practices. This book seeks to investigate and clarify the proper and immediate end of education in its wide ramifications, to crystallize various issues in relation to this end, and to organize educational activities according to its exigencies. We do not propose to draw up yet another long list of "desirable outcomes," rewording the conventional things. We seek to isolate, then to study closely, that purpose to which education as a total process should be directed primarily and immediately.

Professional educators and most thinking people realize that education means more than mastering the three R's and getting a job; yet some few may regard the present analysis of education's purpose as "much ado about nothing." It will be abstract, concerned with ideas —

---

[1] Cf. G. Lester Anderson, "Unsolved Problems in Teacher Education," *The American Association of Colleges for Teacher Education, Third Yearbook* (1950), p. 26.

1

and some of them rarefied. But it is eminently practical because ideas have practical consequences. Training a good doctor involves more than teaching him to use a scalpel and the like. His practical skill is of course important. It is more important that he have the right professional ideas, e.g., respect for human life; otherwise his training will make him, not a good doctor, but a skillful murderer. His idea of human life is abstract; but it has very practical consequences. The difference between the medical attention at the Mayo Clinic and at Dachau is not primarily medical skill, but an idea — respect for human life. Who can say that this idea is unpractical! Educators unquestionably need skills; otherwise they will be quacks. But they need more. They need right professional ideas, a vision of the right purpose for their skills; otherwise they will be wreckers, leading youth skillfully but in the wrong direction, the blind leading the blind to destruction. We do not treat classroom techniques here, important as they are. Rather we treat at length the proper and immediate purpose of all educational skills, along with some of its implications. Once that purpose is seen clearly and understood the educational road is safely cleared for the full-powered use of those skills. Moreover, a criterion is established for judging many vexed questions about the curriculum, courses of study, character formation, discipline, guidance, religious formation in the school, and the like; and these matters are very practical.

Already the question has been voiced several times: "Is this treatise to be about 'Catholic' education or about 'ordinary' education?" An early explanation of this point will not be amiss. No dichotomy is to be made between "education" and "Catholic education"; if made, it would be false. In point of fact, man has no purely natural ultimate end.[2] He has been gratuitously raised by his Creator to a supernatural status which elevates without destroying his purely natural condition; and he has been given a supernatural destiny as his ultimate end. He must either attain this end or fail miserably and irreparably, because he can have only *one* ultimate end.[3] Catholic or Christian education is precisely that education which guides man toward his one, ultimate, supernatural end. Pope Pius XI writes:

> In fact, since education consists essentially in preparing man for what he must be and for what he must do here below, in order to attain the sublime end for which he was created, it is clear that there can be no true education which is not wholly directed to man's last end, and that in the present order of Providence, since God has revealed Himself to us in the Person of His Only Begotten Son, who alone is "the way, the truth and the life," there can be no ideally

2 *Infra*, p. 46.
3 *Infra*, p. 41.

perfect education which is not Christian education.⁴ [The Pope is
here speaking in the strict and undiluted sense of the word "Christian."]

Any other scheme of education would be a preparation for something
that does not exist. All other education outside true Christian education
is a deviation, ranging all the way from incomplete to spurious. Hence
there must be no false dichotomy between "Catholic" and "ordinary"
education, and the proper and immediate end that is to be considered
here is the end to which all education worthy of the name should be
ordained.

It is obvious that this study is begun with a definite point of view,
consisting of definite principles (but not of preconceived conclusions).
For this, no apology is made; however, the following explanation is
offered in order that anyone of different beliefs may appreciate the logic
of the position.

To have no principles is to be blank-minded, not broad-minded. Everybody approaches every problem with a particular point of view. Even
the most articulate relativist is absolutely convinced that there can
never be any absolute truths! The Christian, along with others, is convinced that there are absolute truths. The determined atheist is emphatic
that God and the supernatural order do not exist. The Christian is convinced that they do. The difference between the two viewpoints is not one
of dogmatism versus nondogmatism. Each is equally dogmatic; each has
settled principles. The important point is: which has the *right* viewpoint,
the correct principles?

Hence it is of capital importance to scrutinize one's principles, searching and weighing them in accordance with every rational criterion and,
when they are derived from some higher science,⁵ tracing them back to

---

⁴ Pope Pius XI, *Christian Education of Youth* (Washington, D. C.: N.C.W.C.,
1936), pp. 4–5. Encyclical *Divini Illius Magistri*, December 31, 1929. "Etenim,
quoniam omnis educandi ratio ad eam spectat hominis conformationem, quam is in
hac mortali vita adipiscatur oportet, ut destinatum sibi a Creatore finem supremum
contingat, liquido patet, ut nulla veri nominis educatio esse potest, quae ad finem
ultimum non ordinetur tota, ita, presenti hoc rerum ordine Dei providentia consti-
tuto, postquam scilicet se ipse in Unigenito suo revelavit qui unus 'via, veritas et
vita' est, plenam perfectamque educationem dari non posse, nisi eam, quae christiana
vocatur" (*Acta Apostolicae Sedis,* XXII [1930], 51). This reference will henceforth
be abbreviated to *AAS.*
⁵ The basic principles of some particular science or study are not drawn from that
same science or study. They are drawn from higher sciences or other fields of study
as the case may be. Cf. Fulton J. Sheen, *Philosophy of Science* (Milwaukee: The
Bruce Publishing Co., 1934), pp. 56–57: "Empiricism must use rational principles
which are not of purely empirical origin. The principles it derives from a superior
science, for no science proves its own first principles. . . . The principles of interpretation which experimental science uses are borrowed from a higher discipline, for no
science, says St. Thomas, demonstrates its own principles. Mathematics does not
prove that things which are equal to the same thing are equal to each other, nor does
physics prove the legitimacy of induction. If each science had to prove its own first

4   The Proximate Aim of Education

a firm foundation. These principles being valid, then we can legitimately and scientifically accept them as a point of view. In this sense Brameld aptly speaks of a "defensible partiality."[6]

It is beyond our scope to examine here the credentials for the Christian viewpoint. Suffice it to say that these credentials are open for all who wish to inspect them. The Catholic Church makes a positive claim to be the one Church founded historically by Christ as the custodian of revealed truth and rejoices when her position is searchingly examined. The one thing she fears in this regard is ignorance,[7] because ignorance readily leads to misunderstanding and misrepresentation. Alone in a world seeking answers to the riddles of life, the Catholic Church *claims* to have the answer. One would think that serious-minded and responsible people would inform themselves about her position as a point of general education, would surely investigate her challenging claim systematically and impartially with the same fair-minded thoroughness used to examine scientific claims for new vaccines. Still, many, scholars in other respects, avoid investigating her position and claim from authentic sources.[8]

The approach to this subject of the end of education from the viewpoint of the Catholic philosophy of education by no means implies hostility

principles, and the principles upon which these in their turn depended, there would be an infinity of premises which it would be impossible to traverse, and the human mind could never of itself make that voyage over the sea of an unlimited number of propositions." This interdependence is called the subalternation of sciences.

[6] Theodore Brameld, *Patterns of Educational Philosophy* (Yonkers on Hudson, N. Y.: World Book Co., 1950), p. 559.

[7] Of interest in this regard is the case of Hurter, the German scholar. He planned to write a book on Innocent III (1198–1216) because from his current knowledge he considered that the life of this Pontiff was best calculated to exhibit the pretensions and the dishonor of the Papacy. His detailed study of the Pontiff's life in the course of writing the book led him to become a Catholic. Cf. J. J. Walsh, *The Thirteenth, The Greatest of Centuries* (2nd ed., New York: Catholic Summer School Press, 1909), p. 341. This fact gives historical coloring to the statement of Pope Leo XIII: "There is nothing so hurtful to Christian wisdom as that it should not be known" (John J. Wynne, *The Great Encyclical Letters of Pope Leo XIII* [New York: Benziger Brothers, 1903], p. 189).

[8] Apologetics is the name given to the scientific examination and justification of the whole of religious truth. It establishes and expounds the credibility of Revelation and the obligation of believing it. Since it concerns historicophilosophical matter, it does not give mathematical or metaphysical certitude, but it does give certitude of the moral order and indeed at times metaphysical certitude. Prejudice and passion can inhibit the operation of reason and can lead an investigator to reject the evidence of Apologetics. A simplified manual of Apologetics is Anthony F. Alexander, *College Apologetics* (Chicago: Henry Regnery Co., 1954). M. Sheehan, *Apologetics and Catholic Doctrine* (rev. ed., Dublin: M. H. Gill and Son, Ltd., 1924) is a somewhat more detailed manual. H. Felder, *Christ and the Critics*, trans. by J. L. Stoddard (London: Burns, Oates and Washbourne, Ltd., 1924) is a detailed and scholarly investigation of the credibility of the New Testament. J. L. Stoddard, *Rebuilding a Lost Faith* (New York: Kenedy and Sons, 1923) is a rationalist's own description of his inquiry into the credibility of the Catholic religion.

to educators with different beliefs or contempt for them. Catholic thought is not a destructive lava sweeping down the centuries, obliterating all before it, then solidifying into a cold, hard, immovable mass. More fittingly, Catholicism is the Tree planted near the running waters, assimilating whatever may be true nutriment from its environs — however heterogeneous, spreading its branches, casting its friendly shade, and bringing forth its perennial fruit for all who wish to shelter there. Catholicism respects others in their sincere and unshaken beliefs. It also welcomes genuine scholarship from whatever source because it believes firmly that truth can never be contradictory,[9] that all and any truth is intellectual progress. Hence we welcome wholeheartedly whatever solid contributions non-Catholic educators make toward the clarification of this and all school problems.

Method

The method of the investigation will be positive and analytico-synthetic. It will proceed by a close analysis and development of the truths of Revelation, the principles of philosophy, the statements of the popes, the reasonings of educators. Chapter II will be a general consideration of finality, its notion, validity, importance, and of the division of "ends." Chapter III will scrutinize various opinions about the immediate end of education. Chapters IV, V, and VI will be a consideration of the proper and immediate end of education in the light of Revelation and philosophy. Chapter VII will discuss the many implications of this end. Chapter VIII will be a short summary of the study.

While leaving the full investigation of the Catholic viewpoint to Apologetics, it is altogether fitting that we here devote a paragraph to a consideration of the proposed use of supernatural Revelation and of Scholastic philosophy in the discussion of an educational question.

Supernatural Revelation

Etymologically, "revelation" means the removal of a veil. Hence, generally speaking, it means a manifestation by anyone of something hitherto obscure or unknown. Here we speak of divine supernatural Revelation properly so called, which is God's manifestation to us of some truth unknowable by any actual or conceivable created nature left to its own powers. As St. Paul points out,[10] the manner of the Revelation may vary,

---

[9] Cf. the definition of the Fifth Lateran Council, 1512–1517, in Henry Denzinger *et al., Enchiridion Symbolorum Definitionum et Declarationum* (29th ed., Friburgi: Herder & Co., 1953), n. 738. Cf. also J. J. Wynne, *op. cit.,* p. 154.

[10] "God, who, at sundry times and in divers manners, spoke in times past to the fathers by the prophets, last of all, in these days, hath spoken to us by his Son, whom he hath appointed heir of all things, by whom also he made the world" (Hebr. 1:1–2).

but it always requires some *locutio* properly so called, that is, some action by which an intelligent being immediately and directly manifests his mind to another person. Revelation, then, is more than an illuminating actual grace, more than a divine assistance for the avoidance of error, more even than the mere communication of information.[11] The end of Revelation is that man might believe the truths revealed on account of the authority of God speaking.[12]

Many subdivisions of Revelation are commonly made. It is called supernatural *quoad modum tantum* (literally, in the manner only) when the truth contained in the Revelation could otherwise have been attained by unaided reason, for example, the existence of God; and supernatural *quoad modum et quoad substantiam* (literally, regarding the manner and the substance) when the truth revealed is in itself completely above nature and could never have been attained by the cognoscitive powers of nature, for example, the existence of the Blessed Trinity. It is also divided into *private* and *public* Revelation according as it is directed to particular persons for particular benefit, or to the whole human race or an entire people (such as the Israelites) or to a perfect society. Thus the Revelation made through the Prophets, Christ, or the Apostles and proposed to all by the Church is called public Revelation. Private revelations, no matter how important, do not belong to the deposit of Catholic Faith. In this study we shall be relying on public Revelation (*quoad modum et quoad substantiam*) of which the Catholic Church is the custodian.[13]

There is nothing repugnant to the dignity of a thinking man in the proper use of such Revelation from God, after the fact, the reliability, and the preservation of this Revelation have been established.[14] Does not

---

[11] Cf. *Sacrae Theologiae Summa* (4 vols., Madrid: B.A.C., 1952), I, pp. 93, 96–97. (Hereafter this work will be referred to as B.A.C.).

[12] *Ibid.*, p. 94.

[13] In using this Revelation, it is not enough to take the Bible as a mere human book, and see what it says. As well as a grammar, a dictionary, and the use of rational principles of interpretation, the reader needs to apply to the Bible the Christian principles of interpretation used under the light of divine faith, in order to glean its full and accurate meaning. Says Leo XIII: "It must be recognized that the sacred writings are wrapt in a certain religious obscurity, and that no one can enter into their interior without a guide." That guide is the Church historically commissioned by Christ. Leo XIII, *Providentissimus Deus*, November 18, 1893, trans. in *The Pope Speaks*, II (Autumn, 1955), p. 270. This is only a logical corollary of the fact that the Bible, though written in human words, is the official, inspired word of God, given to the safekeeping of God's official Church — in somewhat the same way as the Federal Constitution, every American's democratic birthright and available to all for reading and study, is nevertheless reserved to the Supreme Court for its official interpretation, no matter how competent private jurists may be.

[14] This is done systematically in Apologetics (cf. note 8) by the searching use of reason according to strictly rational principles. Once rational criteria have established the reasonableness of believing in the authority of the Revealer, man goes *beyond* his

a progressive man use all available knowledge whatever its source — provided only it be reliable — in planning and in problem-solving? Do we not have the wish expressed or implied in our popular literature that maybe "somebody" from Mars could somehow communicate to us information about this planet that we in our condition cannot obtain? And if men of science would welcome knowledge from some reliable "inhabitant" of Mars or Jupiter about his native conditions, why should logical-minded man be unwilling to listen to a like communication from Jahweh, God, about the things that intimately pertain to God? All the recipient need do is to make sure that the communication has actually been made, made through a reliable medium, and accurately preserved; that done, he listens and learns and profits. The process is as simple and logical as that — and as common as daily life; for every day sees messages received from businessmen through their responsible secretaries, skilled knowledge received and accepted by apprentices, train information dispensed to milling crowds by appointed representatives — and these travelers leaving the information desk look anything but insulted and psychologically fettered as they make their way with security to the right train and so the right destination! Hence with a double knowledge, natural and supernatural, and therefore with a double security we proceed to our educational destination, in this case the study of the proper and immediate end of education.

Anyone who would deliberately ignore or even scoff at the invocation of objective Revelation for guidance in education should be careful lest he turn back the clock nearly two thousand years and join the wise fools on the Acropolis who smiled indulgently at Paul. "The sensual man perceiveth not these things that are of the Spirit of God; for it is foolishness to him and he cannot understand. . . . For who hath known the mind of the Lord, that he may instruct him? But we have the mind of Christ."[15]

Scholastic Philosophy

The reliance on Scholastic philosophy likewise needs no apology, only another explanation. It needs no apology because it is itself a legitimate science resting wholly on rational grounds. It needs an explanation be-

---

reason, accepts from the Revealer truths above his own natural capacity; but he is never asked to go *against* his reason. He may not understand how there can be sanctifying grace, but his reason tells him that it is reasonable to accept God's word *that* sanctifying grace exists. So from Revelation he now has, by communication, additional and higher knowledge.

[15] 1 Cor. 2:14, 16. The force of these words is clearly seen in the Greek text: "The natural (or the rational) man receiveth not these things that are of the Spirit of God for it is foolishness and he cannot understand." St. Paul is saying that these things of God are above even the most acute rational examination — seem foolish to it, in fact.

cause misunderstanding and, at times, downright prejudice have clouded or smeared its true features. "Philosophy" is a misused word. Often it is applied to those pet views that an evening cigarette somehow siphons out of man as he relaxes in an armchair — a concoction of milieu prejudice, a few proverbs, hometown experience with illustrative anecdote, socio-economic opinion, half-baked truths, and all with a dash of common sense. This attitude toward life may loosely be called a philosophy of life, but it is not simply and strictly *philosophy*. Philosophy is the science of reality through its ultimate causes, as known by the light of natural reason.

Scholastic philosophy is the name given to a scientific body of truths elaborated by various thinkers from the time of the pagan Greeks. Its development took place slowly from a surfeit of opinion, argumentation, and extended controversy. It is a crystallization from the mixture of the centuries. Into that mixture went, it would seem from the history of philosophy, every conceivable opinion. Out of it, however, was precipitated the crystal, symmetrical and shining clear, that is called Scholastic philosophy. Every truth accepted therein is accepted because of the reasons which prove it, as anyone who takes the trouble to open and read an authentic text can find out for himself. There is no complete agreement on all opinions because philosophers have differed and still differ about the reasons for some of these opinions. It is called Scholastic simply because the university professors of the twelfth, thirteenth, and fourteenth centuries are called Scholastics and they, while disagreeing sharply about particular opinions, considered that it was the soundest system of thought elaborated by the minds of men. Catholic philosophers still accept it for the same reasons — on its own merits; and its rational merits are discernible by all who will take the trouble to investigate it honestly in its authentic sources.

It is not a by-product of religion; yet — to adapt terminology beloved of modern scientific investigation — its proven truths show integration and the very highest correlation with the truths of the Bible, i.e., of objective religion. But why should this welcome "correlation" of independent truths suddenly become a stigma and the basis of an attack whereby this rational philosophy is falsely dubbed "sectarian" philosophy? Undeniably, Scholastic philosophy has been assisted extrinsically by Revelation; but why should the co-ordinated use of the established truths of various fields be intellectually shameful? The pathologist is greatly assisted by X ray. The revelations of the X ray facilitate and guide extrinsically his work; yet they leave him free to proceed untrammeled according to the principles and procedures of his own science. Religion, while it can help and guide philosophy in an external way, leaves it free to proceed untrammeled according to its own principles and methods; and philosophy itself, autonomous yet as it were double-checked and correlated with religion, becomes in turn a guiding beam for other sciences and studies — if only they wish to take advantage of it. If one tenth of the research effort that has produced a plethora of dissertations examining and measuring the *sequelae* of educational theories had been devoted to the investigation of this centuries-proven philosophy and to the application of its rational principles to educational theory, education would not now be swirling amid crosscurrents.

An interesting confirmation of the rational autonomy of Scholastic philosophy came in recent years in unusual circumstances. Queen's University of Belfast is a secular university established by a British Parliamentary Bill of 1908. The statutes permitted theology to be taught, but only by a privately paid lecturer who could not be a member of any board of studies or general faculty board. Later on it was proposed to establish a chair of Scholastic philosophy with a lecturer to be paid from university funds. There was much opposition, popular and professional — despite the favor of some members of the Protestant clergy — on the allegation that it was a use of university funds for the maintenance of theological and religious teaching, and thus was a violation of the non-sectarian statutes of the university. The climax was finally reached when three plaintiffs lodged a joint appeal that went to the Irish Privy Council. The appeal was dismissed by this supreme court on the grounds that Scholastic philosophy was a purely rational system of thought, non-sectarian.[16]

Tributes to Scholastic philosophy from unaccustomed sources are therefore not surprising, even though they may be unusual. For example Dean Inge writes:

> For I am convinced that the classical tradition of Christian philosophy, which Roman Catholic scholars call . . . the perennial philosophy . . . is not merely the only possible Christian philosophy, but is the only system which will be found ultimately satisfying.[17]

A sincere Christian, then, approaches education holding in hand these two bright lights — objective Revelation and Scholastic philosophy. Each is distinct, each sheds its special radiance; but the two, focused on educational problems, place them in perspective and illuminate their darkest recesses. Hence, with this double knowledge from Revelation and philosophy, we hope to clarify, at least partially, the proper and immediate end of education.

Chris DeYoung quotes without reference the remarks of a professor which are sadly verified in educational literature: "No book that attempts to deal with any vital issue or problem in a vital way can be

---

16 Cf. David Kennedy, *Towards a University* (Belfast: The Catholic Dean of Residences, 1946), pp. 63–68.

17 Dean Inge, *God and the Astronomers*, quoted in Fulton J. Sheen, *op. cit.*, xxiii.

published at the present time without balanced sentences in which one pressure group is played off against another, or without the usual dodges of a so-called judicious character."[18] It is sincerely hoped that this book will not merit such a dreadful academic slur. This is not a Trojan-horse presentation of Christian education behind a neo-essentialist or a neo-humanist appearance. It does not modify undeniable supernatural principles just to beguile others.[19] It unashamedly seeks to clarify an admitted educational problem with the twin lights of objective Revelation and rational philosophy. Surely the undisguised statement of a viewpoint is not a disqualification in the mind of an honest reader who seeks an answer to a problem. No scholar should be unwilling to investigate impartially a viewpoint offered seriously, especially one that has produced a dynamic institution as vast as the Catholic educational system in this country.

Review of Literature

Much has been written on finality in general, and on particular ends in education.

Collins[20] investigated at length the metaphysical bases of finality in general, indicating the validity of finality and its significance in all human activity. Without finality there can be no efficient causality, no activity of any sort.

Tos[21] investigated the principle of finality and its implications for education. In education there are several secondary agents operating toward the ultimate end under God, the first cause.

Solari[22] made an analysis of the aims of seventy-seven Catholic colleges for men according to their actual formulation in the respective catalogues. He found that there was much variety in expressing the proximate aims of such colleges.

Many studies of the objectives of particular curriculum subjects have been made, for example by Sheehan[23] investigating the cultural objec-

---

[18] Chris A. DeYoung, *Introduction to American Public Education* (New York: McGraw-Hill Book Co., 1950), p. 498.

[19] *Infra*, p. 76.

[20] Russell J. Collins, "The Metaphysical Basis of Finality in St. Thomas" (unpublished Ph.D. dissertation, School of Philosophy, The Catholic University of America, 1947).

[21] Aldo J. Tos, "Finality and Its Implications for Education" (unpublished M.A. dissertation, Department of Education, The Catholic University of America, 1955).

[22] Frank J. Solari, "An Analysis of the Aims of Catholic Colleges for Men as Expressed in Their Catalogues" (unpublished M.A. dissertation, Department of Education, The Catholic University of America, 1953).

[23] Sister M. F. Sheehan, "Cultural Content of the High School French Curriculum" (unpublished M.A. dissertation, Department of Education, The Catholic University of America, 1937).

tives of French; but such studies have a different scope from one inquiry.

No analysis has yet been made of the proper and immediate end of education as such. Hence is proposed this present study which is, however, limited to an investigation of this end and to some of its principal implications.

CHAPTER II

FINALITY

SINCE this book deals with the end of education, it is fitting that we at once consider closely, even if briefly, the matter of "ends," or, as it is called, finality. This chapter is not an original investigation of finality; that is the work of philosophy. Here we merely draw on philosophy and synthesize its relevant truths. Not all the truths introduced into this chapter will immediately pertain to the central theme of the book; but all will be necessary to have a general appreciation of finality in life and education, which is certainly relevant to this study. Finality lays a rock foundation as a safe highway for education; without it, life and education would be a frustrating treadmill — shifting, changing, but going nowhere. Hence the practical consequences of these abstract truths.

This consideration will require close thought. No one expects an exposition in physics or biology to be casual reading. Finality is equally technical, yet is loftier truth because it is metaphysical. A little attention and reflection as we proceed will introduce the reader into intellectual riches hitherto undreamed perhaps — riches of perspective, wide ramification, and placid security. These are reward enough for mental effort.

In this chapter we can hardly avoid some terminology that is technical and that may seem forbidding, even in a professional book. In the long run, proper terminology is simpler and clearer than roundabout description. It is simpler for the child to learn what and where the teeth are than to be deluged several times daily with "go and clean those white, hard things inside your mouth for chewing, using the little brush you keep for them"! It is clearer for the elocution student to learn what and where the diaphragm is than to be made giddy with gesticulation and circumlocution every time a reference must be made to it. Further, the few technical terms we use designate ideas that every observant and thoughtful reader already has, since philosophy is only the analysis of reality. And these terms not only designate; they sculpture ideas with an artistic precision worthy of Truth's immortal gallery.

There may, however, be some serious students of education who are not accustomed to the vocabulary of philosophy, yet are rightly interested in the proximate aim of education. The summary at the end of this chapter will preserve the continuity of their reading and will give them a spring-board to the rest of the book where many points in this chapter will be illuminated.

The General Notion of End

"Finality" is obviously a derivative of the Latin word *finis*, which means a "boundary," a "limit," a "termination," an "end."[1] End in philosophy has a threefold meaning. It can signify mere termination, or an object, or the purpose for the sake of which something is done. We shall examine each of these and be gratified to see that these notions are familiar from both classical and everyday usage.

End can mean mere termination. This is an obvious meaning. The classical phrases *finem orandi facere*, "to make an end of entreating," and *alicui vitae finem afferre*, "to put an end to someone's life," illustrate this sense of the word.

Webster's New Collegiate Dictionary gives as the third meaning, "The extremity or conclusion of any event or series of events."[2]

In these usages, classical and modern, we have one general notion of the meaning of "end" in Scholastic philosophy. According to one Scholastic usage, *finis* means "limit," "conclusion," synonym of *extremitas, extremum, terminus,* and *ultimum,*[3] with the connotation of terminating something, of being the terminus of some action. In this sense St. Thomas Aquinas says: "Beyond the end there is nothing because the end is the last in anything [activity, series, etc.] and limits it; hence there is nothing beyond the end."[4] Every schoolboy understands the sort of termination we mean when we speak of the end of a lesson.

As well as being a mere terminus signifying the cessation of the activity, end can be considered as the object of the activity, that toward which the activity is orientated. In this sense it specifies the activity as this particular kind of activity and not that kind, so that the activity is de-fined accurately in relation to this object. Two trains in a station may look alike and be on adjoining platforms; we differentiate them care-fully by their destination. This notion of an "object" will be discussed presently.

---

[1] "End," *English-Latin Dictionary* by W. Smith and T. Hall (New York: American Book Co., 1871).

[2] "End," *Webster's New Collegiate Dictionary,* 2nd ed., 1953.

[3] "Finis," *A Lexicon of St. Thomas,* by Roy J. Deferrari, Sister M. Inviolata Barry, and Ignatius McGuiness, Fascicle II (Washington, D. C.: The Catholic University of America Press, 1949).

[4] *Expositio in 12 Libros Metaphysicorum Aristotelis,* Liber X, lectio 5, "Extra finem nihil est, quia finis est id, quod est ultimum in omni re et quod continet rem, unde nihil est, extra finem."

Besides termination and object, *end* carries the third connotation of purpose or aim. Cicero's definition *illud cuius causa aliquis facere aliquid debet* (that for the sake of which someone does something[5]) illustrates this sense. *Webster's Collegiate Dictionary* gives as the fifth meaning for "end" "the object aimed at in any effort; purpose."[6] Scholastics examining this notion of end as an aim, as the purpose of some activity, as that toward which some appetite tends, found with Aristotle that it is truly causal. A man desires to learn; so he goes to school and college; his end in view, learning, leads him to undertake the activity necessary to attain it and so, in a particular sense, causes that activity. A business-man desires to manufacture a particular line of goods; hence he builds a factory to do so. His end in view leads him to undertake the costly activity of building and equipping a factory and so truly causes this activity in a particular sense. If the magnitude of the effect, an equipped factory, means anything, the strength of the causality is considerable. In smaller matters, even in trivia, the same influence operates. An enter-prising man wants to make a set of shelves for his home. He selects the wood, cuts and planes it to size, joins it, *exactly according to his purpose* — as far as his skill allows him; again the causality is apparent. The completed set of shelves not only marks the cessation of his building activity; it is not merely some sort of resultant; it also is that *for the sake of which* he underwent the activity of selecting, sawing, joining, etc. That is why philosophers define the end considered as a cause, *id cuius gratia cetera fiunt* — "that for the sake of which other things are done."[7] Many times we will refer to this notion of end-cause because it is signifi-cant for education.

---

[5] Cicero, *De Inventione*, l. c. quoted in Smith and Hall, *op. cit.*, "End" (subs.), IV, 2.

[6] *Op. cit.*, "End."

[7] We say that the end in view causes the activity in a particular sense, because this final causality is not the only kind of cause operating in this case. In the example given, the wood, etc., which the carpenter uses is the material cause. The principle determining this wood as a set of shelves and not as a pipe or the hundred other things it could have become is the formal cause. In this particular case the form of a set of shelves is an accidental form, that is, an act determining second matter. The man doing the carpentering is the efficient cause, the tools he uses being instrumental causes. Thus "there are four main kinds of causes: *material, formal, efficient,* and *final*. They explain the 'how and why' of a being. The material cause is that 'out of which' something is made. The formal cause is that 'through which' something is made: [it is the act intrinsically determining and specifying the matter]. The efficient cause is that 'by which' something is made. The final cause is that 'on account of which' something is made" (Celestine N. Bittle, *The Domain of Being* [Milwaukee: The Bruce Publishing Co., 1939], pp. 333–334). The elaboration of these varied causes can be found in any standard manual of Scholastic philosophy. The English reader who wishes to study these causes in detail would do well to read Bittle, just cited; then H. Renard, *The Philosophy of Being* (Milwaukee: The Bruce Publishing Co., 1943), pp. 113–162.

Hence, end can mean mere termination, an object, and an end-cause for the sake of which something is done.

A distinction must be carefully drawn between an object and an end-cause. Speaking materially we say that the object and the end can coincide, that is to say, the one and the same good can be an object and also an end — but not in the same respect; because an object and an end are formally and functionally different.

An object understood generally is that to which any operation, any power of acting (namely a faculty), any perfecting disposition of such power (namely, a habit), is ordained. Scholastics further distinguish:

1. *Material object* — whatever is in any way attained by the power or operation. Man is the material object of physiology and also of anatomy.
2. *Formal object* — the precise aspect under which the material object is regarded or attained. Physiology is concerned with the functioning of living organs; anatomy studies the structural make-up of these organs.

We may go on to distinguish:

1. *The proper or proportionate formal object.* It is that which is directly and essentially attained. Color is the proper formal object of sight, as sound is of hearing. The essence of the material thing is the proper formal object of man's intellect in his present state of union of soul and body. The formal object of man's will is the good.
2. *The common formal object.* This is attained by more than one power but in each case through the proper formal object of the power. For example, shape and extension are common formal objects, attained by sight through color and by touch through resistance or pressure. The essences of immaterial things are known by the human intellect and also by the angelic and divine intellects.

The proper formal object specifies the activity or faculty ordained to it. It constitutes the activity or faculty in a definite species, showing it to be a power of a particular kind. So we distinguish the faculty of sight from the faculty of hearing because color is the object of one and sound of the other. This specification is the distinctive function of an object. An object is, therefore, an extrinsic principle pertaining to extrinsic formal causality (not final causality) because on it depends just what the power is and what its operation.[8] A key is described in relation to the lock it fits, and there must be a strict proportion between the key and the lock. The type of key needed can be known from the type of lock it has to

[8] Cf. F. X. Maquart, *Elementa Philosophiae* (3 vols., Paris: Andreas Blot, 1938), III, 2, p. 238.

fit. Even a child knows that the key for a warded lock will differ from the key for a cylinder lock, that the key for the front door is not the right "key" for the combination lock on Dad's safe. This is not a perfect example of a faculty being specified by its object, but it is an illustration from daily life of the way we gauge and type one thing in relation to another.

Now the same thing which is an object can also be considered as that which the rational appetitive power *intends* or which causes the *exercise* of some power of acting. This thing not merely designates the operation as this kind of operation (the function of an object), but, because it is sought as an end, it also determines the appetitive power to be actually exercised here and now. From this latter standpoint it is the "end" — purpose, final cause.

> The proper function of good as an end is not to specify or to con-
> stitute a thing in a definite species or category. . . . The notion of end
> expresses whatever pertains to the execution of some activity since
> nothing happens in the order of execution unless through the influence
> of an end.[9]

Briefly then an object pertains to the specification of a power; the end pertains to the exercise of a particular type of power, namely, an appetite. It is with this notion of end as a cause that we are principally concerned in this chapter. We come now to consider closely this final causality.

The Validity of Final Causality

PRELIMINARY CONSIDERATIONS

This matter of causality is, of course, a metaphysical one. Precisely because it is metaphysical it has bedrock importance for education. Many acts in the educational process pertain to what is ordinarily called cause and effect. Since we are here concerned with one type of causality it behooves us to consider briefly the accurate notion and the validity of causality in general before we proceed to the consideration of final causality.

The Notion of Causality. Broadly speaking, a cause is something which in any way contributes to the production of another thing. We tend to use the word loosely in common speech. But here we need a refined definition, and philosophy gives it to us. A cause is a positive principle from which something really proceeds by a positive and intrinsic influx and on which that thing is dependent in its being. We will now consider each important word of this definition.

---

[9] E. Hugon, *Cursus Philosophiae Thomisticae* (3 vols., Paris: P. Lethielleux, 1936), III, p. 702.

A cause is a "principle," and a principle is defined as that from which something proceeds in any manner whatever.[10] "Principle" implies two things: the principle must be prior to that which proceeds from it; and this priority should be rooted in the things themselves because of some special connection between them.[11] In itself, however, to say that one thing is a principle of another is merely to imply an order of origin; it does not necessarily imply that the one exercises a positive influence on the other.

The definition says "really" proceeds, because there are two kinds of principles — principles in the order of knowledge, such as premises whence something proceeds logically, namely, a conclusion; and principles in the ontological order from which something, some "being," really proceeds. Only this second type of principle is a cause. A logical principle, such as a premise, certainly influences our thinking, but it does not *produce* our thinking so that the act of thinking in its entity really proceeds from it. Hence we insert the word "really" to signify that causes are principles in the ontological order.

The definition says a "positive" principle, because not every ontological principle is a cause. Some principles are negative, a merely negative *terminus a quo*. For example, a human being is generated and so now begins to exist. Before, he did not actually exist. Following this negative state of privation, comes existence; in no sense can this negation or privation of existence be called a cause of the new existence. Only a positive principle can be a cause.

We say "proceeds by a positive and intrinsic influx" because not every positive ontological principle is a cause. It becomes so only when it has some influx into the being of the other thing. A point is the beginning of a line and from this point the line flows. But the point is not the cause of the line. It does not have any influx into the being of the line; it merely marks the inception or a stage in the succession. Whereas a cause is a positive ontological principle whence something really proceeds by an influx into the being of this thing.

"On which it is dependent in being." In regard to created things, the influx from a positive principle into the being of something necessarily implies on the part of this thing a dependence in being or *esse;* for no creature, since it is not its own *esse*, can be its own essential *agere*. Man is not essentially a watchmaker. Hence necessarily there is a real distinction between the agent, principle, and the term of the agent's activity, called the *principiatum*. There is a real distinction between the watchmaker and the watch. So, considering created beings only, there would be no need to introduce into the definition of a cause the phrase "on which it is dependent in being." This dependence would be evident; the

---

10 St. Thomas Aquinas, *Summa Theologica*, I, q. 33, a. 1.
11 Cf. Bittle, *op. cit.*, p. 322.

watch necessarily implies the watchmaker. But because the foundation of this dependence is not the influx into the being of the effect considered in itself, but rather the real distinction between this effect and its cause there is need for the addition of this phrase "with dependence in *esse*" in any definition of causes considered generally.[12]

Of all the things that can be said about the notion of a cause, what is the rock-bottom, never-to-be-omitted idea which makes something a cause of another thing? The precise notion of a cause — as the Scholastics would say, the *formal ratio* of a cause — consists in that perfection of a thing whereby it has something depending on it in regard to being.[13]

Now it is clear how a cause differs from a *principle*. A cause implies a positive influence in those things proceeding from it, whereas a principle implies no such influx. A cause further implies their dependence on it, whereas a principle implies no such dependence. Third, a cause implies some priority in regard to its effect, if not in time, certainly in nature; whereas a principle implies no priority of nature, only an order.[14] Clearly, then, every cause is a principle but not every principle is a cause.

Causality obviously differs from mere *succession;* succession implies no positive influx. One train following behind the other is not being caused to move by the other.

A cause differs also from a *condition,* even from that type of condition which is called a condition *sine qua non.* An ordinary condition is something which facilitates the operation of a cause; a condition *sine qua non* is one which removes those obstacles or limitations without whose removal the cause cannot produce its effect. Thus it has a necessary relationship to the production of the effect but it does not have any positive

---

[12] Cf. F. X. Maquart, *op. cit.,* III, 2, p. 201.

[13] In God, the Father is the principle of the Son's generation by an influx of Being, but there is no dependence of the Son on the Father. God the Father is not the cause of the Son nor is the Son an effect of the Father.

[14] Priority may be of two kinds, logical and real. Logical priority is attributed to a thing which, though *not* preceding the other in time or in nature, has nevertheless within itself the grounds for our *conception* of the precedence of one over the other. Thus in our human way of thinking we conceive of God's "essence" as being prior to His "attributes," e.g., His omnipotence, and as the "principle" of His attributes; whereas there is no succession or division in God.

Real priority is a priority existing in reality and can be threefold: (1) a priority of time, when one thing exists before another, e.g., a father exists before his son; (2) a priority of nature, when the natural entity of the first is presupposed for the other, even though the two may exist simultaneously; for example, a substance is prior in nature to its accidents, but the two exist simultaneously; (3) a priority of origin, when one thing precedes the other and there is a procession from one to the other without however any strict and real dependence on the other. Cf. Bittle, *op. cit.,* pp. 322–323. Thus in the Blessed Trinity the Father is prior in origin to the Son, and the Father and Son are prior in origin to the Holy Ghost. But in neither case is there a priority of nature, since Each has the same divine nature, nor a priority of time, since Each is eternal.

influx into the *being* of the effect. Clear visibility is a normal condition for safe flying and landing, but it is not the cause of the airplane's landing on the airstrip. Throwing a switch in some form or other is a condition for "turning on the light," i.e., for making the filament in the bulb glow; but the electricity is the cause of the easily observed effect.

A cause differs from an *occasion*, which is merely that in the presence of which something usually is done. An occasion is a circumstance or a set of circumstances which gives an opportunity for a cause to produce its effect. So the presence of an audience is an occasion for a pianoforte solo, but obviously is neither the cause nor the condition *sine qua non* of the recital. Schnabel is the cause of the piano-playing; and he could play without the audience.

Since a condition *sine qua non* and an occasion do not have any positive influx into the being of the effect nor imply dependence in being they cannot be called causes *per se;* but since they have some association with the production of the effect they can be called causes *per accidens*. But of themselves they can never sufficiently explain the production of the effect; this always demands the operation of a cause *per se*. Wheel out the piano, assemble an audience — even the biggest; there will be no recital till Schnabel engages the keys with his limpid touch.

So much for the notion of causality. The four main kinds of causes are the material, the formal, the efficient, and the final as noted earlier.[15]

MODERN NOTIONS OF CAUSALITY

A number of modern philosophers weaken or even flatly reject the validity of causes. The existence of true causes cannot be established unless one perceives that the intellect of man can attain a knowledge of the essences of things, because the certitude about the existence of true causes comes from the knowledge of the nature of finite beings and from the knowledge of the actions of creatures through which we know their natures. Hence all those philosophers whose empiricism, positivism, or subjectivism, etc., leads them to discard or vitiate our knowledge of essences will accordingly discard or vitiate the notion of true causality. Many modern writers, even in writing seriously, use the word "cause" to signify little more than a sequence or coexistence of events. This notion was popularized by the English writers, Locke, Hume, and Stuart Mill.

Locke says in effect that we can never understand causality because what our senses observe is only a succession of phenomena. In this latter remark he is profoundly right because our senses of themselves perceive only material objects. But we have other powers besides our senses by means of which we can understand an abstract notion such as causality. Locke showed himself a model of inconsistency in this view because he

---

[15] Cf. Chapter II, n. 7.

believed in the human intellect yet denied the intellect's perception of causality.

Hume, as full-fledged empiricist, reduced all our knowledge to the level of phenomena and, correspondingly, he reduced causality to a mere succession of phenomena in the same order. Hume explains his notion as follows:[16]

> We remember to have had frequent instances of the existence of one species of objects, and we also remember that the individuals of another species of objects have always attended them, and have existed in a regular order of contiguity and succession with regard to them. Thus we remember to have seen that species of object we call *flame*, and to have felt that species of sensation we call *heat*. We likewise call to mind their constant conjunction in all past instances. Without any further ceremony, we call the one *cause* and the other *effect*, and infer the existence of the one from that of the other.

It will be noticed that he traces our notion of causality to our experience of phenomena. But we have all seen the day follow the night "in a regular order of contiguity and succession . . . and we call to mind their constant conjunction in all past instances" but we do not forthwith conclude that the night causes the day! Hume did not believe, however, that regular succession between phenomena in the past (his notion of causality) gave any necessity or certitude to their continued succession for the future. Every time he cut his finger with a knife, he must have been doubly surprised!

Kant admitted the existence of an intellect in man, yet he vitiated the validity of ontological causality by reducing causality to one of his subjective categories of the mind, called *synthetic a priori* — *synthetic*, because the analysis showed that the predicate lay outside the concept of the subject, and *a priori* because its truth was not derived from objective experience nor could be denied by the mind.

The Validity of Objective Causality. Hugon presents the argument thus:[17]

> The concept of cause has objective reality if in truth something outside the mind has an influx of being into another thing and if any thing receives being from another. But it is absolutely certain that existing outside the mind there are things that communicate being to other things and things that receive being from others. Therefore [the concept of cause has objective validity]. The minor is clear. . . . We are absolutely certain, from our internal and external experience, that

[16] David Hume, *A Treatise of Human Nature*, edited by T. H. Green and T. H. Grose, Vol. I, p. 388, quoted by T. V. Moore, *Cognitive Psychology* (Chicago: J. B. Lippincott Co., 1939), p. 368.

[17] Trans. from E. Hugon, *op. cit.*, III, pp. 629–630.

many things begin which were not previously existing, such as animals, men, buildings. But what begins to have existence cannot have it from nothing, because nothing does not determine anything. It cannot have existence from itself, otherwise it would exist and not exist at the same time. Therefore it receives its being from another. [In created things this influx of being necessarily implies a corresponding dependence in being.]

Since outside the mind some beings give and others receive with a dependence in being, it is then clear that at least some true causes exist in reality. But philosophy goes further and enunciates the principle of causality expressing a necessary nexus between a thing and its cause as a universal principle, analytically certain. It is variously formulated and may be expressed thus: "It is necessary that what does not have existence of itself be produced by another."[18] This principle of causality pertains to efficient rather than to final causality and its complete investigation is beyond the scope of our study. It is a metaphysical consideration[19] and to metaphysics we therefore relinquish its investigation. However, from metaphysics, we in education legitimately accept its validity, just as a surveyor legitimately accepts from higher mathematics the formulae that are the basis of his calculations and applications. The findings of experimental psychology as reported by Moore[20] make interesting corroboration for this notion of causality. "We thus see that children between two and three years of age may use the principle of causality objectively and correctly in problems within the realm of their experience."[21]

We have seen the true notion and the validity of causality — important concepts in all human endeavor. Every man hopes that his laborious efforts will produce proportionate results; every teacher in his striving hopes for proportionate educational effects. Whereas the flaccid theories of Locke, Hume, and Kant would eviscerate this striving, Scholastic philosophy stimulates it with the knowledge that his daily efforts are not mere phases in an unpredictable succession, but can be truly causal and therefore truly worthwhile. Man knows that he is not a cork in the sea, that his activity is not ineffectual, inconsequential. He can produce the effects he desires by placing proportionate causes. This is the fundamental optimism of the Scholastic doctrine of causality.

---

[18] Maquart, *op. cit.*, III, 1, p. 238.

[19] A discussion of the validity of this principle of causality is found in R. P. Phillips, *Modern Thomistic Philosophy* (2 vols., Westminster, Md.: Newman Bookshop, 1935), II, pp. 234–239; and in H. Renard, *op. cit.*, pp. 115–124. These authors insist that the validity of causality as a universal principle and as analytically certain rests primarily on metaphysical principles. Only after the metaphysical foundation has been laid can one legitimately invoke experience, whether internal or external. Phillips, *loc. cit.*, p. 235, and Renard, *loc. cit.*, pp. 121–122.

[20] T. V. Moore, *op. cit.*, p. 370.

[21] *Ibid.*, p. 370.

Now we analyze a particular type of causality which is of the greatest importance in education and indeed in all human activity — final causality.

Analysis of Final Causality

The End is truly a cause. Efficient causality really exists. But efficient causality demands the exercise of final causality. Therefore final causality really exists. We will explain this syllogism.

That efficient causality is really exercised is established in philosophy. We accept this conclusion from metaphysics without more ado than merely indicating its metaphysical basis. Efficient causality is needed to explain the change that takes place in beings; for change is a transition from potency to act and since nothing can reduce itself from potency to act — giving itself a new form — an efficient cause is required. Efficient causality is also needed to explain composition, for "diverse things do not come together in unity except through the activity of a unifying agent."[22] Efficient causality is also needed to explain participation of a perfection through composition. Each of the diverse beings cannot have this perfection essentially since beings are distinguished by reason of their essences. This perfection then belongs to one being essentially, and is found participated in other beings accidentally by the efficient causality of the being which has it essentially.[23]

But the efficient cause cannot exercise its causality without the final cause which moves it here and now to act. A potential agent cannot determine itself to a definite act without violating the principle of sufficient reason. A potential agent needs to be determined to a definite act here and now, and this is done through the causality of the end which determines the agent to act in this way to attain the end and not in another way.[24] Hence the final cause is the explanation of the action here and now of the efficient cause; without the final cause there could be no efficient causality. It will be noticed that the end is the cause of the *efficient activity,* not of the determined nature of the agent. An injured man's need on the street does not make any and every pedestrian a doctor, but it does make a pedestrian doctor act here and now as a doctor.

The notion of causality explained above fits perfectly the notion of an end. A true cause is a positive principle of anything from which something really proceeds by way of a positive and intrinsic influx and on which it is dependent in being. But an end is just that; and so it is a true cause. For an end is a *principle;* it is first in intention. A man wishing to go to New York from Washington, D. C., thinks first of New

---

[22] *Summa,* I, q. 11, a. 3.
[23] Cf. Russell J. Collins, *op. cit.,* pp. 54–58, 76.
[24] *Ibid.,* pp. 76–80.

York and then he attends to the devious steps for reaching it. The end is moreover a *positive* principle; it exercises in its own special way (as we shall see) a positive influx by means of which something follows which is dependent on it in being. From the end proceeds the activity of the agent and the effect produced by him, since the end in its special way moves him to his activity. The desire to reach New York moves him to go down to the station, to part with a considerable amount of money, to stay on the train for hours, even though others leave it at Baltimore, Philadelphia, etc. Certainly none of this activity would take place if he had no intention of going to New York. A different end sought would bring about entirely different activity. For example the intention of pruning his roses would put him in the garden, not in the train to New York!

Since the end is truly a cause it will be well to note explicitly its effects as these will depend closely on it.

> The effects of the end are all those things which pertain to the order of execution, both the means willed and the acts of the will regarding these means and the external actions . . . likewise the act of intention towards the end by which the will tends to the end as something to be attained through the means . . . and indeed the simple love of the end *according as it is elicited by the will.* . . . Note that the same love of the end *according as it depends on the end* is not an effect of the end but rather is the very exercise of the causality of the end. And the agent who acts in view of the end is not an effect of the end, but is the subject moved by the end.[25]

This twofold aspect of the love of the end will be developed presently.

Homespun living has many examples to illustrate, inelegantly perhaps but nevertheless cogently, the truth and importance of final causality. The plain fact is that we do things for a purpose; and from the purpose follows the pattern of conduct. When people have not sufficient purpose in life they feel the dragging boredom of life. Man feels the need of purpose both for life in general and for his own particular life, however relatively unimportant for the world his own life may be. In a heartbreak letter to his pleading mother, one of the G.I. prisoners in Korea who elected to stay with the Communists is reported as writing that he now had a goal and a reason in life!

Educational motivation, so much talked about, is nothing else than the operation of finality. How can a teacher who impugns finality logically invoke motivation! Vitiate final causality and motivation loses its cogency; all discussion about it would be verbiage. Motivation simply means that someone now has an end or purpose for studying his physics or Latin.

---

[25] Trans. from J. Gredt, *Elementa Philosophiae* (2 vols., Friburgi: Herder and Co., 1937), II, p. 179.

This end-cause is sufficiently powerful in its causality to counteract and even to conquer the drag of sloth, sleep, or sport — powerful enough to lead him away from television to gerundives.

The question now arises: What precise aspect of the end makes it truly a cause? Classic philosophic terminology would call it the *formal ratio* of the causality of the end.

First of all we wonder: What is it exactly that makes an end a cause in first act, that is, capable of moving the agent to some activity? Is the knowledge of the end, for example, the awareness of New York, the precise aspect of the end that makes it capable of inducing a man to leave his home and endure the buffeting of the normal journey to New York? There are varied opinions about this; but there can be only one conclusion, says John of St. Thomas.[26]

The end is not constituted formally as a cause in first act by knowledge. The reason is clear. A thing is not established *precisely* as a final cause by something which is *common* to many other and diverse things. Something generic in this way cannot be the specific constituent of a thing. But to be known is common to many diverse things. We have knowledge of the proper objects of all our cognoscitive and appetitive faculties, of diverse ends and of diverse ways to one end. Moreover not everything known influences the will to act. Obviously, knowledge of a thing does not establish it as a final cause formally in first act.[27]

While we contend that knowledge of the end is not constitutive of the final cause in first act, we by no means negate the importance of this knowledge; we merely assign it to its proper role, which is that of a condition *sine qua non*.[28] Knowledge of the end is obviously a condition that must be fulfilled before a man seeks the end. *Nihil volitum nisi cognitum.* There may be a remote missionary in Africa who has not as yet heard of penicillin. Tending the sick and injured he may dream vaguely of some wonder drug that would limit infection and hasten healing — ideally applicable to his situation. Even so, he does not lodge a request for penicillin because he does not know it as a reality; in other words, he does not will it because he does not know it as something really existing. This is what John of St. Thomas means when he says that the knowledge required of the end is not only knowledge *per modum applicationis sed etiam per modum existentiae*.[29] We need knowledge not only of the suitability of the end, but also of its existence.

This knowledge of the end is always required but not always in the

---

[26] John of St. Thomas, *Cursus Philosophicus Thomisticus* (3 vols., Turin, Italy: Marietti, 1933), II, *De natura et causis,* q. 13, a. 1, p. 272. Cf. *infra,* p. 190, regarding this notion of first act.

[27] Cf. J. Gredt, *op. cit.,* II, p. 176.

[28] *Ibid.,* II, p. 177.

[29] *Op. cit.,* II, p. 272.

same way. A man knows his own end and then, the condition *sine qua non* being fulfilled, moves himself to that end. In the case of natural agents, the knowledge of the end that is required must not be sought in them — fire does not know that it burns — "but in the thought which gives the agent being, the creative Thought."[30]

Later we will discuss the educational implications of this point about the knowledge of the end. At present the principle is clear. Mere knowledge of something, important though it be, is not enough to endow it with a power of motivation. Knowledge of virtue, of religion, of the school rules does not automatically motivate the corresponding practice. Teachers, administrators, counselors must remember this truth constantly and efficaciously. It will be clear that mere "Christian knowledge," especially if given as part-time or release-time instruction, is inadequate for the formation of the Christian man.

The end is constituted formally as a cause in first act by its own goodness insofar as this goodness is appetible. By way of explanation we note that we are not speaking of goodness insofar as it is the proper object of a particular appetite. Goodness under this special aspect specifies or designates an appetite as being this particular appetite and not another; it determines and announces its proper class as it were. It indicates the *nature* of the appetites without pertaining here and now to the *exercise* of these appetites. And so under this formal consideration good pertains to extrinsic formal causality as we have just seen. But the function of a final cause and therefore of any good considered formally as a final cause, is not to specify or determine the nature of the appetite but to influence its *exercise*.[31] And, we say, the precise constituent of a final cause in first act is goodness, under the particular aspect of *appetibility*, that is, goodness conceived as capable of moving an agent to activity. Close thought will make this clear.

The end is that for the sake of which other things are done. But that for the sake of which other things are done becomes such in first act precisely through goodness; for what is loved so as to become the reason for doing something is goodness. Moreover, this goodness is not something absolute, not transcendental goodness; it is goodness considered as suited to something, befitting it, good *for it*. The very notion of an end is that *for the sake of which* something is done.[32] It is not necessary that this good for the sake of which the agent is moved be truly an ontological good. It suffices that it be an apparent good, an object which the agent's faculties represent as good for him.[33]

---

[30] J. Maritain, *A Preface to Metaphysics* (New York: Sheed and Ward, 1948), p. 128.

[31] Cf. Maquart, *op. cit.*, III, 2, p. 238, and also John of St. Thomas, *op. cit.*, p. 273.

[32] Cf. John of St. Thomas, *op. cit.*, II, p. 274.

[33] Gredt, *op. cit.*, II, p. 175.

It will at once be clear that all successful school motivation must represent the ideals or good proposed as good *for the student*. Even "the honor of the school" must be related to the good of this particular student if its motivating power is to be compelling. It will also be clear how people can do wrong; they see sloth or selfishness or vice as a good in some way for them. If they could be helped to see it as really harmful to them they would not act in this way. This truth will give a tactical clue to the school counselor who believes in an objective law of right and wrong — God's moral law. It will enable him to guide gently a headstrong counselee in a way that is neither immoral nor traumatic.

The end is constituted a cause in second act by being actually sought. "Since the final cause in first act is good *as appetible*, the final cause in second act can only be good as [actually] sought or as desired."[34] For, as John of St. Thomas neatly says: "The proper actuality of a desirable thing is to be actually desired."[35]

The end is a real cause but it exercises its causality by a metaphorical movement.[36] When a man cuts wood he physically breaks the wood. This efficient causality we describe as being physical. The end does not exercise its causality over the agent physically, but metaphorically through its own appetibility. It exercises a certain traction over the agent who seeks it so that the agent is moved to exercise himself in some activity. But the agent cannot exercise an action except by some inclination or appetite which, moreover, cannot tend to something without tending to something definite. This inclination must be made proportionate to the terminus of its tendency, which proportion or modification will give the appetite some special orientation toward its terminus. Now such modification is effected by the appetite's act of love for the terminus.

This act of love is bipolarized as it were; it proceeds from a twofold principle — from the end as attracting and drawing the love, and from the will as eliciting the love. Further, in its dependence on its object it has a twofold relationship — it is specified by the object (but we are not concerned here with this relation) and also it is made *for the sake of* the object; and this is the relation of causality with which we are concerned.

If this act of love orientating the appetite to the terminus be considered on the one hand as proceeding from the appetite, it is called simply an act of the will and an effect of the end. But if it be considered as proceeding from the appetible thing and subordinated to it for the purpose of loving it, it is the very causality of the end being exercised.

St. Thomas speaks of the modification of the appetite by the appetible object.[37] "The appetible object gives to the appetite a certain adaptation

---

[34] Maquart, *op. cit.*, III, 2, p. 238.

[35] John of St. Thomas, *op. cit.*, p. 278. "Propria enim actualitas appetibilis est appeti actu."

[36] *Ibid.*, pp. 278–283, for a profound treatment of this point.

[37] *Summa,* I–II, q. 26, a. 2.

to itself, which adaptation consists in a certain complacency in that object; and from this follows movement towards the appetible object. Because of this change of the appetite by the appetible object, love is called a passion."[38] He points out later that this love denotes, not the movement of the appetite in actually tending toward the appetible object, but the movement whereby the appetite is changed by the appetible object so as to have complacency in the object.

Therefore the end moves, but is itself unmoved. It does not itself produce activity efficiently; hence we say it moves metaphorically, not physically. But the agent loving that end is changed in some way by it and accordingly produces activity. As a result things now really happen and really exist which before did not happen or exist — and this result is due to the influence of the end. Hence, we reiterate, the end is really a cause.

> The true causality of the end . . . is this love which it evokes by the fact that it is known. In the case of "produced," or "elicit," love, this is obvious. [For example, a man comes to know of New York and is captivated by the thought of vacationing there; hence he produces the activity needed to go there.] In the case of "radical," or natural, love which is identical with the agent's being itself, with the very essence of the substance or faculty, the knowledge in question must be sought not in the agent itself but in the thought which gives the agent being, the creative Thought.[39] [Thus fire has a natural "love" of burning, a "love" which is identical with its being. The knowledge of the end is not to be sought in the leaping flames but in the creative thought which made fire to be fire.]

It may be well to note here that love of the end is distinct from desire of the end. The sequence is love, which is complacency in the end; then desire, which follows the love and is a movement toward this end; then joy which is rest in the end.[40]

To sum up: The causality of the end is exercised through its being loved, insofar as this love is considered as depending on the end. If this love be considered as elicited by the will it is not the exercise of final causality but an effect of that causality. The end exercises this causality by a metaphorical motion; nevertheless it is a real cause. The subtleness, the gentleness, and silent power of final causality is apparent.

The end is the first of the causes. This is usually expressed in the dictum: The end is first in the order of intention, last in the order of execution.[41] The point is clear from what has been already said. For the

---

[38] John of St. Thomas, paraphrase of St. Thomas (I–II, q. 26, a. 2), *op. cit.*, pp. 279–280.

[39] Maritain, *Preface to Metaphysics*, pp. 127–128.

[40] *Summa*, I–II, q. 26, a. 2.   [41] *Ibid.*, q. 20, a. 1 ad 2.

first among causes is that which is presupposed by other causes and whose influx precedes theirs; and that is precisely the role of the end, insofar as it exercises a certain traction which leads the agent to act. Thus a man's desire to see New York precedes his activity to go there. A carpenter's desire for a set of shelves precedes his sawing and planing, and precedes the disposition of the material in that particular form. So much for the order of intention. But in the order of execution, the end is last. So, in the above examples, the last thing in all the activity (in this particular series) is the actual reaching of New York, or the finished set of shelves.

Several corollaries flow from this concept.

The end is first in intention and, therefore, if the pursuit of the end ceases the pursuit of the means likewise ceases.[42] If no educational end be proposed, there will be no educational process. This is why the whole matter of the end of education, though abstract and apparently unpractical, is so important. There will be no educational activity of any sort if there be no educational end in view.

The end not merely influences the placing of the means, but also the nature of the means. The distinctive nature of the means depends on the end; "the reason for everything made is derived from the end which the maker intends."[43] Diverse ends demand diverse means. Diverse educational ends will accordingly demand diverse educational means. A school seeking a Christian end must use means different from a school seeking a merely humanitarian end. In the two schools the educational process, despite material similarities, will be formally distinct. The processes will be as divergent as two roads, one climbing a mountain, the other on rolling plains. Hence it can be stated: The end is the guide and measure of the means.

There is another corollary: "When the end is vitiated, in vain are the means repaired."[44] If the end of Catholic education be overlooked or confused or lowered, the educational means naturally lose their full efficacy. In vain will we seek compensation in improved methods, better buildings, and expensive audio-visuals.

A further conclusion is justified: "The best in everything is its end."[45]

All these truths have significant implications for education. They pin-

---

[42] "Cessante fine cessare debet id quod est ad finem" (St. Thomas Aquinas, *Commentary on the Sentences*, 4 Sent. 48, 2, 5 a.).

[43] "Ratio cum cuiuslibet res factae sumitur ex fine quem faciens intendit" (St. Thomas, *Contra Gentiles*, 3, 59). Cf. *ibid.*, 3, 78, and *Summa*, II–II, q. 27, a. 6. Cf. "Ex fine sumitur ratio eorum, quae sunt ad finem" (St. Thomas, *Expositio in 10 libros ethicorum Aristotelis ad Nichomachum*, Bk. 3, 15 d.).

[44] "Remoto fine frustra reparatur illud quod est ad finem" (St. Thomas, 4 Sent. 44, 1, 2.1 ob. 1).

[45] St. Thomas, *Expositio in Librum Aristotelis de Somno et Vigilia*, 4. "Quod est optimum in unoquoque, est finis eius."

point the necessity of an end rightly estimated, clearly comprehended, and continually referred to as the guide and measure of the means.

The Principle of Finality

Omne agens agit propter finem (Every agent acts for the sake of an end) is the traditional and acceptable formula for the principle of finality. Its meaning is that an end is not merely the definite terminus of any activity but is moreover that for the sake of which the agent acts.

A brief commentary on the term "agent" will not be amiss.

In this principle, the word "agent" means more than efficient agents producing transient activity, namely, activity in which there is a communication of actuality from the agent to some other being. It includes also agents capable of immanent activity, not only insofar as this immanent activity may perhaps be virtually or concomitantly transient and productive — which aspect can be included within the notion of efficient causality — but even insofar as this action may be purely immanent, whether entitatively or intentionally. In the vegetable world, for example, the cabbage operates immanently and perfects itself entitatively by growing to its proper status; this immanent activity is entitative. On a higher level man operates immanently in the intentional order by knowing things other than himself. He thus perfects himself intentionally by becoming in some way united with the things he knows. This represents a much higher degree of immanent action and therefore of agents.[46]

Agent then includes more than efficient causes producing transient action. When we say "every agent . . ." we mean every agent capable of transient and of immanent — entitative and intentional — activity. Later on in this study we will need these notions to pass judgment on the self-activity program in the classroom and to discern a quality in good teaching.

This principle of finality is not something founded merely on experience, as an induction; it is founded on being, on the very nature of activity.

Confusion will be removed by recalling that this principle is not concerned with locating the over-all providential purpose of each being in the whole world and of all activity. It does not seek to find what purpose typhoid germs, wasps, and Mont Blanc serve in the world! This investigation would pertain to extrinsic finality. But the principle does say that the wasp in its activity acts for an end — in the sense soon to be explained.

Though the principle says "every agent" it applies to different agents in somewhat different respects. Since being is analogous, the activity of being will likewise be analogous. Hence it must be said that agents act for an end in different ways.

God acts for an end, but He Himself is His own end. Creatures act

---

[46] Cf. Jacques Maritain, *A Preface to Metaphysics*, pp. 111–113.

out of desire and need of something; but God acts, not from need of anything, but from love of His own goodness. Nothing more can be added to His own goodness.

He loves His own goodness perfectly and on this account wishes this goodness multiplied in the only way possible, namely, by a likeness of it. From this follows the advantage of the creature in so far as it receives a likeness to the Divine Goodness. Wherefore we say that God made the creature because of His goodness if we consider the end of the worker, and because of the utility of the creature if we consider the end of the work.[47]

Though God acts for an end there is, however, no final causality involved. God is not subject to the causality of the end, since He is Himself the End.

Rational agents move themselves toward an end *known* as an end, and they are able to choose the means thereto. They are said to act in view of an end *directive formaliter*. A man in seeking food knows not only that he is in quest of a steak but also that this plate of meat is the end-cause of the particular activities needed to attain it. "It is proper to the rational nature to tend to an end, as directing (*agens*) and leading itself to the end."[48]

Irrational animals act in view of an end to which they are directed by another. They can apprehend the end by sense knowledge and move themselves toward it, but they know it only as some material thing for the acquisition of which they act. They do not know it formally as an end. They are said to act in view of an end *directive non formaliter sed materialiter* only.[49] Thus a dog seeks, sees, and gets a bone, unaware that this is the end-cause of his whimpering.

Natural agents devoid of all knowledge act in view of an end determined by another, without themselves apprehending this end in any way. Hence they are said to act in view of the end *executive* only, without any knowledge of the end. These natural agents are determined to a particular end in a twofold way, intrinsically through their nature — thus fire of its very nature burns; and extrinsically through force — thus an arrow is given a certain determination by the archer. In either case the natural agent works executively only. Such determination toward particular goods on the part of both natural agents and irrational animal agents requires an ordination by some rational will; "for particular causes are moved by a universal cause; and so the ruler of a city (who intends the common good) moves by his command all the particular departments

---

[47] St. Thomas, 2 *Sent.*, dist. 1, q. 2, a. 1.

[48] *Summa*, I–II, q. 1, a. 2.

[49] Gredt uses the terminology *executive et apprehensive, at non elective* (*op. cit.*, II, p. 178).

of the city. Hence all things lacking reason are necessarily moved to their particular ends by some rational will which extends to the universal good, viz., by the Divine Will."[50]

It will now be apparent that the principle of finality is an analogous principle, applicable to all agents in a sense identical indeed, but only according to a certain proportion.

An appreciation of the special way a rational agent acts in view of an end can have important educational consequences. The analogies of animal activity can be pressed only so far in regard to human activity. They have only limited relevance for human learning. The human being must *move himself* toward the ends of education. Recognition of this fact does not mean that his knowledge is to be developed in the sense of Idealism,[51] Ontologism,[52] or Innatism,[53] nor that the student direct himself to educational goals independently of any external assistance, guidance, and correction; but this recognition safeguards and preserves in true perspective the essential self-activity necessarily required in all human acts. Hence self-activity, rightly understood and culminating in intentional activity, is a basic principle of all sound education.

Another educational corollary of man's knowledge of the end as such and his self-direction thereto is that throughout his education he should, according to his maturity, be brought to the understanding of the ends of his activity as ends. He should be encouraged to strictly purposeful activity, knowing his end and seeing it as something good *for him*. Every act cannot be a conscious striving for an end, it is true; man learns to act habitually. But even here a periodic, conscious realization of purpose will reinvigorate this habitual activity and prevent it from becoming mere routine. Herein is a philosophical reason why even good people obtain spiritual benefit from missions and retreats, and why the best schools can profit from a regular retreat.

---

[50] *Summa*, I–II, q. 1, a. 2, ad 3.

[51] I.e., in building up a body of knowledge which is simply his own thought unrelated to objective and external reality.

[52] Ontologism, as represented by Malebranche and Gioberti, holds that the intellect does not need to receive created species — indeed cannot — because it immediately and naturally attains the divine eternal ideas according to which all things are created. All created things are then known through these ideas according to the ontologists. It would follow from this theory that all outside instruction and educational assistance would be not only superfluous but completely inept. The educand, under God, would be completely independent in regard to human knowledge. We could well burn down our schools.

[53] Innatism holds that ideas were impressed formally but occultly on the mind in the first instant of our existence. By the exercise of the senses, etc., these impressed ideas pass from a submerged state to an explicit knowledge. This theory, equally false, likewise credits the educand with a less exaggerated but still an unwarranted autonomy. It would not completely eliminate the necessity of schools. But surely the innatist teachers in these schools would be forced to muse at times that, in some of their pupils at any rate, the impressed ideas must be very submerged.

Various formulations have been proposed for the principle of finality but all are not acceptable. The following are to be avoided:

1. "Everything is for an end." This is unacceptable because the concept of "end" connotes the concept of "agent" rather than the concept of "thing."

2. "Every effect is for an end." This formula is inadmissible. As it stands, it would include chance: but an effect which is produced by chance is not produced for an end.[54]

3. "Every being is directed toward an end." This formula is only partially true. Created beings are directed toward an end; but God is also a Being and He is not directed toward an end, since He is independent of all extrinsic cause. Hence this formulation is inadmissible.

The validity of the principle of finality as an ontological principle has been strongly impugned. Some philosophers have completely rejected it — materialists, ancient and modern, such as Epicurus, Democritus, Lucretius, Diderot, Büchner, Haeckel; pantheists such as Spinoza; mechanists and positivists with few exceptions; nearly all evolutionists, notably Darwin and Spencer; Dewey and followers whom it is hard to classify philosophically beyond the label "Deweyites." Other philosophers accept it but only under qualifications which limit or vitiate it.

Despite these divergencies, Scholastic philosophy regards the principle of finality as being a transcendental principle, of itself evident. There may seem a touch of paradox in saying that something denied by these men listed above is of itself evident; but the anomaly dwindles when it is recalled that their speculative denial is the result of an invalid *a priori* position or of an unwillingness to accept the sequelae of finality; and the anomaly disappears when daily life shows that everybody accepts finality in practice, and with good reason. For any agent produces, not any unpredictable and indifferent effect, but an effect which is definite and *per se* proportionate to it (although it can at the same time produce another *per accidens*). An agent which produces this definite effect tends to produce this effect and not another; thus fire tends always to burn, not to freeze, something. But this definite and proportionate effect which the agent tends to produce is a good perfecting the agent and is precisely what is meant by the term *finis* or end.[55]

Moreover, a denial of this principle would lead to absurdity. For an agent would always be producing *per se* a definite and proportionate effect, yet the same agent *would not be tending* toward the production of that effect and the effect would never be intended; so we would have a

---

[54] Cf. Henry Grenier, *Thomistic Philosophy,* trans. by J. P. O'Hanlon (4 vols., Charlottetown, Canada: St. Dunstan's University, 1950), III, p. 247.

[55] Cf. Maquart, *op. cit.,* III, 1, p. 241.

sequence and proportion between an agent and an effect that were not intended and therefore were inexplicable, without sufficient reason — violating the principle of sufficient reason.[56]

Maritain notes that this evidentness of the principle of finality is a case of the second mode of perseity.[57] When the mind understands the two notions "agent," or "being that acts," and "acting in view of an end" it sees at once that the latter concept involves the former as its subject — just as the predicate, "power to laugh," immediately involves "man" as its distinctive subject.

The Division of Ends

John Dewey, if an inference can legitimately be drawn from his writings, would surely object to this subsection even apart from his whole aversion for finality. The man who could describe philosophy as "a show of elaborate terminology, a hair-splitting logic, and a fictitious devotion to the mere external forms of comprehensive and minute demonstration" having "an over-pretentious claim to certainty"[58] might even feel some sardonic gratification at finding his worst strictures verified by the presence of the above subheading. But if Dewey had paid some slight attention to proper division he himself might have been spared the strictures of others: "He is himself a child of chaos and his works are chaos."[59]

Clear division is the handmaid of order, and order leads to clarity. Division of labor leads to order, to smooth system, to efficient production. Proper division of the ends of education leads to orderly understanding, to a valid system, to efficient education in the fullest sense of the term "efficiency." Ask someone to pick up loose grapes and even his two hands will barely hold the equal of a bunch. Let him take the main stalks and his fingers will easily hold several bunches — hundreds of grapes! Likewise, bid a teacher or administrator be attentive to all the picayune ends which are given by the hundreds in several lists with very little real subordination[60] and the conscientious teacher will be driven distraught,

---

[56] *Ibid.*, p. 241.

[57] Maritain, *Preface to Metaphysics*, p. 130. A judgment is evident according to the first mode of perseity when the notion of the subject — its very definition — implies the notion of the predicate. The principle of identity "Being is being" is evident in this way. The second mode of perseity is had when the mind perceives that the predicate, while not implicit in the notion of the subject, nevertheless immediately involves this as its distinctive subject.

[58] J. Dewey, *Reconstruction in Philosophy* (New York: Henry Holt and Co., 1920), p. 21.

[59] Waldo Frank, quoted by James O'Hara, *Limitations of the Educational Theory of John Dewey* (Washington, D. C.: The Catholic University of America, 1929), p. 8.

[60] Bobbitt, analyzing most of the important phases of human activity listed 821 specific objectives for the educator. This mammoth list omitted those educational

moreover will reap only a meager vintage. But establish order among the myriad "desirable goals" in education — hierarchical order according to proper subordination and ramification — and the teacher will be physically able to attain the principal ends that are the main stems from which ramify in profusion the outcomes we all recognize as "desirable goals." To do this we must first understand the different kinds of "ends"; hence this subsection on "Division."

It will be recognized at once that these divisions pin-point concepts that everybody, in a general way, already has. Philosophy is a recognition and honest analysis of reality, not just "a fictitious devotion to . . . external forms."

"End" is capable of many divisions according to the various bases from which it is possible to consider an end. Many of them are self-explanatory, many are beyond our scope here. Very briefly we touch the more important divisions. We are not concerned here with the division of ends considered as the mere terminus or object of any activity in the order of execution. In this case "end" is called the *finis effectus* and can be as multiform as reality; but, as such, is not a cause.

Considered as a cause for the sake of which something is done, i.e., *finis*, "end," is divided into

> *Finis qui:* That which is sought. Thus, a father of a family seeks to make money. Money is the *finis qui* of his activity. This is sometimes called the material or objective end.
>
> *Finis quo:* That *by which* what is sought is attained, viz., the possession of the good desired. Thus the *possession* of the money is the *finis quo* of his activity. This is sometimes called the formal end.
>
> *Finis cui:* The subject for whom the good is desired.

The *finis qui*, *finis quo*, and *finis cui* are not three completely distinct ends. They are different aspects under which end, "for the sake of which something is done," is considered.

The *finis* may be natural or supernatural according as the end sought is something of the natural or the supernatural order.

The *finis qui* can be

> *proportionate:* This is an end proportionate to a created nature; the nature by its own unaided powers is able to attain it. The burning of wood is a proportionate end for fire.
>
> *not proportionate:* This is an end toward which some agent is moved by another, but which is above the unaided natural power of the agent. Always it must be directed and moved to this end by another, just as an arrow is directed toward the target by the archer.

---

objectives concerned with one's occupation in life. See F. Bobbitt, *How to Make a Curriculum* (Boston: Houghton Mifflin Co., 1924), p.8 ff.

According to the order of ends in a series of ends, end (*finis qui*) is divided into

> *proximate* end: An end which is sought immediately, without the seeking of any other end as a means thereto. The relief of a headache is the proximate end for the student taking an aspirin. "One and the same act, insofar as it proceeds once from the agent, is ordained only to one proximate end, from which it has its species; but it can be ordained to several remote ends subordinated one to the other."[61]
>
> *remote* end: An end which is attained only through the previous attainment of other ends; a remote end is attained mediately. *A* attains *B* and through *B* attains *C;* hence, *A* attains *C* mediately. Working on his dissertation may be the student's remote end for taking the aspirin. Note that the relief of the headache is not merely a means. It is itself a good and capable of being an end, though it is itself ordained to a further end. We will recall these notions of remote and proximate ends in considering the proper role of the school in education.

A remote end may be either an

> *intermediate* end: An end to which other ends are ordained but which is itself ordained to a further end. Note that this is itself a good, is of itself desirable, and is therefore a true end; yet it is ordained to a higher end. The production of the dissertation instanced above is ordained toward the further end of graduation.
>
> *ultimate* end: An end to which other ends are subordinated but which is not ordained to any further end.

The ultimate end may be a

> *relative* ultimate end (or *secundum quid*): An end to which all others are subordinated, which is itself not subordinated to any other end in its own order, yet can be subordinated to an end of a higher order.
>
> *absolute* ultimate end: An end to which all other ends are subordinated and is itself not subordinated to any other end in any other order whatsoever.

This absolute ultimate end can be considered formally or materially:

> *formally:* The formal ultimate end is happiness in general.
>
> *materially:* That object in which the formal ultimate end is sought. The true objective ultimate end can only be God since He alone is the universal good. But an individual may select for himself

---

[61] *Summa,* I–II, q. 1, a. 3, ad 3.

some other ultimate end, a false one, and seek to find his ultimate happiness in it.

Considering the degree of influence exercised, the end (*finis qui*) may be

> *primary* (or principal): An end which principally moves an agent and is sufficient of itself to do so. Thus the love of knowledge may be the primary end for a scientist's research.
>
> *secondary* (or accessory): An end annexed to a principal end moving the agent in such a way that the annexed end does not, however, move the agent primarily but only partially. Thus a comfortable living may be a secondary end for the scientist's research.

Note that "whatever has one end *per se* and principally, can have many secondary ends *per se* and an infinite number of accidental ends."[62]
An important distinction must be made between the

> *finis operis:* Literally, the end of the work itself. This is the end to which the activity tends of its very nature, independently of any intention of the agent. This is the material effect of the agent's activity. It follows without being intended of and for itself. Thus, the giving of money to a beggar tends of its very nature to the relief of his indigence, no matter what may be the donor's intention. The watchmaker's activity of its very nature terminates in the production of a watch, whether the motive of his activity be to make a livelihood or to exercise a hobby.
>
> *finis operantis:* Literally the end of the worker. This is the end which the rational agent has in mind when acting. It is the end which the agent fixes for himself by his intentions when he acts; hence this is the formal effect of the activity. Thus he may give some money to a sidewalk beggar with the sole intention of appearing beneficent to the staring passers-by; or he may give plentiful alms in order to alter his income-tax assessment.

A comment on this division is in place.[63] The *finis operis,* also called the *finis effectus* or the object, is never of itself a final cause, but only a material effect of the efficient cause. It simply follows the action and is

---

[62] *Summa Supplem.,* q. 48, a. 2, ad 1.

[63] Some authors introduce a third division here: *finis operationis,* that which terminates the agent's activity, for example, the finished watch; *finis operis,* that toward which the effect produced tends of its very nature, for example, the watch tells the time; *finis operantis,* the watchmaker's livelihood. These distinctions are well made in themselves; but from the viewpoint of the agent and his activity tending toward an object, the further natural purpose of the object once it is effected introduces a new series and is, it seems, irrelevant. Hence we keep the terminology given in the text. Cf. Gredt, *op. cit.,* II, p. 176, and Maquart, *op. cit.,* III, 2, p. 240.

not intended in any way for itself. It does not move the efficient cause
as an end but only as a means. The egoist displaying his beneficence on
the sidewalk for the benefit of passers-by is not in the least interested in
the relief of the cripple's indigence nor moved by it to action. His end
in view is simply and solely his self-display; the relief of the man's
indigence *de facto* effected by his money (*finis operis*) is merely a means
to his real end, the end which really moves him to action, viz., self-display
(*finis operantis*). This example is no general indictment of sidewalk
charity. It is a theoretical illustration of a very practical and widely accepted distinction. Likewise a skilled craftsman may make junk toys or
furniture, an artistic musician may turn out a "rag" song, a writer with
a fine sense of literature may hammer out a "pulp" story — each product
a *finis operis* — with the sole purpose of paying the rent — *finis operantis*
— and with nothing but cynical contempt for the quality of the artifact
produced. The very prevalence in creative(!) circles of the word "pot-
boiler" — plebeian but vivid — is an indication of the widespread, if
implicit, acceptance of the distinction between *finis operis* and *finis
operantis*. The connotation of the phrase "ulterior motive" refers to this
distinction; and world politics and certain peace overtures illustrate it on
a much wider horizon. Later we shall see the educational relevance of
this distinction.

However, the *finis operis* and *operantis* can coincide. In which case the
finis operis, instead of being merely last in execution, now becomes as
well first in intention, that for the sake of which the agent operates, that
which moves him to operate; and thus it now bears a new formality. It
is not merely the terminus of the activity; it is also the cause of the
activity.

The divisions of end, though not exhaustive, are sufficient equipment
for our purpose in this book.

We are now in a position to grasp the significance of the "proper and
immediate end" of something. "Proper" and "immediate" are taken from
different standpoints.

The word "proper" indicates that we are here concerned with an end
which is *per se* and not *per accidens*. Proper is opposed to what is merely
accessory, accidental. The proper end of a chair is to provide suitable
seating for a person, even though it may also serve as a temporary plat-
form from which to scan the high shelves of a cupboard — an end *per
accidens*. Individual parts of a chair may have their own proper end,
e.g., the back supports the person's back, its armrests support the arms,
its crosspieces bind and strengthen the four legs, etc.; but taken as a
whole the proper end of a chair, that to which it tends of its very nature,
is the provision of suitable seating.

The word "immediate" indicates the proximity or propinquity that
exists between the agent and its end. "Immediate" is opposed to what is

remote. The immediate end is that which the agent tends to and attains without the mediation of any other end. This particular end is the first in the line of attainment; no other end is subordinated to this end as a quasi means, although this end may be itself subordinated to further ends, called remote ends. It will be recalled that this proximate end is unique; one agent performing one and the same act can have but one proximate end.[64]

Therefore the proper and immediate end of education will be that end which education, conceived as a whole, should attain *per se* and proximately without the mediation of any other ends. We are concerned here with the proper and immediate end of education considered as morally one process — a moral unity.

What this end is will be discussed in Chapter IV.

The Ultimate End

Since "the whole work of education is intimately and necessarily connected"[65] with the ultimate end, the proper and immediate end of education is along the road to this ultimate end. Before we proceed to this proper end we must first make sure which is the right road, namely, the road leading to the true ultimate end; briefly we survey it.

There is an ultimate end of human life.[66] Among all the ends and series of ends that make up the chain of life, there is and there must be one end which is the last in all series — the ultimate end. This holds true whether end be considered according to the order of intention or of execution; otherwise there would be an infinite series of ends ordained one to the other. However, there cannot be such an infinite series in things essentially subordinated to each other. There cannot be an infinite series of clock wheels each turning the next, without there being an ultimate one on which the others depend.

Man, then, is not aimless in life. He is not flotsam. Philosophers who deny finality should be left in a rudderless ship to drift indefinitely on the Sargasso Sea. Across the sea of life is a final destination — an ultimate end. Man's life is purposeful; it has meaning because it is not merely going, but going *somewhere*. Beyond this ultimate destination, nothing more will or can be sought. Education should correspond to life in tending toward this end. Hence man's education, preparing him for self-navigation as it were, will be purposeful. Surely the education of his life powers will be in accordance with the ultimate end of that life! If educators — parents, teachers, administrators — do not lead children toward that ultimate end, they are not educators but betrayers, no matter how

[64] *Summa,* I–II, q. 1, a. 3, ad 3.
[65] Pius XI, *Christian Education of Youth,* p. 4.
[66] *Summa,* I–II, q. 1, a. 4.

spacious the school and expensive its equipment. Such lavish things would then be only decoys leading youth astray pleasurably.

In every human action a man acts at least virtually in view of a last end considered both formally and materially.[67]

A brief commentary will clarify the meaning of this statement. A "human act" is one which proceeds from what is typically human in man; therefore, it proceeds under the control of man's reason since it is this power of reason which marks him off from the animal as human. Hence, all man's deliberate acts are human acts; whereas snoring, an arm movement in sleep, etc., are not human acts, but are called "acts of a man." The word "virtually" recalls the fourfold mode of human action, viz., actually, virtually, habitually, and interpretatively.[68]

We say "a last end" because an individual can in point of fact choose

---

[67] Gredt, *op. cit.*, II, p. 305.

[68] A man seeks an end "actually" when he here and now thinks about it as he takes the means to attain it. There are three elements in an actual intention: (1) actual knowledge of the end; (2) actual willing of the end; (3) choice of the means and their explicit direction to the end.

A "virtual" intention is one whereby a person actively takes the means to an end, yet in taking these means does not think consciously or actually of the end. A "virtual" intention is of two kinds, explicit and implicit. Again there are three elements in an explicit virtual intention: (1) a previous actual intention seeking the end; (2) the cessation of this actual consideration of the end; (3) but its continued influence on the person's present acts so that these acts are nevertheless directed toward the end. This may seem complex, but it is as simple and common as the householder who decides to walk down to the corner drugstore to buy a paper, then whistles a tune to relish the cool evening air, and notes the car parked by the fire hydrant as he walks along. "An 'implicit' virtual intention is an intention by which an agent does something which, as an imperfect good, of its nature is destined for and tends to a more perfect good as to an end, of which he may or may not have knowledge, unless perchance he, violently and contrary to the nature of his operation, directs his operation to some other end" (Grenier, *op. cit.*, IV, p. 25). A laborer who puts down a basement floor according to the builder's specifications of special thickness, curvature, and strength, without knowing what equipment it is designed to accommodate, is nevertheless acting virtually toward the end intended by the builder.

An "habitual" intention is a habit resulting from a previous intention which now has no influence on the agent's present activity. So when the suburbanite walking for his paper meets a friend just beyond the fire hydrant and accepts his invitation to detour down the side street and see his new color television set, his intention of going to the drugstore is now only an habitual intention. He has not repudiated it, hence some intention remains; but the detour, the admiring inspection of the set, the secret wondering how the friends managed to finance it, the dallying for half an hour to watch the program, have nothing to do with going to the drugstore for a paper; that drugstore intention is now merely habitual. When, however, he eventually leaves and bends his steps toward the store, still thinking about the set, his virtual intention revives without necessarily being actualized again.

An "interpretative" intention is one that does not and never did exist but which presumably *would* exist if the agent were to consider the end, or if circumstances were otherwise. Thus a child born of Christian parents is considered to have an interpretative desire of baptism even before its reason flowers.

for himself that which is not his true last end; even so, all that he does is at least a virtual seeking of this self-chosen end.

We say "formally and materially": man's will is not content to tend toward a merely abstract aspect of good; rather it tends toward an object in the real possession of which this good can be had, since every appetite naturally tends toward its object *as it really exists*. A young man becomes engaged to Mary Ann Somebody, not to an abstract idea of feminine goodness! Yet he becomes engaged to her because he perceives this (feminine) goodness in her! So much for the understanding of the proposition; now for its validity.

St. Thomas brings home the truth of this point in his characteristic, simple profundity:[69] if the good which a man seeks is not itself the perfect good, he must seek it as something tending to the perfect good, because the beginning of anything is always ordained to its completion — the beginning of perfection is always ordained to the complete perfection, which is had in the ultimate end.

The cogency of this argumentation has something of the intangibility but undeniability of the fresh air. It is inescapable. Whoever would build stairs going nowhere? Instinctively in the longest chain of stairs, we look for the landing or the level that terminates the chain; and every step leads to that landing. How then do some philosophers theorize that maybe there is a chain of human action leading nowhere and that life is just an unceasing human treadmill! It is clear that man cannot and need not always seek his ultimate end *actually* in all that he does. Experience bears this out. That is why we insert the word "virtually"; because the virtual seeking of the end keeps the universality of his tendency toward the ultimate end within the limitations of human powers. Thus the last end is the irresistible and inescapable magnet toward which all man's actions tend.

An important corollary of this truth is that no human act, considered practically, can be indifferent to the last end.[70] Considered in the abstract, namely, just insofar as it is ordained to an object, acts such as walking, eating, talking, singing can be morally indifferent, i.e., neither conformed nor unconformed to man's last end, and therefore neither good nor bad. But considered in the concrete, since every agent acts for an end and every action is subject to circumstances, no human act can be indifferent to man's last end. Man's every human act will either tend toward it or away from it, and accordingly be either moral or immoral. This naturally includes all those human acts that make up man's educational process, as we shall discuss later, in an important question.

---

[69] Cf. *Summa*, I–II, q. 1, a. 6.

[70] Cf. Gredt, *op. cit.*, II, n. 883, 1. Also, at greater length, C. Boyer, *Cursus Philosophiae* (2 vols., Bruges: Desclée & Co., 1939), II, 458–464; and Grenier, *op. cit.*, IV, p. 100. These authors expound the teaching of St. Thomas in this regard.

No man can, at one and the same time, act efficaciously for two diverse, absolute ultimate ends.[71]

"End" is here understood materially, i.e., the good which concretely is considered as the ultimate end of the agent. Good in the abstract obviously cannot be multiple.

The validity of this proposition is clear because such ends would be wholly incompatible and it would be impossible for man's will to tend wholly and efficaciously toward each as though each were its perfect good, just as it is impossible for him to walk in two different directions at once.

Eclecticism in education, as in other things, may be sound in regard to means and intermediate ends, depending on the intrinsic reasons for the eclecticism. But there is a tendency in education toward an eclecticism in philosophy, and correspondingly in methods, whereby the attempt is made in varying degrees to blend in one school-system ideas and therefore methods tending toward radically different ends. Such a tendency is philosophically unsound. Therefore, a system of discipline designed to lead a child to a naturalistic end, e.g., some sort of evolutionary self-expression conceived as the educational ultimate, can never have even a partial place in what purports to be Christian education. To attempt to give children a Christian education and at the same time to mold them on a naturalistic system of discipline would be to seek to direct them efficaciously toward two diverse, ultimate ends; and that would be philosophically foredoomed. But it may happen that some principle or technique in a naturalistic system of school discipline is accepted in Christian education because justifiable on sounder reasons, e.g., the encouragement of normal self-expression; in this case, however, the similarity is not formal, only material or apparent — as would be the similarity between a gangland and a government execution.

The ultimate end is the same for all men.[72] In regard to its formal aspect, i.e., the realization of perfect happiness, the last end is obviously the same for all, since all men seek their own happiness. But in regard to the good in which this is to be realized, all men in point of fact do not seek the same last end; some seek wealth, some pleasure, and so on.

The ultimate end is not to be found in created goods.

1. There are those who place it in something external to themselves such as in wealth[73] or in reputation[74] — honor, power, etc.

Wealth in the form of luxurious living cannot be the true ultimate end because such luxuries — mink coats, Cadillacs, splendid estates — are *for something else,* namely, the sustaining of life, however remotely. Wealth in the form of money is even a step further removed from man's true end

---

[71] Cf. Grenier, *op. cit.,* IV, p. 30. Also cf. *Summa,* I–II, q. 1, a. 5.

[72] *Summa,* I–II, q. 1, a. 7.

[73] *Ibid.,* q. 2, a. 1.

[74] *Ibid.,* a. 2, 3, and 4.

because money is *for* the purchase of natural wealth *for* the sustaining of life; and something that is for something else cannot be the ultimate. Surely the fate of American Confederate and Japanese Occupation money is sufficient historical commentary on mere money as man's ultimate end.

Reputation in whatever form is something extrinsic to a man and cannot bring him intrinsic happiness. Of its nature, honor is only a public recognition, not a constituent, of excellence; in these days it may be only a witness to the number of figures in a man's income! Power has even less relation to intrinsic excellence and the Hitler war bears witness to the world-wide recognition of the difference between power and intrinsic excellence. These things are clear to all thinking people. Yet on the shaded stage of life, man's material imagination, projecting his irrepressible yearning for happiness, has from time to time deceptively spotlighted these tinseled goods in roseate hue; and so the world has had its Epicureans, its Napoleons, its misers. It has also had St. Benedict Joseph Labre, whose life was a symphony in rags — a proof in object lesson of the philosophical conclusion that man's ultimate happiness is not to be found in external goods.

The clarity of this concept can easily be dimmed in a prosperous society, and its institutions can be correspondingly affected. But the truth remains as a beacon for sound education. Graduation to material prosperity and repute is not the total goal of education.

2. The objective ultimate end is not to be found in internal goods within man's own nature, whether of body or soul. Bodily goods, such as health, athletic prowess and agility, longevity, muscular physique, are of themselves inept as an ultimate end.[75] Man is puny in these things compared to various animals. But the basic reason for the exclusion of such substitutes is that man's body is ordained to his soul as co-operator in human activity and by nature is destined for a minor role in this human activity; its conservation and beauty can no more be the ultimate end of human action than the preservation and painting of a ship can be the ultimate fulfillment of its builder's purpose and the captain's role. The function of both body and ship is purely ministerial.

This truth, well understood, will throw light on the attitudes that should govern hygiene and physical education in education circles. The Nazi use of the educational system to assist the development of a physical super race was, among other things, a philosophical deordination, inevitably disastrous for true education.

3. The true ultimate end is not to be found in bodily pleasure.[76] However passing sweet the sugar of sensuality, is man to have an ultimate end that brute animals can fully share? Such pleasure is only the resultant of a good apprehended by a bodily sense. Even the highest

[75] *Ibid.*, a. 5.
[76] *Ibid.*, a. 6.

pleasure cannot constitute man's ultimate happiness, because pleasure of its nature is only a proper accident resulting from some good; it is never a constituent of happiness. "No pleasure can make up happiness; rather it must always follow humbly in the wake of happiness, like a train-bearer following a bride," writes Fr. Farrell.[77] Pleasure has been the Inchcape Rock[78] for many a life. Schools, colleges, writers, "educationalists" that permit and even encourage bodily self-indulgence in the name of self-expression and self-development are forming their students to a habit of living which cannot bring them to their true end — which in fact will only freewheel them to the destruction of all that is best in human activity. One naturally doubts if any educator worthy of the name will be found to advocate complete Hedonism; that is not the danger since the majority of men would recognize it for what it was. Rather, the danger is in that partial Hedonism which wears the cloak of "self-expression," or "natural tendency." Injected into human nature, where original sin has already upset the balance of control, even small doses can be lethal, especially where life-giving Christianity,[79] a divine remedy, is rejected or diluted. Clark and McKillop, in speaking of basic human needs, include among them the need for sexual gratification;[80] and they add, "if any one of them is not satisfied, the organism will not function normally." Here in a popular educational manual is palpable error which, if translated into theory and practice — as presumably it is meant to be — can have far-reaching and disastrous consequences. The teaching of the Catholic

[77] Walter Farrell, *A Companion to the Summa* (3 vols., New York: Sheed and Ward, 1939), II, 12.

[78] In Robert Southey's ballad "The Inchcape Rock," Ralph the Rover jeeringly removed the warning bell which the Abbot of Aberbrothok had hung on the dangerous rock, and later was himself wrecked on it. Cf. B. E. Stevenson, *Home Book of Verse* (2 vols., New York: Henry Holt and Co., 1940), I, 1617–1619. This poetic ballad is adduced as a fitting symbol of the guiding and warning function of the Church. Her warnings cannot be disregarded, in education or anywhere else, with impunity.

[79] "I am come that they may have life, and may have it more abundantly" (Jn. 10:10).

[80] H. Clark and A. McKillop, *An Introduction to Education* (New York: Chartwell House, Inc., 1951), p. 73. The error in this attitude begins with the failure to distinguish between a tendency, which is a capacity, and the actual gratification of that tendency. The sexual *tendency* is an integral part of the human organism and its functioning; the physical gratification of that tendency, as Clark and McKillop presumably envisage it, is not. The sexual instinct cannot accurately be regarded as merely an animal instinct. Because of the unity of personality, it must be considered along with the love of which the whole man is capable. When that love is focused and dedicated at a higher supernatural level so as to exclude a merely physical gratification, its fulfillment is not thereby negated, but rather sublimated. Similarly the dedication of earth's first fruits to the Creator in ancient times meant that these fruits, far from being frustrated in function, fulfilled their purpose far more profoundly and nobly than had they been used "naturally" as ordinary nourishment.

Church has always been as the tolling of the bell against the treacherous rocks of self-indulgence, and her tones have simply been the echo of Christ. But we in this era of liberalism have seen educators belittle or silence that tolling as surely as did Ralph the Rover — with the same rueful results, clearly visible in the moral wreckage of youth all about them. Matthew Arnold and C. S. Lewis have written of the immorality of the "better" English schools.

4. The ultimate end of man is neither his own soul nor a good belonging to the soul.[81] His soul considered *in itself* is in potency to further perfection, e.g., knowledge, and hence cannot be the *ultimate* end. Any good *inhering* in the soul would be a participated and therefore a limited good, likewise incapable of the perfection befitting the ultimate good.

However, in regard to the *finis quo* or the *attainment* of the last end,

> something of man pertaining to his soul does belong to his last end, since he attains happiness through his soul. Therefore the thing itself which is sought as the end, is that which constitutes happiness and makes him happy; but the attainment of this thing is called happiness. Hence we must say that happiness is something belonging to the soul; but that which constitutes happiness is something outside the soul.[82]

No created good can satisfy man.[83] Only universal good can content his spiritual will just as only universal truth can be the adequate object of his immaterial intellect. But the universal good is not found in any created thing since creatures have goodness by participation and therefore with limitation.

It is apparent that true education must be concerned with more than earthly prosperity and contentment, desirable as these are in themselves. Any home or school that would direct all its educational effort to the attainment of these created goods and nothing more would be urging youth toward a mirage. Apropos of all these false ultimate ends we can profitably make the further reflection: Man is a rational creature apprehending the end *as an end* and moving himself accordingly; it follows that somewhere in his education he should be brought to the formal consideration of the pseudo ends and of the true end of human life.

The ultimate end is to be found only in the uncreated good, God. "God alone can satisfy the will of man, according to the words of Ps. 102.5: 'Who satisfieth thy desire with good things.' Therefore God alone constitutes man's happiness"[84] as his ultimate end.

In the natural order, natural happiness is man's ultimate end (relative). This of course is not perfect happiness, which can be had only in

---

[81] *Summa*, I–II, q. 2, a. 7.
[82] *Loc. cit.*

[83] *Summa*, I–II, q. 2, a. 8.
[84] *Loc. cit.*

the possession of God. It is the ultimate human perfection, but it does not comprehend every good. It is merely the highest good that man can attain in his present condition, and it can be attained in this life. St. Thomas calls it imperfect happiness.[85] This natural happiness which man can attain in his present condition consists in virtuous operation proper to himself, i.e., in the most perfect acts that he as man can produce.[86] The ancient thinkers had a dictum: *Omnis res est propter suam operationem* — Everything exists for its own operation. If the philosophical reader wonders how man as a substance can exist for his activity, which is an accident,

> Cajetan's answer is profound. *Omnis res est propter suam operationem, scilicet propter semetipsam operantem.* Everything exists for *itself* in *operation*, for inasmuch as it is in operation, it attains its ultimate actuality[87] [italics added].

For this natural happiness, goods of the body such as health, food, clothing, etc., the operations of his vegetative and sensitive powers, the society of friends, are all quasi-instrumental requisites. Obviously, no sound system of education can neglect them. Education must avoid the extremes of neglect and excess; each is inimical to happiness. Great riches and abundance are never required for happiness. The lofty operations of man's reason and will are possible without such abundance. Indeed, such abundance is prejudicial to his happiness because, by entangling him in the care of material goods and by making him dependent on the co-operation of others for their administration, it lessens his self-sufficiency. Doubtless, this is a dehydrated, philosophical consideration. It might evoke cynicism along millionaires' row and in sunless Wall Street, but perhaps it is best demonstrated there! It is the bedrock truth. The life and words of Christ confirm and moreover wonderfully vivify these dry philosophical concepts. "Lay not up to yourselves treasure on earth: where the rust, and moth consume, and where thieves break through and steal. . . . For where thy treasure is, there is thy heart also."[88] Clearly, education, in its guidance of youth regarding natural goods, must steer a middle course between the two extremes of neglect and excess.

As we have seen, no created good can satisfy man as his ultimate end. Natural happiness is only his relative ultimate end. Only the uncreated good, God, can fully satisfy him, and it is this good which is his true

---

[85] *Summa*, I–II, q. 4, a. 6 and 7; also q. 5, a. 5.
[86] Cf. Grenier, *op. cit.*, IV, 38–42. This operation will therefore be rooted in his specifically rational faculties, viz., his intellect and will, and will attain the most perfect objects they can in this life, viz., the natural knowledge and love of God. Cf. Gredt, *op. cit.*, II, p. 326.
[87] Maritain, *Preface to Metaphysics*, p. 125.
[88] Mt. 6:19, 21.

ultimate end. Only in the possession of this uncreated good can he find complete happiness. He may seek his ultimate happiness in other goods; all will fail him.

The ultimate end is God SUPERNATURALLY attained. Hypothetically, this possession of the ultimate good could have been possible for man in a state of natural beatitude in a future life, in which state his natural desire for happiness would have been satisfied. In that event, knowledge of God would have been provided him by created intellectual species representing the divine nature analogously, after the manner of, yet more perfectly than, the intellectual species of this life. From Revelation, however, we know that man is no longer limited to the natural order and its purely natural ends. No state of mere natural beatitude awaits him after death.

God, with incomprehensible love and gratuity, has raised man to a supernatural level, has given him a supernatural ultimate end, which is none other than the vision and possession of God Himself as He is in Himself in heaven — *Deus sicuti est,* according to the terminology of theology. This special vision of God is expounded by St. Paul when he says we shall see God "face to face";[89] and by St. John, "we shall see him as he is."[90] We find a reference to it also in the words of Christ: "Blessed are the clean of heart; for they shall see God."[91] This face to face vision of God is called the *Beatific Vision* and it is the true ultimate end for all men without any satisfactory alternative. Attain it they must, or fail miserably and irreparably and be ever outside that irradiant divine happiness, suffering eternally the consequences of the deliberate spurning — as free agents — of their elevation to the level of the Godhead and their invitation to share His heavenly riches:[92] "Lay not up to yourselves treasures on earth. . . . But lay up to yourselves treasures in heaven."[93]

---

[89] 1 Cor. 13:12.   [90] 1 Jn. 3:2.   [91] Mt. 5:8:

[92] Mt. 25:34, 41, 46. "Then shall the king say to them that shall be on his right hand: Come, ye blessed of my Father, possess you the kingdom prepared for you from the foundation of the world. . . . Then he shall say to them also that shall be on his left hand: Depart from me, you cursed, into everlasting fire which was prepared for the devil and his angels. . . . And these shall go into everlasting punishment: but the just, into life everlasting." There is no third choice.

Very few people openly repudiate the Bible. Many conveniently ignore it. As a bound book they treat it with respect — and gild its edges! Hence it is fashionable even in educational literature to refer to it piously, if platitudinously. But as an opened book — historical, authentic, pertinent — whose pages teem with varied and explicit directives, divine directives, it is so often ignored.

The great dilemma stands, however. If its positive truths and directives be hocus pocus to be merely disregarded, why such piousness about that "great textbook of life," etc. If it be true, its statements, such as the quotation above, sound very important, personally important, and worthy of efficacious attention.

[93] Mt. 6:19, 20.

These considerations point up the logic of Pius XI's insistence:[94]

It is therefore as important to make no mistake in education, as it is to make no mistake in the pursuit of the last end, with which the whole work of education is intimately and necessarily connected. In fact, since education consists essentially in preparing man for what he must be and for what he must do here below, in order to attain the sublime end for which he was created, it is clear that there can be no true education which is not wholly directed to man's last end.

All this gives the reason for our insistence that no false dichotomy is to be made between "ordinary" and "Catholic" education.

The ultimate end, then, of a man's education, as of all his human acts, is the possession of God in the Beatific Vision. Indeed, education is very intimately connected with this last end, since it is essentially a preparation of man for the living of this life in such a way that he attains the Beatific Vision in the next life. Catholic education is not narrowed or made contemptuous of this life by having its ultimate end located in the next life according to the supernatural order. Rather it is immeasurably enriched and extended, because it has another dimension running off this earth into infinity. Behold the breadth and the importance of Christian education!

Summary

"End" can signify a termination, an object, a purpose for the sake of which something is done. We are chiefly concerned here with end as a purpose for which something is done, i.e., as a cause.

Broadly speaking, a cause is something which in some way contributes to the production of another thing. Strictly speaking a cause is a positive principle from which something really proceeds by a positive and intrinsic influx and on which it is dependent in being; the precise notion of a cause is to be found in that perfection of a thing whereby it has something depending on it in regard to being. Cause and effect differ from mere succession. A cause differs radically from a condition — even a condition *sine qua non* — and from an occasion, since neither of these has any positive influx into the being of the effect; at the most they can be called causes *per accidens*. The four kinds of causes *per se* are material, formal, efficient, and final. An example will illustrate the difference between a cause, a condition, and an occasion in regard to the one effect. Carnegie Hall is illuminated. A recital by Schnabel may be the occasion; pressing the switch is a condition; electricity is the cause. Locke, Hume, and Kant have been prominent among modern philosophers in impugning

---

[94] Pius XI, *Christian Education of Youth*, pp. 4–5.

the true notion of causality; but the validity of causality, accepted even by the Greeks, stands unshaken. The world is not a chaos of random activity; there are true causes producing true effects. It is consoling to the teacher to know that his planned activity need not be barren.

The end is truly a cause and its effects are the simple love of the end precisely insofar as it is elicited by the will, the act by which the will tends to the end as something to be attained through the means, and all those things which pertain to the order of execution — the means willed, the acts of the will regarding these means, and the external actions. The end is formally constituted as a cause in first act, not by knowledge (which is merely a condition *sine qua non*) but by goodness insofar as this goodness is appetible; it becomes a cause in second act by being actually sought. The end exercises its causality by a metaphorical motion; nevertheless, it is a real cause. Indeed it is the first of causes, because, though last in the order of execution, it is first in the order of intention. Being first in the order of intention gives the end a certain pre-eminence. The end is the best in everything and is the guide and measure of the means; their distinctive nature in any operation depends upon the end. The end of education will be the cause of the educational activity leading to that end and will be the guide and measure of that activity. Clearly, the educational activities of both home and school will differ according to the ends proposed. It is both important and practical, therefore, to find the true end of education.

The principle of finality is traditionally and best formulated: *Omne agens agit propter finem.* Every agent acts for the sake of an end, "agent" being understood to include every agent capable of both transient and immanent activity. This principle has also to be understood analogously of God, men, animals, and natural agents having no knowledge. Its validity, though impugned in diverse ways by some writers — materialists, pantheists, positivists, evolutionists — is in practice an accepted part of daily life. It is of itself evident according to the second mode of perseity; its denial leads to absurdity and to a violation of the principle of sufficient reason. Since every agent acts for an end, the teacher and the student must have a clear and compelling end in order to teach and to learn.

The principal divisions of end were noted.

The proper and immediate end of education is that end which education, conceived as a whole, should attain *per se* and proximately without the mediation of any other ends.

With the ultimate end "the whole work of education is intimately and necessarily connected."[95] The proper and immediate end of education is

---

[95] Pius XI, *loc. cit.*

along the road to this ultimate end which, then, must be rightly understood. To understand it better, we surveyed these points:

There is an ultimate end of human life.

In every human action a man acts at least virtually in view of a last end considered both formally and materially.

No man can, at one and the same time, act efficaciously for two diverse, absolute, ultimate ends.

The ultimate end, considered formally, is the same for all men; it is the realization of perfect happiness. But in what is this happiness to be found? (This is what is meant by the ultimate end considered materially.) In point of fact people seek this happiness in various created goods, but in doing so they are mistaken.

The ultimate end is not to be found in created goods.

a) Not in external goods — wealth, reputation, etc.

b) Not in internal goods whether of body or soul. Health, bodily development and preservation, bodily pleasure are inept and even dangerous as an ultimate end. Neither the soul nor any good inhering in it can be the ultimate good that should be sought in life or in education.

N.B. In the natural order, happiness is man's ultimate end (relative). This natural happiness consists in virtuous activity proper to him as man; yet it is an imperfect happiness. For this natural happiness goods of body such as health, food, clothing, the operation of vegetative and sensitive powers, the society of friends are all needed. We classify these as quasi-instrumental requisites. No sound system of education can neglect them. In them, however, the extremes of neglect and excess must be avoided; each would mar happiness.

The ultimate end is to be found only in the uncreated good, namely, God. Only God is a good without limitation. Only in God, therefore, can man be completely happy.

The ultimate end is God SUPERNATURALLY attained. Hypothetically, it could have been possible for him in the next life to attain the uncreated good in a natural way in a state of natural beatitude. In point of fact, however, he has no such natural end awaiting him in the next life. For man depends absolutely on his Creator, God; and God, with incomprehensible love and gratuity, has elevated him to a supernatural status by sanctifying grace, communicating to him a share in His own divine nature, giving him a *supernatural end* of ineffable happiness — the Beatific Vision. This alone is man's true, objective, ultimate end. Here alone can he find his perfect happiness. Attain this end he must, or fail irreparably and suffer eternally in hell for having freely spurned the extraordinary generosity of the divine invitation to heaven's riches.

With stakes so high and consequences so disastrous "it is important to make no mistake in education . . . since education consists essentially in preparing man for what he must be and for what he must do here below, in order to attain [this] sublime end."[96]

We saw in passing some basic implications for a number of educational issues: motivation, its nature[97] and qualities;[98] guidance and counseling;[99] the irreplaceable necessity for clear aims[100] a consoling truth for those schools whose ideals are clear but whose funds are low; the grades of self-activity;[101] the essential limitation of all comparisons from animal to human learning;[102] student understanding of educational aims;[103] the simplification of these aims;[104] eclecticism;[105] self-indulgence and false "self-expression" in education.[106]

Now, with our general concepts of end sharpened and arranged like a surgeon's instruments, we shall dissect the proper and immediate end of education. We will begin by considering the opinions of various people about this end and thus "by indirections find directions out."[107]

---

[96] *Loc. cit.*
[97] *Supra*, p. 23.
[98] *Supra*, pp. 25, 26.
[99] *Supra*, p. 26.
[100] *Supra*, pp. 28–29.
[101] *Supra*, pp. 29–30.

[102] *Supra*, p. 31.
[103] *Loc. cit.*
[104] *Supra*, pp. 33–34.
[105] *Supra*, p. 41.
[106] *Supra*, pp. 41, 43.
[107] *Hamlet*, Act II, Sc. 1.

CHAPTER **III**

OPINIONS ABOUT THE END
OF EDUCATION

IT IS manifestly impossible to consider or even to list all the opinions expressed by theorists and teachers about the ends of education. Nor can we here give an adequate historical conspectus of the development of even the principal opinions. We present only some of those opinions offered by prominent movements and men. Rather than confine ourselves to contemporaries, we have thought it useful to review briefly the con- tribution made by some early educators of the modern era — the Humanistic Realists, Sense Realists, Rousseau, etc. We have selected the opinions for consideration insofar as they provide special viewpoints whose analysis will be helpful in emphasizing what we believe to be important aspects of the proper and immediate end of education.

Any adverse remarks made in assessing these opinions are intended purely as critical and in no way as invidious.

Humanistic Realists

Rabelais (1483–1553), Mulcaster (1531–1611), and Montaigne (1533– 1592), insofar as they can be grouped together, are considered as Humanistic Realists.[1] Humanistic Realism was a reaction against the ultraliterary aspects of Humanism. It would make the end of education a practical adjustment to reality chiefly through study of the classics, since the classics were considered to be exhaustive founts of reality in all its aspects. Thus the knowledge of reality it so highly prized would be sought chiefly, but not exclusively, in the classics. The educand's acquisition of the spirit and meaning of the classics was the special immediate work of education.[2]

Certainly we agree that the end of education must not be an imaginary

---

[1] Cf. Patrick J. McCormick and Francis P. Cassidy, *History of Education* (3rd ed. rev., Washington, D. C.: The Catholic Education Press, 1953), pp. 440–453.

[2] J. Redden and F. Ryan, *A Catholic Philosophy of Education* (Milwaukee: The Bruce Publishing Co., 1951), p. 63. Cf. Pierre J. Marique, *History of Christian Education* (3 vols., New York: Fordham University Press, 1926), II, pp. 200–205.

or an artificial one; it must be rooted in reality. The vital question is: What is the exact notion of reality? And what is the precise, particular good which is sought as the proper and immediate end of education as such? In regard to the emphasis on the realistic study of the literary classics a phrase of Pugin's could well be adapted to the effect that there is a danger lest reality would be only the grandmother, not the mother, of knowledge.

Sense Realism[3]

Francis Bacon (1561–1626) is the first name that comes to mind in speaking of the Sense Realists. Ratke and Comenius are notable followers. Sense Realism would make education an adjustment to reality through the practical mastery of nature, by understanding nature's laws and developing its potentialities.

The same crucial consideration of reality arises here as it did above. Insofar as Bacon and his followers were occupied with nature they were in touch with only the half of reality, because man *de facto* has been elevated to a supernatural order and put in touch with a supernatural reality. Man has been given a supernatural reality as his true, absolute, ultimate end.[4] And since every other end is sought in virtue of the ultimate end and must be ordained to it,[5] it follows that man's education cannot have an exclusively natural end, since that would be in a different sphere. One might as well try to reach the sea by heading inland. This consideration excludes *ab ovo* any aim of education that is exclusively natural, no matter how it is camouflaged or tinseled. Therefore when Spencer, some two centuries after Bacon, said that the aim of education was complete living[6] he gave us acceptable words but an unacceptable idea because he meant the words to express a notion of complete *material* living.

Insofar as Bacon concentrated on the *knowledge* of reality — "I have taken all knowledge to be my province"[7] — he was concerned with only the half of man's perfection; man is capable of more than knowledge. He has other powers besides the powers of knowledge. Are not his willing and doing to be guided and perfected by his education? Bacon's overemphasis on knowledge is positively unacceptable.

"*Scientia et potentia humana in ipsum coincidunt,*" he wrote.[8] "Knowledge is power" sums up his attitude. But knowledge can be misguided

---

[3] McCormick and Cassidy, *op. cit.*, pp. 455–473.
[4] *Supra*, p. 46.
[5] *Supra*, p. 39.
[6] Cf. H. Spencer, *Education: Intellectual, Moral, and Physical* (New York: D. Appleton and Co., 1886).
[7] Cited by Marique, *op. cit.*, II, p. 214.
[8] *Ibid.*, p. 215.

power unless something more is given the educand than mere knowledge. Knowledge without moral formation is simply a weapon in the hands of a criminal. The reason is that man's intellect, being of its nature limited by its partial dependence on the senses for its operation and being moreover darkened by original sin, is unable to grasp what is true and good so perfectly that his will necessarily adheres to it. Hence in this life to *know* what is right and objectively good does not necessarily mean to *do* what is right and to seek what is good. Therefore a man's education as a total process must be seriously concerned with more than the attainment of mere knowledge, even though this were to include the highest levels of knowledge — even metaphysics. His deficiency shows itself not merely in errors of the intellect but in the bad tendencies of his appetites.[9]

The proper and immediate end of education must, then, be concerned with more than natural reality, and more than mere knowledge.

Rousseau

The name of Rousseau (1712–1778) is almost synonymous with the movement in education called Naturalism. Naturalism can, of course, have many forms. With Rousseau it represented a sloughing of what he regarded as conventions (some of them rather fundamental!), freedom from social inhibitions, and the unhindered following of the caprices of nature, higher and lower, until such time as morality would be learned by natural consequences. *Emile* is the book that expounded this twaddle. Freed from some of its worst excesses, the germ of this theory entered education's blood stream and produced a condition that is, in part, still with us.

Historically, some good ideas and techniques have followed in the wake of Rousseau. Whatever is good in these has a value independently of Rousseau's basic principle, because his self-indulgent and capricious back-to-nature viewpoint is unsound.[10] The end of man's education, as we saw in considering Bacon, cannot be purely natural. Rousseau's concept of this reign of nature is untenable even from natural reason, apart altogether from supernatural considerations. To allow man in his human acts to be dominated by the whim of lower passion is to subject a higher order to a lower, to permit his immaterial powers to be dominated by his material powers. It is a deordination, contrary to simple reason. It would, moreover, be a will-o'-the-wisp satisfaction that could never lead him to true happiness.[11]

Rousseau's own life is a practical refutation of his theories. If he

---

[9] Cf. St. Thomas Aquinas, *Comm. in Eth., op. cit.*, Bk. 6, lect. II.

[10] *Supra*, p. 52.

[11] *Supra*, p. 42 f.

lived his life in America today and practiced the things he wrote, he would surely be barred from respectable homes and be on the black lists of courts and child-welfare agencies!

The proper end of education is not to be found in the return to the so-called state of nature.

Developmentalism

In general, the proximate end of education for writers with this viewpoint is a degree of personal perfection self-educed from one's innate natural endowment. The development is to take place in a permissive atmosphere provided by the agencies of education. Each of its prominent advocates has his own particular modification; and some are more optimistic than others regarding the child's innate endowment, the nature and manner of his development, etc. It will readily be seen that this view has a suggestion of Rousseau's naturalism; historically, it has a link with his views. Basedow, Pestalozzi, Froebel, and G. Stanley Hall are prominent among those who can be regarded as subscribing to this general view. These are big names in European and American education, men of sincerity and dedication, men who made many notable contributions to modern education.

Developmentalism, however, in this sense is naturalistic and unsound. It is not all bad; neither is it all good. We do not have to accept the bad nor be blind to it because of the good. By making the proper distinctions we can retain the good, which is gold in its own right, and discard the dross.

It is entirely acceptable but incomplete to say that education is a process of self-development whose proper object is a degree of self-perfection. That is just another way of saying that education is immanent human activity whose term is the perfection of the agent.

It is, however, wrong to understand the educand's "innate, natural endowment" in such a way as would postulate the entire goodness of newborn human nature, requiring only a kindly freedom to develop and bloom like the rose.[12] This viewpoint overlooks the fact that man is born in original sin and hence is wounded in his nature,[13] that his intellect is darkened (not a startling assertion for teachers, surely) and his will weakened. Thus the child is born neither wholly good nor wholly bad

---

[12] "In view of the original soundness and wholeness of man, all arbitrary (active) prescriptive and categorical, interfering education in instruction and training must, of necessity, annihilate, hinder, and destroy" (F. W. Froebel, *The Education of Man*, trans. by W. N. Hailmann [New York: D. Appleton and Co., 1887], p. 9, quoted in McCormick-Cassidy, *op. cit.*, p. 551). In this viewpoint expressed so simply by Froebel we have the genesis of the extreme antiauthoritarianism attitude.

[13] *Vulneratus in naturalibus* is the accepted theological phraseology.

Therefore it can be said on the one hand that educational guidance is needed, on the other that education need never be pessimistic.

It is likewise wrong to understand the child's innate, natural endowment in such a way as would *include* his elevation to the supernatural order of grace, thereby vitiating the absolute gratuity of that elevation. Froebel believed in some sort of special divine spark possessed *naturally* by man.[14] This is a tinge of Pantheism.

It is wrong to understand this "self-educed" development in a way that is almost evolutionary,[15] or even as an ordinary natural process independent of grace as the principle of salutary acts.[16]

It is wrong to understand the "degree of perfection" to which the educand is to develop as a status of purely natural perfection or a mutilated supernatural perfection, as will be clear from what has already been said about man's gratuitous orientation to an objective supernatural end. He has no absolute natural ultimate end.

The words of Pope Pius are relevant and precise:[17]

> Every method of education founded, wholly or in part, on the denial or forgetfulness of original sin and of grace, and relying on the sole powers of human nature, is unsound. Such, generally speaking, are those modern systems bearing various names which appeal to a pretended self-government and unrestrained freedom on the part of the child, and which diminish or even suppress the teacher's authority and action, attributing to the child an exclusive primacy of initiative, and an activity independent of any higher law, natural or divine, in the work of his education.

The proper and immediate end of education cannot be a degree of personal perfection self-educed from one's innate natural endowment, even if a permissive atmosphere provided by the agencies of education be regarded as a necessary condition of that development. One might as well try to build a patient to health by transfusions from his own

---

[14] Cf. McCormick and Cassidy, *op. cit.,* pp. 550–551.

[15] It is interesting to note that the legitimate meaning of the very word "education" is to rear, to nourish, to bring up. "The term *education* is derived from the Latin verb *educare,* and not from the Latin verb *educere* (to lead, bring forth or out), as is commonly supposed. Thus, Quintilian wrote: *Si mihi tradatur educandus orator.* Thus, Cicero: *In dedecore natus, ad turpitudinem educatus.* Thus also Plautus: *Ille homo hominis non aliit, verum educat, recreatque*" (Redden and Ryan, *op. cit.,* p. 22).

[16] Salutary acts demand a supernatural principle whence they spring and supernatural assistance from God. Only salutary acts are meritorious for heaven. The matter of the act can be any naturally good act — e.g., eating, sleeping, working, studying, recreating oneself in a normal way — directed and elevated by grace. It would be erroneous to think that only acts of religion, such as praying, etc., can be salutary acts.

[17] Pius XI, *Christian Education of Youth,* p. 24.

sickly blood — even if a "permissive atmosphere" be provided by a warm hospital bed and the best of attention.

John Dewey

Dewey despised the concept of finality. He was absolutely opposed to "the rigid clamp of fixed ends." This phrase gives an interesting clue to his whole attitude.

When he did approximate to the formulation of something like an end of education — because even Dewey, despite all his expressed contempt, could not evade the metaphysical necessity for finality — he expressed himself thus:

> The object and reward of learning is continued capacity for growth.[1]
> There is nothing to which education is subordinate save more education.[19]
> Keeping constant the part of the individual in the life process the determinant aim of education is "social efficiency in a democracy."[20]
> In our search for aims in education, we are not concerned, therefore with finding an end outside of the educative process to which education is subordinate. Our whole conception forbids.[21] [In other words the educational process has no end outside itself; it is its own end.
> Education . . . is a process of living and not a preparation for future living.[22]

Other statements expressing his views in other words could be gathered from his voluminous writings because his writing was consistent with his basic outlook in that he dipped his pen in the mood of the moment. The above statements may be summarized thus: Education is its own end; education is ordained only to more of it; it is foolish to look for fixed ends, especially if it be question of future realization, for education is in and for the present; its determinant aim is "social efficiency in a democracy." Education cannot be its own end. Only God can be His own end. Clearly, Dewey has no understanding of true finality and has nothing positive to offer toward the accurate solution of our problem.

Briefly we treat of the end of education as more education, the fear that finality means fixity, and the emphasis on social efficiency in a democracy.

Dewey's insistence on continued, never ending educational growth as

---

[18] J. Dewey, *Democracy and Education* (New York: The Macmillan Co., 1937) p. 117.

[19] *Ibid.*, p. 60.

[20] James O'Hara, *op. cit.*, p. 56.

[21] J. Dewey, *Democracy and Education*, p. 117.

[22] J. Dewey, *My Pedagogic Creed* (New York: Kellogg & Co., 1897), p. 7.

ts own object and end is a sterile thing. Progress does not consist in
oing, going, going; but in going somewhere, going to the right place
r condition, and going in the best way. Education, like every process,
nust have some ultimate end which it seeks incessantly and in which
t will finally rest. Along the way, it will have its own proper end and
erhaps intermediate ends, all desirable for their own sake, yet all
teppingstones to the absolute ultimate end in the next life in which
he agent will find rest and happiness. Acceptance of finality does not
nean, as Dewey seemed to fear, that at some precise moment the
tudent would close all his books irrevocably, declare his whole educa-
ion accomplished, and take up a life of golf or daily trifles. Its
acceptance does not prevent the retiring professor from saying, "Forty
years a teacher, but all my life a student"; neither did it dissuade
he monk Cassiodorus from writing yet another book, *De Orthographia,*
n his ninety-third year.

Dewey seems to fear moreover that the acceptance of the principle
f finality would clamp life and education to an ironlike rigidity; at
ther times he implies that ends accepted and retained would somehow
aint and corrupt, like old milk turned sour. This fear seems reducible
o a notion of end as some particular good *in concreto* which could, like
hariots, powder horns, or papyri, become obsolete as a goal worthy of
roductive activity. This is of course a pathetically imaginative attitude
oward finality, a head-in-matter view that has not yet glimpsed the
tars of transcendent truth; for finality, as purest metaphysics, belongs
loft in the farthest universe of intelligible truth. As we have seen,
inality indeed indicates the one, ultimate, objective good in which
mmutably man's happiness is found; but it does not restrict man
igidly to the pursuit of some *particular* objective goods — which of
heir nature are limited in goodness. Finality does assert that man in
ll his acts seeks his good as an end, but does not assert that there is
 list of some twenty or thirty immutable, particular, existing goods
vhich alone he may seek, neglecting all others. For example, we see
he verification of finality in man's quest for food; but we do not
hereby limit him to sauerkraut only and always — and unimproved!

The fact that there is one, ultimate, universal, immutable good and
hat man in all his activity should seek those particular goods which
est lead him to this ultimate good in heaven does not imprison him
n rigid mental bars. He who gains All is not confined and not pitiable;
nd the happiest progress consists not in going anywhere in any manner,
ut in going to the right place in the best manner.

C. S. Lewis, in a masterly address worthy of a great *littérateur* and
 venerable university, inaugurated his lectureship at Cambridge with
vords that are particularly relevant for Dewey. "How has it come
bout that we use the highly emotive word 'stagnation,' with all its

malodorous and malarial overtones, for what other ages have called 'permanence'?"[23] We, in vindicating finality and examining the proper and immediate end of education, are not concerned about stabilizing rigidly the particular, concrete goods and "values" that bedeck the contemporary scene. But, without neglecting the tangible things of life, we are looking in the realm of intelligibles for the abiding values that will give our education *"permanence."*

Dewey speaks of social efficiency in a democracy as *the* aim for education. This cannot be. Even if he understood "end" in the true philosophic sense, this aim would still be unacceptable.

Man is indeed a social being by nature since, to attain happiness in life, he has an indispensable need of society. This need is felt in regard to his health — care in infancy, sickness, and old age; in regard to protection against enemies and dangers of various sorts; in regard to the skills, sciences, and arts in life which no man alone could adequately foster; in regard to the counsel and instruction needed to live virtuously. From all these natural exigencies, it is clear that he is placed by nature in a condition that needs society.

There is, however, some discussion as to the details of the relationship between the individual and society; for example, whether or not the proper ends of the individual man can be *per se* directed to the ends of civil society, where these ends are considered as intermediate ends or a relative ultimate end.[24] We do not propose here to enter into this discussion.

But there is no doubt whatever about the subordination of the proper ends of man, and therefore of his education, to the natural ends of society where these are considered as the absolute ultimate end. Such a subordination cannot be; because man, elevated to the supernatural order, cannot have a natural end as his absolute ultimate end. Pius X gives authoritative expression to the mutual relationship of man and society:

---

[23] C. S. Lewis, *De Descriptione Temporum* (Cambridge, England: Cambridge University Press, n.d.), p. 16. In rich language he depicts the cultural gulf between contemporary man and man of the first eighteen centuries A.D. — the widest gulf in all European history.

[24] Cf. Grenier, *op. cit.,* IV, pp. 367–373. Holding a different view are: R. Garrigou-Lagrange, "Subordination of the State to The Perfection of Man According to St. Thomas," *The Philosophy of Communism* (New York: Fordham University Press, 1949), No. 3; also Jacques Maritain, *The Rights of Man and the Natural Law* (New York: Charles Scribner's Sons, 1943); also R. J. Harvey, *The Metaphysical Relation between Person and Liberty* (Washington, D. C.: The Catholic University of America Press, 1942); also J. H. Hoban, *The Thomistic Concept of Person and Some of its Social Implications* (Washington, D. C.: The Catholic University of America Press, 1939).

In the plan of the Creator, society is a natural means which man can and must use to reach his destined end. Society is for man and not vice versa. This must not be understood in the sense of liberalistic individualism, which subordinates society to the selfish use of the individual; but only in the sense that by means of an organic union with society and by mutual collaboration the attainment of earthly happiness is placed within the reach of all. . . .

Man cannot be exempted from his divinely-imposed obligations toward civil society. . . . Society, on the other hand, cannot defraud man of his God-given rights. . . .[25]

Elsewhere, the same Pope utters words which serve as commentary and reinforcement for the above. He says that it is a "basic fact that man as a person possesses rights which he holds from God and which must be protected against any attempt on the part of the community to deny them or hinder their exercise or suppress them."[26] Therefore, any subordination of man's proper ends to a social good that is exclusively natural is false as we saw in considering Bacon; and this is precisely Dewey's viewpoint. It is, accordingly, to be repudiated. Orientate the person to the state in a naturalistic way — call it democracy, call it any name as sweet as the rose — and you submerge him in waves that could easily rise to totalitarianism. In passing, we can admire the wonderful balance that the Christian view preserves between man and society. The two are perfectly harmonized; but man is always the root of the harmony.

There is also another reason why the cliché, "Social efficiency in a democracy," is unacceptable. The utterance of the reason would be regarded in some quarters as shocking;[27] but it is the cold truth. It has never been proved that democracy is the only legitimate, or even the best form of government for all men of all races in every age. It is merely one legitimate genus of government specially suited to certain races at certain stages of development. The word "genus" is used designedly to provide for the fact that it is hard to get international unanimity among democracy's protagonists for the acceptance of a precise, specific statement of

[25] Pius XI, *Divini Redemptoris, AAS,* XXIX (1937), trans. in *The Ecclesiastical Review,* XCVI (1937), pp. 494–495. Another English translation may be had in a pamphlet edition by the America Press. For an excellent commentary on this passage, *vide* John P. Lerhinan, *A Sociological Commentary on "Divini Redemptoris"* (Washington, D. C.: The Catholic University of America Press, 1946), pp. 91–103.

[26] *Mit Brennender Sorge, AAS,* XXIX (1937), 159.

[27] Democracy developed strongly as a vogue in education between 1930–1940, becoming almost a substitute for religion, clothed with a religious terminology as a "creed," a "faith," an "ethics," with quasi commandments in the form of "ten abiding values." Cf. especially Gordon C. Lee, *An Introduction to Education in America* (New York: Henry Holt and Co., 1952), pp. 34, 79, 97, 476, 489.

how ideal democratic government should be organized. Different form of government are legitimate "as long as they are of such a nature as to insure the attainment of the common good."[28] Therefore democracy, as something arbitrary and partially relative to race and milieu, cannot be the proper end of that education which befits man *as man*. This is no treason, not an attack on Congress, certainly not a subtle plea for Kremlin rule. It is simply that honest recognition of reality that keeps men and trends sane. Gold is a precious thing in its own natural order and is valued and sought by all. Democratic welfare is likewise a precious thing in its own order — a legitimate and highly acceptable form of government, justly valued and desired. But elevated to a pedestal as a creed, a doctrine, a faith, an ultimate ideal, it becomes merely another golden calf to which, amid educational clamor and confusion, some offer a devotion and a service that is inept for good because inordinate.

Much more could be written in analysis and refutation of "Deweyism" on finality, but it would have to be a general reiteration of epistemology and metaphysics; it would, moreover, be the mere flogging of a limping horse already on its way to the educational museum, there to be preserved and studied for its very oddity. Neo-Realists, Essentialists, Educational Idealists, Humanists, even irate parents and disillusioned teachers are hurrying it along.[29]

The proper and immediate end of education cannot be a *per se* social or nationalistic aim. This proper end must not be conceived as something that will give rigidity to education. Its quest is simply a search for those educational values that befit man *as man* and that are as permanent and as universal as his human nature.

Theodore Brameld

It is difficult to assess Brameld's thinking and to assign it a proper place in the general consideration of finality. To attempt to clothe

---

[28] Lerhinan, *op. cit.*, p. 97.

[29] "Progressive education is being spanked. The chastisement is not taking place quietly in the family woodshed. It is open to the public, and all who care to lend a hand are cordially invited to participate. Professional educators, popular writers, and 'just plain folks' are responding with a will, and the general applause drowns the feeble cries of the victim." This was written by a Progressivist, P. F. Valentine, "Progressive Education — A Defence," *Educational Forum*, V (1941), 277. Cf. the mention of parental dissatisfaction in some quarters, Howard Whitman, "The Struggle for Our Children's Minds: Our Schools — Afraid to Teach," *Colliers* (March 19, 1954), 34–40.

"It is plain that lay opinion of the Progressive school as herein evaluated is heavily weighted on the adverse side. . . .

"In the light of these considerations, it seems safe to conclude that the progressive school has not as yet been accepted wholeheartedly by the general public" (Sister Mary Ruth Sandifer, *American Lay Opinion of the Progressive School* [Washington, D. C.: The Catholic University of America Press, 1943], pp. 198–200).

Brameld in Scholasticism would be impossible, and at the same time an unwarranted liberty; for he is very definitely not Scholastic — "non-perennialist" he would probably say. His thought is in a different world. It is essentially relativistic. There can be no question, then, of indicating precisely what, in his view, is the proper and immediate end of education. He would proudly claim that he has no view on the matter and therein he would regard himself as the glimmer of hope against a dark, stifling, reactionary background of perennialism.[30] We will try to represent his views in his own words as far as possible.

Reconstructionism, as he entitles his views, is by no means a finished philosophy;[31] hence, the goals of education have not been "fully delineated" nor "will ever be, to everyone's satisfaction."[32] Yet it is important to have clear ends.[33] It is imperative that we "specify the goals of our culture" and for this reason he says that it is "imperative that we specify the ·ends of human nature."[34] However, he seems to eschew the notion that man is "a goal-seeking animal"; he gives this concept the headline "INADEQUACY OF A BELIEF LONG HELD" and goes on to say that "no single view could better illustrate how philosophic beliefs always hover in the coldly impartial atmosphere of laboratories."[35] His idea of a goal is not of something to be attained as an outcome, but something which interacts actively with the means thereto so that "while the end-in-view conditions and refines the functions needed to arrive at its consummation, these functions constantly remake and hence determine the nature of the outcome itself";[36] thus "the response is constituted by the stimulus and the stimulus by the response."[37] He insists that the end and the means — and above all the end — are never to "crystallize or absolutize in such a way as to become a criterion of the other."[38] Hence the "key interest . . . [is] not the product, but . . . the process or *method,* which we call intelligence."[39] Thus is safeguarded the human being's primary concern "with the ongoing present of continuous means-ends-means-ends-means. . . ."[40] He notes that this interactivity of aims and means is a principle central to Progressivism; but he identifies himself with it. These references will show unmistakably the basic cleavage between Reconstructionism and Scholasticism in the very notion of end.

The goals of education, as Brameld understands "goals," are arrived at by social consensus, which, though not *the* criterion of truth ("experimental intelligence"[41] is also indispensable, he says), is nevertheless the most important single criterion for the *"crucial purposes of goal-seeking*

---

[30] T. Brameld, *op. cit.*, p. 82.
[31] *Ibid.*, p. 83.
[32] *Ibid.*, p. 443.
[33] *Ibid.*, p. 604.
[34] *Ibid.*, p. 441.
[35] *Ibid.*, p. 438.
[36] *Ibid.*, p. 439.
[37] *Ibid.*
[38] *Ibid.*
[39] *Ibid.*
[40] *Ibid.*
[41] *Ibid.*, p. 456.

and *future-making*."[42] Without this consensus whereby "they are agreed upon by the largest possible number" of people, experiences most vital in the social life of any culture are simply not true.[43] He draws his goals from the findings of various sciences and branches of learning, and his first mention of them is anything but convinced. In fact he proposes them very dubiously under the names of the men who he considers championed their importance and, as it were, proposed them for social consensus: "The utopian Fourier was already on the right track. . . . The political-economic philosophers, Marx and Engels, are proving to be sound . . . [regarding the necessities of life]. The psychiatrist, Freud, is right . . . [regarding the need for love]. The sociologist, Thomas, is influential . . . [regarding man's four deepest wishes]. The anthropologist, Malinowski, is convincing in his analysis of 'freedom.' . . . The sociologist, Lynd, is likely to be right in his analysis of human 'cravings.' . . . The social psychologist, Lewin, is gaining experimental verification . . . for his theory of 'need-like tensions.' . . ."[44]

This is the genesis of the list of goals which later in his book[45] he presents with a little more conviction in the following order:

a) Sufficient nourishment
b) Adequate dress
c) Shelter and privacy
d) Sexual expression
e) Physiological and mental health
f) Steady work, steady income
g) Companionship, mutual devotion, belongingness
h) Recognition, appreciation, status
i) Novelty, curiosity, variation, recreation, adventure, growth, creativity
j) Literacy, skill, information
k) Participation, sharing
l) Fairly immediate meaning, significance, order, direction.

Then he seeks for an all-inclusive value to serve as a measuring stick for the present and a normative criterion for the future — a value that will exclude none of the above human wants but will embrace all crucial values in one great synthesis.[46] He finds it in *social-self-realization*. This, he says, is the supreme value. "Through it, economic, political, educational, and personal goals, as well as scientific, esthetic, and religious goals, are sought, interwoven, and fulfilled."[47]

In assessing Brameld's viewpoint from the Scholastic position it is idle to discuss particulars. The real cleavage is in fundamentals; a chasm lies

---

[42] *Ibid.*, p. 457.
[43] *Ibid.*
[44] *Ibid.*, p. 442.

[45] *Ibid.*, pp. 477–478.
[46] *Ibid.*, p. 480.
[47] *Ibid.*, p. 481.

between the two positions. Hence the conflict must be fought out on fundamentals. Brameld's world is naturalistic; he does not recognize God efficaciously, and a fortiori he takes no real cognizance of Revelation. We do both, for reasons advanced in Apologetics.[48] Brameld's position crumbles with the naturalism on which it is based. His relativistic, pragmatic, experimental criterion of truth — another of his favored planks — must likewise be referred to Metaphysics, where it is shown to be mere flotsam at the mercy of whatever casual currents flow in contemporary society. His criterion is in no way worthy of man who was man 5000 years ago and today is essentially the same rational animal. Common sense makes this (social) consensus appear a very dubious norm when one thinks of the difficulty of obtaining even educational consensus, thinks moreover of those yearly conventions wherein little new is agreed to except the next convention's date.

It is apparent that we cannot accept his mercurial concept of end as something never to be stabilized, never to be made a criterion for the means to its attainment; and our reasons will be clear from the pithy propositions quoted in the previous chapter, viz., the end is first in the order of intention, and the end is the guide and measure of the means. Brameld's view would seem to imply that arrival or nonarrival at New York is not a criterion for judging success of efforts to reach New York; or that MacArthur's orderly capture of the Inchon peninsula was not a criterion for judging his success in planning the tactics of capture. It seems that Brameld's unwillingness to stabilize the end as a product and/or a criterion springs from his failure to distinguish between the end in the abstract and in the concrete, between the formality which is sought and the objective material thing in which it is sought.[49] Perhaps he would fear for example that "adequate dress" as a fixed value and end would somehow bind us to the wearing of the toga or the animal skin of former ages, without the freedom of modification.

Most of the particular values he lists we would and do wholeheartedly accept — if they be properly understood. We would make of them educational accessories, certainly not ultimates, not even proper and immediate ends. Education ordained *directly* and exclusively to the attaining of these values would be an education ordained directly to those external goods of wealth and reputation and those internal goods of body and soul that we have already excluded as ultimate ends in the previous chapter.

His supreme value is social-self-realization! To man's self-realization according to his nature and supernature, we say an emphatic yes; to *social*-self-realization, whereby man fulfills his role in the brotherhood of man according to Christian charity under the Fatherhood of God, again

[48] *Supra,* Chap. I, n. 8.   [49] *Supra,* p. 57.

yes. But this meaning is a world apart from the naturalistic, pragmatic sense in which Brameld proposes the term as the end of education; and in that sense we cannot choose but reject it. We have already, in discussing Dewey, considered the unacceptability of man's intrinsic subservience to a purely social end.

Little light regarding the proper and immediate end of education is to be found in the pages of Reconstructionism.

William Chandler Bagley

Bagley has an exalted ideal for education. For him it is a vital issue, and teaching is a delicate and complex art. The earnestness in his writings is apparent. His general viewpoint is know as Essentialism.

Naturally Bagley does not use our terminology of finality, but it seems that his concept of the proper and immediate end of education is expressed equivalently in these words:

> It is the prime task of education to see to it that the useful modifications of conduct that have been accumulated with the experience of the race are transmitted safely from generation to generation.[50]

> The paramount problem of education becomes, therefore, the *conservation of experience;* and the materials of education are the controls of conduct which represent the resultants of that experience. Of these controls, not all are worthy of perpetuation. Changing conditions bring changed needs and demand new adjustments. Thus the task of selecting for survival the essential elements of experience is one of the most troublesome constructive problems of the educator.[51]

He classifies these modifications of conduct whose communication and transmission is the prime task of education as habits and skills, knowledge, ideals and emotionalized standards, and attitudes.[52]

We commend Bagley for his concern about drifting values and for his genuine desire to salvage the essential heritage of humanity. But the essential heritage as he sees it is humanitarian and hence naturalistic; the criterion for selecting the essentials that are to survive is largely a common consensus, usually implicit and tainted with Relativism. Suppose a particular society was dedicated to wife-beating! Consensus or no consensus, we hold that this would be a violation of the objective norm of charity which is rooted absolutely in God and which is independent of all human consensus.

---

[50] W. C. Bagley, *Educational Values* (New York: The Macmillan Co., 1915), p. 14.
[51] *Loc. cit.*
[52] W. C. Bagley, *Education and the Emergent Man* (New York: Thomas Nelson and Sons, 1934), pp. 76–77.

Bagley's viewpoint is unacceptable on another score. By stressing the social heritage, by declaring that "folkways and mores are social institutions" — and he expressly mentions respect for life, property, and marital fidelity as an example of these "mores" — by declaring that the "so-called human rights are in no sense 'natural' rights [but] are social in their origin and in their significance"[53] he intrinsically and ultimately orientates man, and therefore his education, toward a social good; and this is unacceptable, as we saw in considering Dewey. For us, then, Bagley's prime end of education is falsely founded and is inadequate. Yet because the essential pattern of social and private conduct that Bagley wishes to conserve and transmit is fundamentally and extensively Christian, he is *de facto* largely saved from the potential errors of his viewpoint. And we welcome the blow he strikes for Christian cultural heritage.

The proper and immediate end of man's education cannot be the transmission to the educand of the human "essentials" conceived as the refined residue of social experience.

Frederick S. Breed

Professor Breed offers no explicit answer to the question of the proper and immediate end of education. As a New Realist his thinking is strongly colored with Scientism and he has little patience with philosophizing. He would submit even the field of values to the scientific method.[54] Hence we can only look for an equivalent expression of his view.

He seems to give it in the following words:

> The central task in education is the guidance of learning. A method of instruction is nothing more than a way of performing this function. What learnings shall we cultivate, and how? No other educational problem outweighs this one in importance. More broadly still, no other social problem seems to surpass it in importance. It is the crucial question as to what is to be our general educational and social orientation in the nation, and no question is worthy of more attention today on the part of educational leaders.[55]

How is this guidance to be effected? What is to be its norm? Science. Nothing is exempt from the measuring of science.

> Things and their relations, man and his reactions, including the purposive and the ethical, all come within the comprehensive grasp of science. It evaluates human procedures in terms of results. . . . In this sense educational objectives are determined by scientific investigation.[56]

[53] *Ibid.,* p. 24.
[54] F. S. Breed, *Education and the New Realism* (New York: The Macmillan Co., 1939), p. 18.
[55] *Ibid.,* p. 12.   [56] *Ibid.,* p. 19.

Yet he concedes:

> Whatever view one takes of learning and its guidance, one will have
> to build in part upon assumptions and supplemental hypotheses the
> consequences of whose acceptance cannot be accurately forecast. Such
> assumptions are constructive factors in every field of knowledge.
> Ultimately, in the absence of conclusive experimental evidence, one
> says to himself something like this: I *favor* emphasis on liberty rather
> than on discipline . . . because I *believe* such a policy will produce more
> competent humans and a better commonwealth; and it will do this,
> moreover, because proceeding thus seems to be more in harmony than
> any other policy with our present knowledge of the nature of the
> world and man[57] [italics added].

Breed justifies this attitude by saying that "in the social field no less
than in the religious, faith is an indispensable factor."[58]

This is his view, then. The guidance of learning is the central task of
education. Science provides that guidance — in part. Where science is inadequate, "assumptions and supplemental hypotheses" take over — "I
favor . . . because I *believe* . . . and proceeding thus *seems*." This he calls
faith and justifies by the mere name.

We wholeheartedly agree to the importance of the guidance of learning, but cannot agree that this guidance in and of itself is the central task
of education. Guidance of learning! Learning what? Ma Barker guided the
learning of her children — as professional pickpockets! She guided them
so well that it was some time before the family went to jail and their
effects went to the F. B. I. museum. The mere insistence on guidance is
not enough; it is the norms of guidance that count. Surely that to which
learning is guided is more important than the actual guiding. "The best
in everything is its end."[59] The spectacle is more important than the
ticket of admission and the signposts guiding the way; these exist for
the sake of the spectacle! We are concerned in this investigation with the
end to which learning is to be guided. Knowing it, we can then guide the
educand, just as knowing the location of the shop we can guide someone
else to it. But Breed does not indicate exactly whither he would guide
the educand. Hence, in truth, it must be said that he bypasses the real
issue. His house would have stairs leading the educand up to nowhere —
except clouds.

Breed does indeed indicate the general area in which his values and,
therefore, the end can be found, namely science and "faith." We shall
briefly consider each.

Physical science, if it stays science, can only deal with measurables, that
is, things in some way quantified. It cannot deal directly with im-

---

[57] *Ibid.*, p. 21.   [58] *Ibid.*   [59] *Supra,* Chap. II, n. 45.

measurables, e.g., with philosophical essences, with universals, with trans-cendentals, because all these things pertain to intelligible truth. While it can count the number of good actions when these are overt, it cannot tell us the nature of goodness or judge the goodness of the act since it cannot touch the ultimate end in relation to which goodness is judged. You cannot put kindness into a test tube and heat it to 100 degrees Centigrade! Furthermore science has nothing to say about the super-natural order — its existence, its nature, its acts — because the two are in entirely different realms. One might as well try to weigh a smile on the kitchen scales; and even that would make more sense than trying to put an angel or the love of God under the microscope!

The "faith" which Dr. Breed proposes as justification for the personal "assumptions and supplemental hypotheses" by which learning can be guided is — may we say it without harshness — even more sterile. Some people have "faith" in a rabbit's paw, some had it in Al Capone, some in Hitler. The label "faith" means or proves nothing here. Faith in what? This is the significant issue. And here the answer in all truth must be: Faith in what is colloquially called a "hunch" is Breed's refuge in the higher altitudes of conduct where his science fails him — faith in a personal impression![60] "I favor . . . because I believe such a policy will produce more competent humans and a better commonwealth . . . and pro-ceeding thus seems . . ." Hitler "favored" the confiscation of Czechoslo-vakia and Austria because he "believed" that "such a policy" would "produce more competent" Germans and "a better commonwealth" for the pure-blood German race; and who is to call his faith wrong? Logically, not Breed, except on the basis of his own assumption of "faith" — which also might be equally wrong. Breed's proposed "faith" is no criterion for the guidance of learning. It is entirely subjective.

Catholics have a faith in God on the basis of objective, public revela-tion whose fact and authenticity are historically verifiable according to the most rigorous internal and external criteria. But because we invoke it in solving educational questions we are alternately ignored, pitied, or criticized. Breed simply spells the word and pins it to "assumptions and supplemental hypotheses" that are ultimately personal whims — "I favor . . ." He does it without a literary blush. Yet in this practical twentieth century he is given a place as a leader in educational thinking, as a man devoted to science and in no way a sentimentalist.

Many writers of several schools of thought would quarrel with "guid-ance of learning" as being incomplete on another score for education's

---

[60] Faith in its religious sense has suffered sadly from contemporary Nominalism. Robbed of its rich, clear-cut, theological meaning, it is now used as a cover-all for any surge of sentiment. It is the "nice" word to use and, if spoken, is preferably to be uttered with a mellow warmth of tone, irrespective of its designation — the reference could easily be to "faith" in the fidelity of pets!

central task. They would want "guidance in *doing*" to receive equal or even greater emphasis. This consideration again evokes finality, because the important thing is not just "doing," but doing the right and proper thing; and this can only be judged objectively in relation to an end.

We therefore propose the conclusion that Breed, by a defect in regard to objective finality, misses the real issue in discussing the central task of education.

The Ethical Culture Aim

Under this general heading, we include all those statements of the primary aim of education that emphasize conduct and character, such as: the fostering of "worthy ideals,"[61] "desirable attitudes,"[62] "the good life,"[63] "high ideal and ethical standards,"[64] "spiritual values,"[65] "lofty sentiments of self-regard,"[66] "life-good-to-live,"[67] and many other similar expressions.

This section of the chapter is not meant as a contemptuous indictment of all these educators in their well-meaning attempts to express the correct aim of education. Their earnestness is unquestionable, and their desire to advance education is deserving of the highest praise. But this is the place for a critical appraisal of expressed aims; and the truth is unavoidable. Many of these aims are vague; insofar as they are specific, some are naturalistic and therefore inadequate; others invoke a mutilated religion. We cannot treat each of these points exhaustively here, but an indication of their caliber will not be irrelevant; it will moreover help us to appreciate the logic, the fullness, and the warmth of the Catholic position.

Many of these ethical culture aims are vague: Crow and Crow plead for spiritual values in education, yet say that these "defy definition." They cannot specify these values we are to seek.

Most of these "ethical" aims are naturalistic: Some of their protagonists speak of religion, but their fundamental Naturalism remains. Thus, among educators Bagley represents a conservative and a so-called elevated attitude! He would even advocate the teaching of "religion." But he has

---

[61] A. G. Hughes and E. H. Hughes, *Learning and Teaching* (London: Longmans, Green and Co., 1948), p. 192.

[62] L. D. Crow and A. Crow, *Introduction to Education* (New York: American Book Co., 1950), p. 55.

[63] *Ibid.*, p. 251.

[64] *Ibid.*, p. 479.

[65] *Ibid.*, p. 478.

[66] Hughes and Hughes, *op. cit.*, p. 194.

[67] William H. Kilpatrick, *Philosophy of Education* (New York: The Macmillan Co., 1951), p. 147.

no belief in the afterlife[68] and his teaching of religion is purely naturalistic.[69]

Such naturalistic aims are, to say the least, objectively inadequate. For man's Maker has chosen to give him, quite gratuitously but quite certainly, a supernatural end. Mere Naturalism leaves him far short of his supernatural heights. He might as well try to fly in his boots.[70] This Naturalism is inadequate on another score, too. It leaves man, already clouded in intellect and fickle in will, unequal to the task of coping with the preternatural enemies of his salvation. No doubt such a consideration would evoke immediate amusement in some halls of learning. But if Christ is the Great Teacher,[71] why not pay respectful attention to His teaching! Especially since it is preserved authentically for us — more authentically than Plato's *Republic* and Cicero's *Pro Milone* — in "that great textbook of life,"[72] the Bible! In the Bible we find the Great Teacher saying that the attempt to build virtue while rejecting His words is foredoomed; it would be like "a foolish man that built his house upon the sand . . . and great was the fall thereof."[73] And surely experience illustrates how easily naturalistic religion collapses in the first puff of adversity. Why spurn the words of a great teacher in a great textbook! Christ is either what He claimed to be, God, and therefore to

---

[68] Bagley, *Educational Values.*

[69] Bagley, *Education and the Emergent Man,* pp. 151–154.

[70] We do not here depreciate the law of nature stamped by God in the heart of man to direct him to his proper end and made known to him by right reason. This "natural law," as it is called, is simply the reflection of the Eternal Law. Obviously, God's Revelation in no way repudiates it; Revelation rather clarifies, reinforces, completes, and elevates it in a way altogether beyond the power of unaided reason to dictate. Those who through no personal fault have not been reached by Revelation — the "good tidings," from God — can, by faithfully following this natural law, find a safe and satisfactory path to virtue and to God. Their sincerity is such that they fully carry out what they know is required of them and they would also hear and heed God's positive Revelation if they knew it to be such. They therefore seek God and fulfill His Positive Law implicitly; and the providence of God guides and supports their efforts to live a good life. Their ignorance is not blameworthy, and hence the Catholic Church always has the deepest respect for their sincerity. But whatever about their subjective sincerity and good faith, objectively mere natural standards and natural virtue are inadequate, and hence could not be accepted as the norm and ideal for education.

An entirely different situation is the conscious avoidance, rejection, or mutilation of God's positive Revelation, an unwillingness to investigate it honestly and thoroughly lest plain reason demand the acceptance of its consequences. This attitude, ranging from deliberate ignorance to contemptuous rejection, in no way deserves the extenuation of "good faith," and the compensation of God's supreme providence. Such chosen Naturalism is disastrous both in private life and in education.

[71] Chris A. DeYoung, *op. cit.,* p. 316.

[72] *Loc. cit.*

[73] Mt. 7:24–27. Cf. the comment regarding the Bible in Chap. II, n. 92.

be heard and followed with attention as truly the Great Teacher; or He is an imposter, a fraud, a confidence man, claiming to be what He was not, and therefore in no way to be hailed as the "Great Teacher." The choice and the consequences are clear. A middle position is untenable for anyone with logic enough to ring a fire alarm at the sight of billowing smoke.

The words of Pius XI apply pointedly to this naturalistic ethical culture quest:

> So today we see, strange sight indeed, educators and philosophers who spend their lives in searching for a universal moral code of education, as if there existed no decalogue, no gospel law, no law even of nature stamped by God on the heart of man, promulgated by right reason, and codified in positive revelation by God Himself in the ten commandments. These innovators are wont to refer contemptuously to Christian education as "heteronomous," "passive," "obsolete," because founded upon the authority of God and His holy law.[74]

Even where the ethical aims are religious in their connotation, some of them invoke a mutilated religion. Horne, who is known to be genuinely religious, is one of these. But he errs in a belief about the perfectibility of human nature unaided by grace, a confused idea of the nature of God and unnecessary vagueness regarding the hereafter.[75] In the light of the Revelation given to man, these deficiencies are lamentable. Faith is a seamless garment. Since it is accepted on the authority of God the Revealer, one cannot pick and choose among the truths of faith without substituting one's own or another's whim as the final authority, thereby destroying faith as a supernatural adhesion to God on God's authority, and laying a defective foundation for man's life and education. Hence we must deplore and reject all religious ethical-culture aims except those that are founded both on nature and on the *whole* of objective, public Revelation.[76]

The proper and immediate end of education is not to be found among the so-called "ethical culture" aims.

Summary

With the Realists we agree that the proper and immediate end of education must be a real end that will fit men for dealing with reality; but our interest in the classics does not lead us to regard them as our

---

[74] Pius XI, *Christian Education of Youth,* pp. 24–25.

[75] Sr. Agnes Endres, "The Educational Philosophy of Herman Harrell Horne" (unpublished M.A. thesis, Department of Education, Catholic University of America, Washington, D. C., 1934), p. 76.

[76] *Supra,* 5 ff, 46, 49.

principal contact with reality. This end of education must be concerned with more than merely natural reality, no matter how veneered or tinseled, and more than a mere knowledge of reality, even though it be knowledge of the highest level. It is patently not to be found in habits of self-indulgence, euphemistically called a return to a state of nature.

This end of education is indeed a degree of self-perfection necessarily involving the educand's immanent activity at all levels; but this must not be understood as a perfection exclusively self-educed from the educand's innate natural endowment, even if the provision of a permissive atmosphere by the agencies of education be regarded as a necessary condition of that development. Nor can this self-perfection be called a social-self-realization in Brameld's pragmatic, naturalistic sense.

Educational growth cannot be its own end as Dewey would wish; nor can his "social efficiency in a democracy" be invested with the dignity of a proper end of the education of man *as man*.

Nor can the end be the transmission of "essentials" where these are understood as the working conclusions of social experience. True, education should deal with those things that are essential; but these will need to be determined by a better than pragmatic or relativistic criterion.

The vague, subjective faith posited by Breed is hopelessly inadequate as a criterion of the essentials of reality. The faith we propose as a criterion to complement reason is not vague, not arbitrary. It is faith in God's objective, public Revelation.

The ethical-culture aims point up an important consideration; but they fail to cope with it because in varying degrees they are vague and inadequate, being either wholly naturalistic or, as mutilations of complete Revelation, heretical.

Hence no end of education that is naturalistic can be accepted; no mere sampling of religion suffices.

We have reviewed some opinions about the aim of education. We come now to a consideration of the Catholic, that is, the Christian,[77] view of the proper and immediate end of education.

---

[77] Henceforth in this book we use these two words "Christian" and "Catholic" correlatively for the following reason: We know indeed that "Christian" is a word that has come to mean many things and to be appropriated by diverse groups who feel no illogicality in using the same name. It has come to be one of the "nice" words of the language, its mere utterance spreading a halo; and hence many variant groups desire the reflected glory of the name. But, properly speaking, a "Christian" is "one who believes or professes or is assumed to believe in Jesus Christ, and the truth as taught by him," says *Webster's New Collegiate Dictionary*, 1953. Since Jesus Christ founded a Church and declared and urged the unity of His teachings, it follows that only the Church which *historically goes back* to the group of men He organized as Apostles in the first century and efficaciously accepts *all* His teaching, merits to be called His Church, i.e., the Christian Church. Culling from His words such quotations as please one and ignoring or rationalizing the others do not make one personally a Christian any more than using an American jeep in Burma

makes one an American. It is only by the acceptance in accredited circumstances of the proper baptism that Jesus Christ stipulated and by the pledge of loyal allegiance to the *whole* of his doctrines that one is made truly a Christian; just as it is only by fulfillment of the stipulated citizenship requirements as received from accredited officials and by the oath of allegiance to the *whole* of the constitution (not just to a few advantageous articles) that one is made an American citizen.

Likewise the sudden adoption of the name "Christian" and some Christian emblems by an infant group in the sixteenth, eighteenth, or twentieth century is no more a valid historical title to Jesus Christ's apostolic commission (Mt. 28:18–20: "And Jesus coming, spoke to them, saying . . . going therefore, teach . . . baptizing them . . . teaching them. . . .") than would the twentieth-century adoption of a Roman name and some Roman emblems by a U.S.A.F. group be a valid historical title to continuity from Julius Caesar!

The Catholic Church alone has the public historical continuity with Christ and His doctrinal integrity. The evidence on which she bases this claim is to be found in Apologetics (cf. Chap. I, n. 8); and the Church welcomes the serious investigation of this evidence. Without such a thorough investigation, no scholar who values his scientific impartiality can reject this claim.

This is not written in a spirit of polemical malevolence. Educational issues are so important and yet so clouded that a frank statement of what one believes to be the truth is a service that everyone should give in no matter what minor capacity — and should likewise receive. Here, then, is merely a cold, academic statement for clarity's sake of what seems to this writer to be the proper and full meaning of the word *"Christian."* Henceforth, we shall be using the word frequently with this full and meaningful connotation. Cf. n. 59, Chapter IV.

CHAPTER IV

CATHOLIC VIEW OF THE
PROPER AND IMMEDIATE END
OF EDUCATION

PIUS XI states clearly and authoritatively:

The proper and immediate end of Christian education is to co-operate with divine grace in forming the *true and perfect Christian,* that is, to form Christ Himself in those regenerated by Baptism, according to the emphatic expression of the Apostle: "My little children, of whom I am in labour again, until Christ be formed in you" (Gal. 4:19). For the true Christian must live a supernatural life in Christ: "Christ who is your life" (Col. 3:4) and display it in all his actions: "That the life also of Jesus may be made manifest in our mortal flesh" (2 Cor. 4:11).[1]

Pius XII, speaking to the Union of Italian Teachers, told them to take as their ideal the formation of "the *perfect Christian.* By the perfect Christian we mean the Christian of today, the child of his own era . . . a citizen and not something apart from the life led in his own country today."[2]

Pius XII in his "Counsels to Teaching Sisters" said: "According to the

---

[1] Pius XI, *Christian Education of Youth,* pp. 35–36. The Italian original, *Rappresentanti in Terra, AAS,* XXI (1929), 758, states: "Fine proprio e immediato dell'educazione cristiana è cooperare con la grazia divina nel formare il vero e perfetto cristiano: cioè Cristo stesso nei rigenerati col Battesimo, secondo la viva espressione dell'Apostolo: 'Figliuolini miei, che io nuovamente porto in seno fino a tanto che sia formato in voi Cristo.' Giacchè il vero cristiano deve vivere la vita soprannaturale in Cristo: 'Cristo che è la vita vostra,' e manifestarla in tutte le sue operazioni: 'affinchè anche la vita di Gesù sia manifesta nella nostra carne mortale.'" The official Latin version *Divini Illius Magistri, AAS,* XXII (1930), pp. 49–86, reads: "Eo proprie ac proxime intendit christiana educatio, ut, divina cum gratia conspirando, germanum atque perfectum christianum efficiat hominem" (p. 83). In this and the following quotations the phrases referring to the "perfect Christian" have been italicized.

[2] Pius XII, address to the Union of Italian Teachers, September 4, 1949. Translated in *Catholic Action,* XXXI (October, 1949), 18.

Catholic concept, the object of the school and of education is the formation of the *perfect Christian.* . . . Your entire school and educational
system would be useless were this object not the central point of your
labor."³

Pius XII elsewhere said: "The substance and aim of Christian education is the formation of the human being, reborn in Baptism unto the
stature of a *perfect Christian.*"⁴

When Pius XII declared St. John Baptist de La Salle the patron of all
teachers and students, he quoted the remark of St. Bonaventure: "The
only true educator is one who can kindle in the heart of his pupil the
vision of beauty, illumine it with the light of truth, and infuse virtue."⁵
This quotation is doubly valuable; it bears witness to the thought of the
thirteenth century as expressed by one of its towering scholars; it is
quoted with approval and reinforced by a greater authority, the man who
holds by demonstrable historical succession the supreme teaching commission conferred by Jesus Christ. This statement quoted from St.
Bonaventure is undoubtedly less specific than the previous ones. But in
the context of Scholastic philosophy and Christian theology, no one can
doubt the dimensions of the words "beauty" — connoting integrity, due
proportion, and clarity;⁶ "truth" — "I am the way, and the truth";⁷
and "virtue" — morally good acts, both natural and supernatural.

What of the authority of these papal words? Are they just one
scholar's opinion? Are they meant as positive statements? Are they enduring or just relative? Are they localized, not generally applicable to
the prevailing conditions in English-speaking countries?

Papal pronouncements are made in any of a dozen ways and may be
classified according to form and according to content.⁸ Some have reference to a particular group or circumstance; others are general pronouncements. The inscription, form, contents, and wording will always make
clear the extension of the pronouncement as a whole. Even in a pro-

---

³ Pius XII, "Counsels to Teaching Sisters," September 13, 1951, *AAS*, XLIII
(1951), 742–743. ". . . secondo il senso cattolico lo scopo della scuola e dell'educazione
è di formare il perfetto cristiano. . . . Tutto il vostro sistema di scuola e di
educazione sarebbe vano, se questo scopo non fosse al centro dell'opera vostra"
(translated by the N.C.W.C., Washington, D. C.).

⁴ Pius XII, *Nuntius Radiophonicus,* March 23, 1952, "The Right Formation of
Christian Conscience in Youth," *A.A.S.,* XLIV (1952), 271. "Contenuto e scopo della
educazione cristiana è la formazione del nuovo essere umano, rinato nel battesimo,
a perfetto cristiano."

⁵ Pius XII, *A.A.S.,* XLII (May, 1950), 631. "Ille solus verus est doctor, qui potest
speciem imprimere et lumen infundere et virtutem dare cordi audientis."

⁶ *Summa,* I, q. 39, a. 8.

⁷ Jn. 14:6.

⁸ Cf. the Most Rev. Amleto G. Cicognani, *Canon Law* (2nd ed. rev.; Westminster,
Md.: The Newman Bookshop, 1934), pp. 80–96.

nouncement relative to some group or circumstance, however, the Pope may make statements that are positive assertions, or at least indications, of his mind about general matters, and the words and content of such statements nearly always identify them as such. The important thing to remember is that the Church's teaching commission exercised authoritatively through the Pope is not restricted in its exercise to his infallible pronouncements when, as the technical phrase has it, he teaches *ex cathedra.*

Christ's injunction to teach all nations was not limited by any qualifications. The Church has been commissioned by God to teach with authority on matters of faith and morals. It has been promised the guidance of the Holy Spirit. In rare cases, the fullness of this guidance is invoked in a solemn definition of an article of faith.[9]

In speaking of education, as quoted above, the Popes were speaking of something intimately connected with the virtuous life and the last end of the educand, something pertaining to his salvation. They have explicitly stated that basic educational issues are vitally important — "it is therefore as important to make no mistake in education, as it is to make no mistake in the pursuit of the last end. . . ."[10] Hence, no Catholic can whittle away the stature of these educational pronouncements.

Elsewhere Pius XI has spoken clearly about this very matter of the acceptance of papal pronouncements. The context is about the Church's social teaching; but since he is speaking formally of official pronouncements on important matters as such his words are precisely relevant here:

> How many are there who profess adhesion to Catholic doctrines on such matters as the authority of civil society and the due respect to be shown it, on the rights of property, on the rights and duties of farmer and artisan, on capital and labor, on international affairs, on the mutual relations between Church and State, on the rights and prerogatives of the Holy See, the Roman Pontiff, and the Episcopate, and finally on the rights of Christ Himself, the Creator, Redeemer, and Lord of individuals and nations? Yet despite these protestations, they speak, write, and habitually act as if the doctrines and injunctions many times promulgated by the Supreme Pontiffs — and especially by Leo XIII, Pius X, and Benedict XV — had lost or almost lost their original force.
>
> This indeed is a kind of moral, legal, and social modernism, which, along with dogmatic modernism, we strongly condemn.

---

[9] John F. Cronin, *Catholic Social Principles* (Milwaukee: The Bruce Publishing Co., 1950), p. 56. Cf. Joseph C. Fenton, "The Doctrinal Authority of Papal Encyclicals," *American Ecclesiastical Review,* CXXI (1949), 136–150, 210–220.
[10] Pius XI, *Christian Education of Youth,* p. 4.

It is therefore necessary to keep in mind those doctrines and injunctions we have mentioned. All should awaken in themselves that fervent spirit of faith and of charity which alone can lead to the clear understanding of these truths and to their observance.[11]

When the Pope says that the proper and immediate end of education is Christian perfection, he is carefully and seriously stating something which he considers important, something that has been equivalently reiterated several times. Any evasion of this statement, therefore, is unworthy of a Catholic. It would also be unhistorical, because the Popes have only formulated the accumulated Christian tradition. Even as far back as the seventh century, in the one hundred and twelve Cathedral schools that had been established in Frankland alone by 614,[12] "the moral and spiritual formation of the student was of paramount importance."[13]

Non-Catholic educators who may not indeed recognize *a priori* the special guidance of the Holy Ghost given to the Popes for the fulfillment of their special teaching office, will at least respect and perhaps heed the statements of the Popes as men who are scholars in their own right.[14] Their official papal utterances are always models of meaningful, terse wording, as anyone who reads an encyclical will clearly perceive. Their statements, then, about the end of education are worthy of the scholarly respect and the serious consideration of everyone.

CONSIDERATION OF CHRISTIAN PERFECTION

We will now discuss the meaning of Christian perfection at some length, in order that it may be accurately understood. Words matter little — they merely form a platitude; but the concepts behind the words matter much. Only from a full understanding of the meaning and connotations of the concept "Christian perfection" can we proceed reliably to its thorough and balanced implementation.

Some non-Catholic readers may feel that so far we have merely stated our view in reliance on papal authority, without adducing convincing proofs. From the consideration we now unfold along with the objections

---

[11] Pius XI, *Ubi Arcano Dei,* December 23, 1922, *AAS,* XIV (1922), 696.

[12] E. P. Cubberly, *Syllabus of Lectures on the History of Education* (New York: The Macmillan Co., 1904), p. 58. Nobody can suspect this writer of being so biased in favor of Catholic education as to invent favorable facts.

[13] McCormick and Cassidy, *op. cit.,* p. 214.

[14] As librarian in the Ambrosian library, Milan, Achilles Ratti (the future Pius XI) earned respect and acknowledgment for himself in the learned world for his prodigious historical research in the *Acta Ecclesiae Mediolanensis,* his share in the *Missale Ambrosianum Duplex,* and his editorship of *San Carlo Borromeo e il III Centenario della sua Canonizzazione.* Pius XII's versatile scholarship is well known. And these men, writing as Popes, have at hand for consultation the *periti* who compose the twenty-one bureaus that assist him in his pontifical functions.

and discussions will appear the fittingness of Christian perfection as the proper and immediate end of education.

Our consideration will be under two chief headings: (1) "God's General Plan for Man's Perfection: Restoration in Christ"; (2) "Analysis of Some Aspects of Christian Perfection."

1. *God's General Plan for Man's Perfection: Restoration in Christ*

God created man as the masterpiece of the world; but man rebelled against God's arrangements and brought disasters on himself. Instead of casting him off, God has planned his restoration through the redemptive life and death of Jesus Christ. Man is to perfect himself through Christ.

Since perfection in Christ is a supernatural thing and the word "supernatural" will be used extensively throughout this chapter, we will begin by noting the precise meaning of the word. Its correct understanding is vital for our consideration. The medieval Nominalists vitiated the true notion of the supernatural by vitiating the true notion of the natures of things. They thereby confused the clear difference between the natural and the supernatural — the distance between two areas only vaguely located on the map cannot be accurately measured; and this vague confusion has prevailed in various modern usages of "supernatural."

Nominally, the word means something which is "above nature." What is nature? Nature in general signifies more than the essence of a thing; nature is the principle and cause of the motion and rest of the thing in which that principle exists fundamentally and essentially, and not accidentally.[15] Thus a man's essence makes him what he is, different from a bird or a piece of granite; it refers to his *being*. Nature refers to *acting;* nature is essence considered as the principle of activity. Hence, through his human nature, a man acts like a man and not like a bird; his nature is something fundamental to him — not something put on and off like a Sunday suit. Sometimes, however, nature is used in the sense of all the created essences or principles of activity taken collectively and forming the universe of which we are a part; and so in this collective sense we speak of "nature" and the poets write their lyrics in its praise.

God, according to our human way of expressing things, also has His proper nature — we call it the divine nature. But "nature" used without qualification is taken to refer to created nature. "Natural" is the adjective indicating that which is according to or due to some nature taken individually, or according to nature taken collectively; hence it is "natural" for a man to laugh; but not natural for a fish to laugh. Natural then is taken to mean whatever is due to some created nature in any of

---

[15] Aristotle, *Phys.*, 1, II, c. 1.

several ways: (1) *constitutively* or essentially, i.e., whatever is required for constituting some being in species — for example, it is natural for man to have a rational soul; (2) *consecutively,* i.e., according to powers which flow from the essence of the thing — for example, it is natural for man to have an intellect and a will; (3) *according to exigency,* i.e., as required in some way by it — for example, air and nourishment are required for organic life, society for man; the divine support is always required for the continued existence of a created being. Things in these three categories are called natural in the sense of being due to nature. There is another category whereby things are called natural (4) *meritoriously,* i.e., according to the deserts of an intellectual creature through the free operation of his faculties. When, through the operation of his free faculties, a man attains some end, this end is said to be meritoriously natural and *due to the person.*[16] A keen student merits his diploma; it is due to him.

Since order is the apt arrangement of means to the ultimate end and requires (*a*) an agent, (*b*) an end to which the agent tends, (*c*) the means through which he attains the end, and (*d*) some law regulating and controlling his use of means to the end, the natural order about which we speak so often may be designated as the apt arrangement of natural means to a natural ultimate end.[17]

"Supernatural," meaning "above nature," can now be understood in relation to all that has been said of "nature" and "natural." It refers to something which is above whatever is constitutive of a created essence, consequent upon a created essence, and required by or due to a created essence in some way. Hence something is supernatural if it is above the essence, powers, exigencies, need, merits of a created nature; it is obviously a gratuitous gift to the created nature. For example, sanctifying grace is supernatural because it constitutes man in a state that is in no way due to his created being. To see God just as He is, is supernatural because it altogether exceeds the natural powers of seeing that flow from any created nature. The glorification of man's body and soul in heaven is supernatural because it altogether exceeds the exigencies of man's body and soul, and his natural merit.

The "supernatural order" correspondingly is the apt disposition of means essentially supernatural toward a supernatural end. This order will also connote the four elements considered above in regard to the natural order. In the case of man as elevated to the supernatural order there will be: (*a*) the primary agent, God, considered now as the author of grace and the secondary agent, man, as elevated to a higher level of operation by grace; (*b*) the ultimate end, namely, the face-to-face vision of God, *just as He is;* (*c*) the means — objective and subjective, for example,

---

16 Ad. Tanquerey, *Brevior Synopsis Theologiae Dogmaticae* (9th ed., Paris: Desclée & Co., 1949), n. 659.

17 *Ibid.,* n. 661.

objective revelation and the exercise of the infused virtues respectively;
(*d*) the law regulating the means to the end, namely, the whole body of
Divine Positive Law superadded to the natural law.[18]

The word "supernatural" may be understood in a relative or imperfect
sense called *secundum quid,* to indicate something which is according to
one created nature but is nevertheless above another created nature. This
is what we mean by the word "preternatural." Thus to know everything
intuitively without any reasoning is natural for an angel, but preternatural for a man. To recite verses is natural for a man but preternatural
for a parrot.

Supernatural in an absolute sense, called *simpliciter,* refers to something
completely above all existing and possible created natures, even the
highest. In this sense it may be further divided into what is supernatural
quoad substantiam and supernatural *quoad modum.*[19] Supernatural *quoad
substantiam* (literally, "in regard to the substance") refers to something
supernatural in its very being, intrinsically supernatural; for example,
grace, the hypostatic union, and the glory of heaven. Supernatural *quoad
modum* (literally, "in regard to the manner") refers to something natural
in its being but supernatural in its mode. It may pertain to efficient
causality; for example, in the raising of the dead Lazarus to life, natural
life was supernaturally given to him. It may be ordained to a supernatural
end and so pertain to final causality, for example, a devout mother's
care for her sick child or a teacher's work in the classroom becomes
supernaturalized when ordained to a supernatural end.

We are now in a position to understand the significance of saying that
the Christian perfection which is proposed as the proper and immediate
end of education is essentially a supernatural perfection belonging to the
supernatural order. It is a perfection which is above the essence, powers,
exigencies, and merit of any created nature and effort. Parents, teachers,
administrators must be deeply convinced of this. That it is actually supernatural will be made clear by a consideration of the general divine plan
of human perfection, and of the elements it involves. In this plan there is
an historical dimension that we cannot disregard. God's plan is indeed of
a piece; there was nothing evolutionary about it. Christ was the center of
His design for the perfection of man. But God spread His plan across
the centuries so that not only essentially but also historically Christ
should be seen as its center.

In its broadest outlines the over-all plan is this: God created and richly
endowed man; man fell and was helpless in his fallen state; God restored
man and gave him an adopted sonship through the satisfaction of Jesus
Christ, the Second Person of the Blessed Trinity; with the grace of
Christ man must actively pattern himself on the likeness of Christ and

---

[18] *Ibid.*
[19] This distinction has already been mentioned above in regard to Revelation.

enter heaven as an image of Christ — not an infantile image but the full measure of the stature of Christ. A brief elaboration of each of these details will help us to glimpse the splendor of God's over-all plan for our perfection and to appreciate the chasm that separates naturalistic from Christian education.

CREATION OF MAN

God created man as a natural image of Himself[20] and richly endowed him. He gave him a complete nature with a harmonious balance between all his natural powers. He also gave man preternatural gifts of *freedom from concupiscence*,[21] of special *knowledge*,[22] of *immortality* consisting in immunity from death,[23] of special *extrinsic happiness* consisting negatively in *impassibility*[24] — freedom from the bodily inconvenience of fatigue, hunger, heat, cold, sickness, decrepitude, injury — and consisting positively in the possession of the truly good things of life.[25] He gave him also a certain dominion over the lower creation.[26] God did more, much more. By sanctifying grace He elevated man to the supernatural order

---

[20] Gen. 1:26–28.

[21] Theologically certain. Gen. 2:25; 3:7, 11, as interpreted by Tradition. This concupiscence is to be understood strictly as the tendency of the appetite toward a sense good of the senses, *despite the dictates of reason;* cf. B.A.C., *op. cit.,* II, p. 766. Sometimes this freedom from concupiscence is called the gift of integrity; cf. *B.A.C., loc. cit.* At other times "the state of integrity" is used to indicate the whole of Adam's natural gifts, and even to indicate the state of original justice.

[22] Theologically common and certain from Rom. 5:12–19; 1 Cor. 15:21–22 as interpreted by Tradition. The fulfillment of Adam's commission, Gen. 1:28–30 and 2:15, implies this knowledge also. Cf. B.A.C., *op. cit.,* 801. Some authors consider that Gen. 2:19–20 does not prove that Adam was given a preternatural gift of knowledge. Cf. Tanquerey, *op. cit.,* p. 369.

[23] Wisd. 2:23–24; Gen. 2:16, as interpreted by Tradition and defined by the Council of Trent. Adam was mortal insofar as he was able to die without, however, being under the necessity of dying. He was immortal insofar as he was able not to die, without any implication that he *could not die* under any circumstances. This immortality was conditioned on his will of sinning or not sinning. Under the latter condition of remaining free from sin, it was truly impossible for him to die. Cf. B.A.C., *op. cit.,* II, 782–783. "Sic Adam erat *mortalis* quatenus poterat mori, at non quasi deberet necessario mori, et *immortalis* quatenus poterat non mori, at non quasi non posset mori. De facto moreretur vel non moreretur pro libera eius voluntate peccandi vel non peccandi. At ea *immortalitas* non est concipienda mere ut *factum non mortis* . . . sed ut vera *impossibilitas moriendi* sub conditione non peccandi."

[24] This is de *fide* and is proven from Gen. 3:16–19. Even reason indicates that freedom from death would naturally seem to imply freedom from those things that would remotely lead to death. Cf. B.A.C., *op. cit.,* II, 794–795.

[25] This is theologically common and certain from Gen. 2:8–17 as interpreted by Tradition. Cf. B.A.C., *op. cit.,* II, 794–795.

[26] This, according to B.A.C., *loc. cit.,* is theologically common and certain, from Gen. 2:19.

with the right and means of entering heaven. The state of complete nature, adorned — with the preternatural gifts and elevated to the supernatural order, we call the state of original justice. Thus was Adam endowed — the masterpiece and lord of the natural universe.

> And the Lord God had planted a paradise of pleasure from the beginning: wherein he placed man whom he had formed. And the Lord God brought forth . . . all manner of trees, fair to behold, and pleasant to eat of: the tree of life also in the midst of paradise. . . . And the Lord God took man and put him into the paradise of pleasure, to dress it, and to keep it.[27]

FALL OF MAN

But man fell. Adam and Eve by their conscious, personal sin — a grave sin of proud disobedience — lost their supernatural grace and elevation to the supernatural order, lost too, their preternatural gifts; and so death and suffering came into the world. Human nature itself was in some way affected. It was partially disrupted by the enormity of the sin in which created nature deliberately flouted its Creator on whom it depends absolutely for its being. It was not intrinsically corrupted, as Luther conveniently imagined.[28] It was nevertheless wounded "perhaps intrinsically but at least extrinsically."[29] The harmony of its natural powers was disrupted. Through this sin Adam's whole being was changed for the worse.

The taint of his fall fell on his descendants, for all except Mary, the Mother of Christ, were born in original sin — a condition proper to each, incurred by each in his very propagation, whereby each receives from his parents a nature deprived of original justice and wounded in its powers, since these powers "in a certain way lack their proper order by which they are naturally ordained to virtue."[30] St. Thomas enumerates these wounds as a partial darkening of the intellect, a proneness to evil in the will, a weakness in fortitude, and the upsurge of concupiscence.[31]

---

[27] Gen. 2:8–15.

[28] Notice the intrinsic pessimism of Luther's view. Eleven centuries earlier Pelagius, followed by many since, erred on the side of wild optimism and presumption by denying original sin and vitiating the supernatural order.

Here, as in so many cases, the Catholic Church, by adhering accurately to Divine Revelation, threads a safe passage between Scylla and Charybdis. She saves man from the despairing pessimism of intrinsic corruption; she saves him from a bubble optimism that would float him to destruction. She leaves him humbled by his fall but truly hopeful, as we shall see. Even ordinary experience bears out the falsity of the two extremes. Daily life tells us that everyone is not intrinsically corrupt in nature (who could believe it of a baby?), that everyone is not wholly perfect with unimpaired powers. This whole matter has important educational consequences.

[29] B.A.C., *op. cit.*, II, 743.

[30] *Summa,* I–II, q. 85, a. 3.

[31] *Ibid.*

Mankind fell under a certain ascendancy of the devil who had conspired its ruin. Moreover, it had to leave the blissful shelter of Paradise to face the labor and storms of life.

It is important for the educator to remember that original sin has wounded but not intrinsically corrupted human nature. The remembrance of this theological truth will preclude many educational excesses — such as Developmentalism, already treated — and will save the teacher from a despairing pessimism as well as from a bubbling optimism. We shall invoke this truth later on in seeking the solution to some practical problems.

MAN'S SUPERNATURAL HELPLESSNESS

After Adam's fall, he and his descendants of themselves had no chance to reinstate themselves. They could not give themselves what they did not have, nor procure it. The lost supernatural status was entirely above their natural essence, powers, exigencies, and merits. They were helpless; they had no key to heaven's closed door. Even natural prayer, uttered with all the intensity of man's combined powers, could do nothing to deserve the restoration of the lost supernatural gifts, because there is absolutely no proportion or approximation between the effort made and the effect desired. Man might as well lift up his arm to move the moon. And so the bright clear sunshine of man's day on earth became heavily, but not hopelessly, clouded.

MAN'S RESTORATION THROUGH CHRIST

God gave him hope by a startling promise. In the mysterious words of Genesis, "I will put enmities between thee and the woman, and thy seed and her seed: she shall crush thy head and thou shalt lie in wait for her heel,"[32] He promised a Redeemer, Someone who would in some way repair Adam's fall, heal wounded nature, and give again to man a title to enter heaven — *if he wished*. Mankind clung to that promise. It was kept alive formally and explicitly by the Hebrew people and was echoed faintly in diverse ways in the traditions of other peoples. Gradually God made known various prophetic details about this Redeemer who would come, characteristics that would unerringly identify Him when He came. Hebrew history pointed toward Him; and in the fullness of time He came. He was Jesus Christ, the Second Person of the Blessed Trinity, and therefore a Divine Person, truly God. In a unique union He took to himself human nature complete in its essence and powers, typical in everything except sin and whatever would be a consequence of sin. He was therefore one Divine Person with two natures, divine and human, truly God, truly man, "full of grace and truth."[33] He was a bridge between mankind and

[32] Gen. 3:15.   [33] Jn. 1:14.

God, able to atone to God for men because He was truly one of them, acceptable to God in His atonement because He was God. This was the Redeemer, the Saviour,[34] who came at Bethlehem as the fulfillment of the gratuitous Divine Promise made in the dawn of mankind: but He came *incognito* — born of Mary, a woman from a village. Hence, His life was one of reverses and persecution. Superficial and perverse people could not or would not distinguish between the reality of His dignity and its accidental pomp. So Christ by His own permission was eventually brought to His Passion and Death, an adequate and abundant atonement for man's sinful debt to God. "There is now therefore no condemnation to them that are in Christ Jesus who walk not according to the flesh."[35] Now was heaven opened again to man — *if he wished*. Now could man call on the inexhaustible merits of the risen Christ to obtain what his own unaided prayers and efforts could not obtain. Thus, through Christ, *God restored man* to the supernatural order, *but somewhat differently*.

Our restoration in Christ has various elements. Each is itself a subject for an entire theological study. We treat them here with as much brevity as will give an appreciation of the facets of our perfection in Christ. They must not be understood as distinct or separable; rather they are different views of the one pearl of great price as we turn it this way and that in the light of Revelation.

Grace. The gift of *supernatural grace* is the first of the elements in our restoration through Christ, and grace is a supernatural gift infused by God into the rational creature with reference to eternal life. Later on we will treat grace in some detail with the prerogatives that accompany it. Here it is enough to say that grace elevates man to the supernatural order and in some mysterious way — who can confine and measure the works of God! — gives him a supernatural likeness to God, ennobling, deifying without warping his own nature. By grace he enters a new life, a supernatural one, to be lived in Christ, with Christ, and for Christ.

God has restored to man the gift of sanctifying grace; but he has not restored to him the preternatural gifts that were lost to humanity by Adam's fall. Man's will, therefore, remains fickle; his intellect remains darkened; he still must fight his disorderly inclinations. God, of course, was under no obligation to restore to man a purely gratuitous gift that man had willfully lost.

And there is a special providence in the withholding of these preternatural gifts. Man is vividly reminded of his fall and his natural helpless-

---

[34] Lk. 2:11. Very pertinent here is the reiteration of the adage: To those who believe in God no explanation is necessary; to those who do not believe, no explanation is possible. God as omnipotent *could* do it. As infinitely merciful, He *did* it of His free will. We know He did it from the internal and external signs that serve as criteria for the fulfillment of His startling promise and are examined in Apologetics.
[35] Rom. 8:1.

ness; never can he hold his head high in self-sufficiency without ex-
periencing painfully the hollowness of his pride. He is to rebuild his own
perfection as a facsimile of his former preternatural excellence, enlightening his mind by instruction, strengthening his will and restoring in part
the balance of his inclinations by the practice of virtue. To aid him in
this he has abundant and overflowing supernatural means; his solace, his
food, his unfailing friend in his effort is Christ Himself. His special and
perpetual helper is Mary, the Mother of God. And for each and the least
effort he makes in accordance with these supernatural means he receives
merit and an increased reward in heaven, a reward that outweighs even
his most intensive efforts. The labors of daily life now have an eternal
significance. "I reckon that the sufferings of this time are not worthy
to be compared to the glory to come."[36] Thus under God man heals his
own weakness; then is richly rewarded for his labor, in heaven.

Divine Indwelling. Intimately related to the possession of sanctifying
grace is the indwelling of the Holy Trinity in the soul of each man. This
indwelling is a formal effect of sanctifying grace, and it is more than the
mere omnipresence of God; yet it is not a substantial pantheistic union.
It is the privilege that every man can have through the merits of Christ,
whereby he is a temple and God is his Guest. "If anyone love me he
will keep my word, and my Father will love him and we will come to him
and will make our abode with him."[37] It should be remembered that the
Holy Spirit is not a passive, inactive guest in our souls. His divine touch
gives the increase and fruit to our spiritual growth. Later we will consider
the special equipment through which He works in us. This element of
our restoration through Christ has valuable implications as we shall see.

Divine Adoption. By a formal effect of sanctifying grace man also
becomes an adopted son of God.

> Dearly beloved, we are now the sons of God.[38]

> Behold what manner of charity the Father hath bestowed upon us,
> that we should be called, and should be the sons of God.[39]

> You have received the spirit of adoption of sons whereby we cry:
> Abba (Father).[40]

> For the Spirit himself giveth testimony to our spirit, that we are
> the sons of God.[41]

We commonly say how fortunate is a waif adopted into a good home.
God's adoption of us as part of our restoration through Christ is much
more gratuitous and wonderful. Adoption requires a similarity of nature

---

[36] Rom. 8:18.   [39] 1 Jn. 3:1.
[37] Jn. 14:23.   [40] Rom. 8:15.
[38] 1 Jn. 3:2.   [41] Rom. 8:16.

as a prerequisite — properly speaking, a man cannot *adopt* a fish! But the divine adoption bridges an infinitely greater chasm between God's nature and ours. God Himself through sanctifying grace brings about the likeness of nature required as a prerequisite for adoption. Again, human adoption is external, effected by the will of the one adopting and by legal declaration; whereas God adopts us with an outpouring of internal gifts. Hence much more fittingly do we call God "our Father who art in Heaven" than the adopted waif calls its foster parent "father." Human adoption means sustenance and support, but almost invariably the attainment of the inheritance comes only after the death of the parent. In the divine adoption, however, we enter at once into the divine inheritance;[42] and in it, wonderful to say, we are coheirs with Christ. St. Paul says: "And if sons, heirs also; heirs indeed of God, and joint heirs with Christ."[43] Our dignity as adopted sons of God is one of the glories of our restoration through Christ. We take our place in the house of God as sons and princes.

Christ Our Exemplar. There can be no doubt about it, Christ is our Exemplar. Each man is called to become in some degree, but nonetheless certainly *alter Christus,* another Christ. This is clearly and forcibly shown in the Scripture.

> Whom he foreknew, he also predestinated to be made *conformable to the image of his Son;* that he might be the first-born amongst many brethren [italics added].[44]

> Put ye on the Lord Jesus Christ.[45]

> To me, to live is Christ.[46]

> Let this mind be in you, which also was in Christ Jesus.[47]

Pius XII emphasizes this characteristic of our restoration in Christ:

> Let those then who glory in the name of Christian all look to our divine Saviour as the most exalted, and most perfect exemplar of all virtues; but then let them also by careful avoidance of sin and assiduous practice of virtue, bear witness by their conduct to His teaching and His life, so that when God appears they may be like unto Him and see Him as He is.[48]

Natural man is already a created, natural image of the Word, the Second Person of the Blessed Trinity. This reflection of God is clearly seen in the

[42] Cf. B.A.C., *op. cit.,* III, 623–624.   [45] Rom. 13:14.
[43] Rom. 8:17.   [46] Phil. 1:21.
[44] Rom. 8:29.   [47] Phil. 2:5.
[48] Pius XII, encyclical, *Mystici Corporis,* trans. (Washington, D. C.: N.C.W.C.), n. 46.

nature of the human soul. However, nature is only, as it were, God's footprint on earth — remote and imperfect compared with God as He is in Himself. But now through Christ he is to mold himself into a far more perfect image of God whereby even in this life he may become a wondrous supernatural likeness of Christ. Death will be its unveiling; heaven its crowning. Men are providentially destined to enter heaven only as perfected in the likeness of Christ their Redeemer — as other Christs. God the Father, seeing the multitude of the saints "of all nations, and tribes, and peoples, and tongues,"[49] with the Lamb "in the midst,"[50] will see in the varied glory of that throng the participated supernatural perfection of His own Beloved Son in whom He is well pleased[51] and whom He thereby exalts.[52]

Here then is the destiny, the potential glory of every child, and the end-product of his development — to become an image of Christ, in some way another Christ.

In terms of causality, Christ our Model is an exemplary cause of our perfection.

An exemplary cause is defined as "the form which an artificer uses as a pattern in his operation,"[53] or the form in imitation of which a thing is produced according to the intention of an agent that determines an end for itself.[54] The exemplar, considered proximately, is the idea as it exists in the mind of the artificer, whether he be painter, sculptor, or skilled craftsman; this idea is the concept or *species expressa*. The exemplar, considered remotely, signifies the external thing existing in reality and used by the artificer to form the idea on which he now patterns his activity. It is clear then that the person of Christ is the remote exemplar of our activity: our ideas of Christ are the proximate exemplars of our perfection. But here a very important philosophical distinction is to be noted and applied: "Not every concept or *species expressa* is an exemplary idea; only a practical concept, or a *species expressa* which represents the thing as *able to be imitated*,"[55] is an exemplary idea. Here is one philosophical reason why academic knowledge alone does not lead us to fashion ourselves according to the good which is known. Hence it is not enough for the student to acquire mere knowledge of Christ, in other words, to acquire mere concepts, mere information, mere history about Christ. These do not automatically make Christ the exemplar of his conduct and lead

---

49 Apoc. 7:9.
50 Apoc. 5:6.
51 Cf. Mt. 3:17.
52 Phil. 2:9.
53 Grenier, *op. cit.*, III, p. 216.
54 Cf. St. Thomas, *De Veritate*, q. 3, a. 1. "Forma quam aliquis imitatur ex intentione agentis determinante sibi finem."
55 Maquart, *op. cit.*, III, 2, p. 215.

him to fashion himself as an image of Christ. If Christ is to be the exemplar, on which all will *de facto* model themselves, He must be known, not just as a figure whose life and sayings are references, but as a model that can and should be imitated, as One who, while flawless in Himself and His own perfections, presents a pattern that is within reach of our supernaturalized efforts. Therefore, educators should present Christ and the saints in this way as exemplars, able to be imitated. Christ is *the* Exemplar; His Immaculate Mother and the saints as his heroic and closest followers are also our exemplars mediately, like moons shedding a reflected light. In this regard we see the natural and spiritual wisdom of saints such as St. Vincent de Paul and St. Alphonsus de Liguori who strenuously opposed the florid panegyrics of the saints so fashionable in their day — and so often an excuse for literary affectation and egotism. They insisted that panegyrics should not only honor God in the praises of his saint but should move people to imitate the saints as exemplars under Christ.

Considered materially, the exemplary cause pertains in some way to efficient causality insofar as the exemplary idea as it were completes the power of the agent by constituting it in first act for the production of the effect. (Later we will explain the notions of first and second acts.)

It also pertains in some way to final causality insofar as it is that for the production of which the agent acts. We say "in some way" since the exemplar is seen by the agent, not precisely as something to be *attained,* but rather to be imitated. The artist does not kidnap the model; rather he paints his likeness.

But considered formally, exemplary causality is reducible to formal causality as an extrinsic formal cause: "formal" since the exemplar determines in the agent's mind the form or likeness or the "thisness" of the thing to be done, and such an influx pertains properly to formal causality; "extrinsic" because the exemplar is through imitation the external determinant of the kind of effect produced. We would be surprised to see a student artist copying the Mona Lisa to paint a spray of flowers; we would expect to see a Mona Lisa likeness. Da Vinci's original would then be the extrinsic formal cause of the student's copy.

Christ, the Word Incarnate, is not merely man's efficient and final cause; as his Supreme Exemplar, He is man's extrinsic formal cause, both naturally and supernaturally — although in different respects.[56] This, according to Prat,[57] is the meaning of St. Paul's words that all things are by Him, in Him, and for Him.[58]

---

[56] The Word of God, the Second Person of the Blessed Trinity, is the Exemplar of the natural creation. The Word Incarnate, Jesus Christ, is the Exemplar of man's supernatural perfection.

[57] Fernand Prat, *The Theology of St. Paul,* trans. by John L. Stoddard (2 vols., London: Burns, Oates & Washbourne, Ltd., 1927), I, 291.   [58] Col. 1:16.

88 *The Proximate Aim of Education*

Behold then the depths of the philosophical and theological riches found in Christ; likewise, the depth and nobility of our work as educator in assisting the educand to his perfection in Christ.

The Mystical Body. There is still another element of man's restoration in Christ; it is the call to the membership of the Mystical Body of Christ so often referred to by St. Paul. The Mystical Body means this: Christ true God and true man, is the new Adam, the Head of the human race that He has redeemed. He and the baptized constitute one body with its own special solidarity. This is called His Mystical Body.

Christ is its Head on several titles: by reason of His excellence, whereby He is immeasurably above all creatures; by reason of His government whereby He guides and regulates and directs the society of members; by reason of His intimate personal relationship with each, gently influencing the inmost thoughts and desires of each; by reason of the similarity of nature whereby He and we share the same human nature; by reason of our conformity to Him, a conformity founded on the common sharing of human nature but perfected by our personal efforts to fashion ourselves as special images of Christ; by reason of His plenitude of supernatural perfection in which we are to participate; by reason of His positive influence over the whole Body and its members, "since He distributes every single grace to every single person according to the measure of the giving of Christ."[59]

All men are called to enter this Mystical Body and therefore all men are potentially its members. But actually it is entered only through baptism. The Mystical Body of Christ is actually the Catholic Church which, juridically founded and presided over by the Supreme Pontiff, is the Church of Christ, the Church of charity, and the universal family of Christians.[60] Baptized souls are incorporated into this Body and participate in its supernatural life in various degrees.

The union of the members under Christ is a real union. Yet it is not a substantial union, which would submerge them. It is, however, more than a moral union,[61] as Pius XII emphasizes.[62] "Mystical" is to be understood as designating a supernatural, remarkable reality. In the Mystical Body

---

[59] Cf. Pius XII, encyclical, *Mystici Corporis*, nn. 36–50.

[60] Cf. Pius XII, *AAS*, XXXI (1939), p. 250. The Pontiff expressly warns that it is false to create a dichotomy between the juridic Church and the Church of charity. "Perperam secernitur Ecclesia iuridica ab Ecclesia caritatis. Non ita, sed illa Ecclesia iure fundata, cuius caput Pontifex est, eadem est Ecclesia Christi, Ecclesia caritatis, universaque christianorum familia." Notice the usage of the word "Christian"; cf. n. 79, Chap. III. Pius XII reiterates the same doctrine in the encyclical *Mystici Corporis, op. cit.*, n. 64.

[61] A moral union or a moral body is an extrinsic union of free members who are joined together in the quest of one end and, by mutual co-operation, in the attaining of this end. The faculty of a school is a moral union.

[62] Encyclical, *Mystici Corporis, op. cit.*, n. 61.

over and above the unity arising from the common tendency toward a common end, there is "a distinct internal principle which exists effectively in the whole and in each of its parts, and whose excellence is such, that of itself it is vastly superior to whatever bonds of union may be found in a physical or moral body."[63] This principle is the Holy Ghost[64] Who is accurately called the quasi soul of the Mystical Body — "soul" insofar as the Holy Spirit efficiently and, as it were, formally produces in the Church the manifestations of life similar to those produced by the human soul in the human body; and "quasi" to indicate the analogy of the term, since the Holy Spirit does not inform the Mystical Body substantially.[65]

Through this union we live in Christ, share His goods, and in some mysterious way complete His life and suffering. We are one with Him. "Saul, Saul, why persecutest thou me?"[66] Christ said in the apparition to the man who persecuted the first Christians: "I am Jesus whom thou persecutest."[67] "For as the body is one and hath many members: and all the members of the body whereas they are many, yet are one body: so also is Christ. . . . Now you are the body of Christ and members of member."[68] In the light of all that has been said, we can appreciate the pregnant phrase in which St. Augustine indicates the culmination of our efforts to perfect ourselves in Christ; "And there shall be one Christ loving Himself."[69]

Christ is the Head of the Mystical Body. But men pertain to this Body in diverse grades. The blessed in heaven are irrevocably its members in the most perfect way possible. On earth nobody can belong actually to the Mystical Body of Christ unless he is baptized and professes the true faith as a member of the true Church founded by Christ. Such a believer who happens to be in mortal sin is indeed a member, but imperfectly. While all other men on earth pertain to the Mystical Body potentially, those sincere people who through no fault of their own are not members of the Catholic Church pertain to it proximately by an implicit desire.

There is a special solidarity between Christ the Head and each of His members. This solidarity has some of the features of a partnership, but is more mysterious, more perfect. This "partnership demands an intricate succession of mutual interaction and co-operation, a relationship of mutual cause and effect repeated over and over again; and yet Our Lord's part in the partnership on earth was completed nearly two thousand years ago, while our part has still to be performed."[70] Here we have a solidarity

---

[63] *Ibid.*, n. 61; also n. 55.

[64] *Ibid.*, n. 61.

[65] B.A.C., *op. cit.*, I, 819.

[66] Acts 9:4.

[67] Acts 9:5.

[68] 1 Cor. 12:12, 27.

[69] *Et erit unus Christus amans seipsum.* St. Augustine, *In Epistolam ad Parthos,* Migne, *Latin Patrology,* XXXV (1845), 2055.

[70] E. Boylan, *This Tremendous Lover* (Westminster, Md.: The Newman Bookshop, 1947), pp. 21–22.

that transcends "not only space, but time also, defying even the external sequence of events."[71] A clear example of this transcendence is the case of our Lady who was preserved free from original sin through the merit of Christ's Redemption some fifty years before the supreme act of that Redemption. Every moment of the life of Christ is in contact in some way with every moment of the life of the member — of the educand; and His power goes out[72] to that soul: yet He touches each soul differently So close and real — but not as of earth — is this contact, this union, that St. Paul says: "And I live now not I; but Christ liveth in me. And that I live now in the flesh: I live in the faith of the Son of God, who loved me and delivered himself for me."[73] Indeed this is the operation of a dynamic union between Christ and member, and a marvel of our restoration in Christ. Boylan, casting around for some similitude to help us grasp even dimly the spiritual reality of our time-defying union with Christ, likens it to the modern technique in the making of a film, whereby a part may be "dubbed in" to a film already made, allowing the same actor, or one temporarily absent to fill in the missing role.

Our part in Christ's life is being played *now;* the re-running of the film starts with our Baptism and ends with our death, and we have to fit in our actions in the place left vacant for us in the original taking of the film and to make our part harmonize with Christ's when He lived His part.[74]

This may seem exaggerated until we recall the vigorous words St. Paul uses to express the close identification of our life with Christ's life. We are to be baptized in His death,[75] to suffer with Him,[76] to be crucified with Him,[77] to die with Him,[78] to be buried with Him,[79] to rise from the dead with Him,[80] to be made alive in Him,[81] to live with Him,[82] to be glorified with Him.[83] Thus does the inspired St. Paul paint the closeness of our ineffable union with Christ in the Mystical Body.

This union with Christ is, moreover, bilateral; and here is deeper mystery. We configurate our lives on Him: He adapts His restoration in some way to *us* according to His adequate knowledge and unlimited love of us; He treats each differently because each person is in a sense unique — unique in his strengths and weaknesses and failures. He completes our perfection — He is our perfect Complement; we, the members of His Church, mysteriously but really complete His Mystical Body.

---

[71] *Ibid.*, p. 21.
[72] Lk. 6:19.
[73] Gal. 2:20.
[74] Boylan, *op. cit.*, p. 45.
[75] Rom. 6:3.
[76] Rom. 8:17.
[77] Rom. 6:6.
[78] Rom. 14:8.
[79] Rom. 6:4.
[80] *Ibid.*
[81] 1 Cor. 15:22.
[82] Rom. 6:8.
[83] Rom. 8:17.

It can even be said in a certain sense that He needs us; and here we quote Pius XII:

> Because Christ the Head holds such an eminent position, one must not think that He does not require the Body's help. What Paul said of the human organism is to be applied likewise to this Mystical Body: "The head cannot say to the feet: I have no need of you." It is manifestly clear that the faithful need the help of the Divine Redeemer. . . . Yet this, too, must be held, marvellous though it appear: *Christ requires His members.* First, the person of Jesus Christ is borne by the Supreme Pontiff, who in turn must call on others to share much of His solicitude. . . . Moreover Our Saviour does not rule the Church directly in a visible manner, and so in carrying out the work of Redemption He wishes to be helped by the members of His Body. This is not because He is indigent and weak, but rather *because He has so willed it* for the greater glory of His unspotted Spouse. Dying on the Cross He left to His Church the immense treasury of the Redemption; towards this she contributed nothing. But when those graces come to be distributed, not only does He share this task of sanctification with His Church, but He wants it in a way to be due to her action. Deep mystery this, subject of inexhaustible meditation: that the salvation of many depends on the prayers and voluntary penances which the members of the Mystical Body of Jesus Christ offer for this intention and on the assistance of the pastors of souls and of the faithful, especially of fathers and mothers of families, which they must offer to Our divine Saviour as though they were his associates [italics added].[84]

The plain sense is that Christ needs each child for the completion of His Mystical Body. He needs the co-operative work of parent and teacher for the perfection of each child. And as St. Paul says, "I fill up those things that are wanting in the sufferings of Christ, in my flesh, for his body which is the Church."[85] Parents and teachers are to "fill up" His body by the Christian formation of the child. Let educators realize their spiritual dignity and responsibility.

Not only is there this solidarity between Christ and His members: there is a superadded link between member and member. "And if one member suffer anything, all the members suffer with it: or if one member glory, all the members rejoice with it."[86] The members need one another supernaturally no less than naturally. "And the eye cannot say to the hand: I need not thy help: nor again the head to the feet: I have no need of you. Yea much more those that seem to be the more feeble members of the body are more necessary."[87] So real is this supernatural

---

[84] Pius XII, *Mystici Corporis*, n. 44.
[85] Col. 1:24.
[86] 1 Cor. 12:26.
[87] 1 Cor. 12:21–22.

link that the members of the Mystical Body are to "be mutually careful one for another."[88]

It will be apparent that the Christian conception of education adds one more reason — and a conscience reason — for that social consciousness and participation so ardently desired by many educational writers.

Yet, despite the solidarity of the members there is also a supernatural diversity that underscores both the uniqueness and the interdependence of each member. This the educator must never forget. Christ Himself spoke in parable of the graded distribution of "talents" — to one five, to another two, to another one.[89] In his Epistle to the Corinthians, St. Paul devotes a chapter[90] to the diversity of spiritual gifts among the members of Christ's Mystical Body — "diversity of graces,"[91] "diversities of ministries,"[92] "diversities of operations,"[93] apparent diversity of honor whereby some members seem the more honored and some the less;[94] "are all apostles? are all prophets? are all doctors?"[95] Yet all of these diverse members are bound together, have need of each other, form one Body under one Head; for "all these things one and the same Spirit worketh, dividing to everyone according as he will."[96]

There is already a natural social bond between all men: but by the incorporation into Christ's Mystical Body that is part of our spiritual restoration, there is, between students and educational personnel, a supernatural social bond more sublime, more far-reaching, more efficacious for good, more enduring. This is the doctrinal basis for the delightful family spirit uniting faculty and students that is found in some high schools and colleges and should be found in all. It is a cordial relationship wherein mutual respect is preserved, a natural cleavage is bridged, and mutual confidence is fostered.

We have seen the principal elements of our restoration in Christ: our elevation to the supernatural order, without however the restoration of the preternatural gifts; a supernature of sanctifying grace, the indwelling of the Holy Spirit in the soul; our adoption as sons of God and coheirs of Christ; the giving of Christ as the perfect Exemplar whose likeness we are to become; the incorporation into the Mystical Body; the bilateral union with Him and with the other members in a real, vital, fruitful union that transcends all natural ties. With good reason does the Church glorify God for having wonderfully established and more wonderfully renewed the dignity of human nature;[97] and truly Christ, though God, is the First-Born, the Eldest Brother of men, the Center of the world historically, intentionally, dynamically.

[88] 1 Cor. 12:25.
[89] Mt. 25:15.
[90] 1 Cor. 12.
[91] 1 Cor. 12:4.
[92] 1 Cor. 12:5.
[93] 1 Cor. 12:6.
[94] 1 Cor. 12:23–24.
[95] 1 Cor. 12:29.
[96] 1 Cor. 12:11.
[97] Cf. the prayer for the blessing of the water at the Offertory of the Mass.

Historically, the centuries before Him (B.C.) were focused on Him as the "desired of the ages." The history of the centuries after Him (A.D.) was modified by His influence: culturally in art, architecture, music, literature; politically in the Holy Roman Empire and the concept of Christendom;[98] militarily in the Crusades of the centuries; socially in the civilizing influence of Christianity, and in such institutions as the right of asylum and knightly chivalry; educationally in the gigantic, varied school system sponsored directly and indirectly by Christianity since the remote days of Protogenes at Edessa, Justin at Rome, Pantaenus at Alexandria — dark days when persecution still glowered on the near horizon and struck with lightning speed.

Christ is the center of man's world *intentionally* because as man's Exemplar He is the intentional form according to which men of good will pattern their free operations.

Dynamically, Christ is the centripetal force of the world, efficaciously drawing all right-minded men — "And I if I be lifted up from the earth will draw all things to myself";[99] and in different respects He is the centrifugal force with a plenitude of power — sending men forth to live Christian lives in society, sending them out of their homes to the farthest apostolate to "teach . . . all nations."[100] It is little wonder that the thinking of the early Christians was penetrated with the consciousness of Christ,[101] and that Christian literature should be studded with beautiful Christological passages similar to these from St. Ambrose.

> We have therefore all things in Christ . . . Christ is all to us. If you desire to cure your wounds, He is the Physician; if you burn with fever, He is the fount of living water; if you are oppressed by injustice, He is Justice; if you need help, He is Power; if you fear death, He is Life; if you desire heaven, He is the Way; if you would escape the darkness, He is the Light; if you seek nourishment, He is Food. Taste therefore and see how sweet is the Lord. Blessed is the man who trusts in Him.[102]

> Christ is grace, Christ is life, Christ is the Resurrection; he who rises will find Christ reigning.[103]

Education must be deeply and efficaciously centered in Christ; otherwise it would be out of touch with transcendental and eternal reality. The

---

[98] Cf. Hilaire Belloc, *Europe and the Faith* (New York: The Paulist Press, 1920).
[99] Jn. 12:32.
[100] Mt. 28:19.
[101] Cf. J. Lebreton and J. Zeiller, *L'Eglise Primitive,* Vol. I of *Histoire de l'Eglise,* ed. by A. Fliche and V. Martin (24 vols., Paris: Bloud & Gay, 1946), pp. 259–267.
[102] St. Ambrose, *De Virginitate,* XVI, 96, quoted in F. Cayré, *Manual of Patrology* (Paris: Desclée & Co., 1936), I, p. 543.
[103] St. Ambrose, *Expositio Evangelii Secundum Lucam;* from J. P. Migne, *Patrologiae, Cursus Completus (Latina)* (Parisiis, 1844 seq.), XV, 1668 c.

Catholic teacher, even amid the humdrum of algebraic exponents and chemical formulae, must never, despite discouragement, lose his Christian focus in regard to the child's destiny and his own part in it.

In noting the place of Christ in our perfection it is altogether fitting that we notice at His side Mary His Mother. She, by the will of God, was and is morally necessary for our restoration in Christ.

> Mary, bearing the Savior in her womb, can be said also to have borne all those whose life was contained in the life of the Savior. All we therefore who are united to Christ and as the Apostle says are members of His Body, of His flesh, of His bones (Ephes. 5:30) have issued from the womb of Mary as a body united to its head. . . . She is our Mother, spiritually indeed, but truly the Mother of the members of Christ, which we are.[104]

Those whose minds have been narrowed by Naturalism and discolored by the experience of human jealousies fail pitifully in trying to assess the disposition of God's providence in regard to Mary. Spiritually deaf, dumb, and blind, they emerge from their little earthly molehills and try to comprehend the length, breadth, height, and depth of the supernatural order; almost invariably their attempted comprehension is quantitative, additive, fractional. And one of the first points of failure is in estimating the role of Mary in the Christian life.

They fear, in a quantitative estimate, that she is given too much honor — as though the honor given her were a fraction to be taken from Christ but, mind you, not to be exceeded! She can never, however, be given too much of the right kind of honor, which is *hyperdulia*. Too much honor never adds up to worship or, technically, too much *hyperdulia* never adds up to *latria*. Love, honor, and devotion to Mary can be intensified to the *nth* degree without detracting from the worship due to God alone who Himself honored Mary surpassingly. He created her and lifted her to her eminence; He first loved her; He revealed her divine Maternity to us; He assumed her, body and soul, into His heaven; He crowned her in immeasurable glory. By His will she is inseparably and ineffably united with Christ in His life, His redemptive work, His glorification, His sanctification of the human race. Man's sanctification in Christ comes, by His will, through His Mother Mary as the Mediatrix of Grace. Any attempt to separate Him from her is to out-Herod Herod in snatching the

---

[104] Pius X, encyclical, *Ad diem illum,* February 2, 1904, *Actae Sanctae Sedis,* XXXVI (1903–1904), 453. "Ita ut Salvatorem habens Maria in utero, illos etiam dici queat gessisse omnes, quorum vitam continebat vita Salvatoris. Universi ergo, quotquot cum Christo iungimur, quique, ut ait Apostolus, *membra sumus corporis eius,* de carne eius et de ossibus eius (Ephes. 5:30), de Mariae utero egressi sumus, tamquam corporis instar cohaerentis cum capite. . . . *Mater quidem spiritu. . . , sed plane mater membrorum Christi, quod nos sumus"* (S. Aug., *L. de S. Virginitate,* c. 6).

child from the mother, and is to fail dismally. Devotion to Mary is not, then, a spiritual hobby which one may choose or neglect, not a side-chapel appendage; it is by God's design indispensable for our perfection in Christ. No Catholic school can fail to inculcate deep solid devotion to Mary, and be worthy of its title. Entirely to be commended then are those schools where the Rosary is said each day in the classroom, as, for example, in the schools conducted by the Marist Brothers.

The final element to be considered in man's restoration through Christ is man's own *co-operation with Christ.* For convenience, however, we defer the treatment of this point to the next chapter, and now consider some special questions that arise in regard to Christian perfection.

2. Analysis of Some Aspects of Christian Perfection

We have seen in an earlier chapter that it is for man to move himself to his end as a free agent; this requires, as a condition *sine qua non,* knowledge of the end. We have also seen that the proper and immediate end of education is perfection in Christ. We come now to analyze some aspects of this perfection in order that the educator may understand better the end of his activity and hence proportion more prudently the means to this end. In all these considerations we merely synthesize and apply for the teacher's benefit the pertinent truths of Revelation as elaborated extensively in theology. With full right education draws on theology for its higher principles as was discussed in Chapter I. Here as elsewhere we do not speak of the teacher in an exclusive sense as though these matters applied to him and not to parents, administrators, and all other educators. For convenience we refer simply to the teacher. This is fitting, too, because the teacher can readily appreciate educational issues and tune parental opinion.

We shall examine the core of Christian perfection, the degree of charity required, the variation of charity, and finally the call to this perfection in Christ.

A. THE CORE OF CHRISTIAN PERFECTION

A thing is said to be perfect when nothing proper to it is lacking. The full and complete perfection of something implies not merely the essence of that thing but the complexity of things that compose its normal integrity.[105] Good eyesight is part of the integrity of a man's physical perfection; without it we could not say that physically a man was completely perfect. Full Christian perfection will likewise demand a complexity of well-ordered elements. For the time being we are not concerned with all of these; but we are seeking for that element which constitutes the core of man's perfection in Christ.

[105] Cf. *Summa,* I–II, q. 4, a. 5.

There have been and are many erroneous notions about the nature of perfection — some of them clearly defined and explicitly proposed, others vague and pervading, noticeable yet evasive like a taint in the air. Sometimes wrong or shallow notions are given to children in Catholic schools.

Christian perfection obviously cannot consist essentially in the pantheism of Theosophy or Immanentism, however subtly that be expressed, e.g., as the consciousness of our divine identity.[106] It does not consist in a "broad, nicely balanced human culture that is 'well-informed' on actual problems and careful to grasp those phases of Christianity which are most attractive to a lofty nature."[107] Mere natural culture, even if it preserves the terminology of Christianity, cannot be the essence of a supernatural perfection; it is the concept, not the name, that matters. Absurd as it is, sometimes in popular literature and readers' columns, "goodness" or union with "God" is credited to the cultivation of the arts or to "moments" one may have in listening to a symphony or in admiring sea or landscape. These and kindred views show the extent of the religious sabotage wrought gradually by the subjectivism of the Reformation. Christian perfection does not consist essentially in Intellectualism[108] even though this be as lofty as contemplation; of itself, "knowledge puffeth up: but charity edifieth."[109] Christian perfection does not essentially consist in being courageous in the face of different difficulties, in doing what is "hard." Virtue consists in doing what is good rather than what is difficult; but, other things being present, the difficulty of the act increases the merit of the act.[110] Patience is an admirable virtue and always commands respect. But patience, restraint, self-control, even in the most trying circumstances, are not the essence of perfection. When the Scripture says, "Patience hath a perfect work,"[111] it refers to a patience ruled by the higher virtue of charity.[112] Perfection is not to be found in any or all acts of philanthropy, or humanitarianism. "If I should distribute all my goods to feed the poor, and if I should deliver my body to be burned and have not charity it profiteth me nothing."[113] Perfection is not found formally in austerity; so future generations are spared the gloom of

---

106 Cf. R. Garrigou-Lagrange, *Christian Perfection and Contemplation According to St. Thomas Aquinas and St. John of the Cross,* trans. by Sr. Timothea Doyle (St. Louis: B. Herder Book Co., 1937), p. 130, quoting Father Mainage, *Les Principes de la Theosophie,* 1922. Henceforth Fr. Garrigou-Lagrange's book will be referred to in these notes as *P. & C.*
107 *Ibid.,* p. 131.
108 *Ibid.*
109 1 Cor. 8:1.
110 "The principle of merit resides in charity. . . . It is more meritorious to accomplish easy things with great charity than to perform very difficult acts with less charity" (Garrigou-Lagrange, *P. & C.,* p. 133, n.). Cf. St. Paul, 1 Cor. 13:2.
111 James 1:4.
112 Cf. *Summa,* II–II, q. 184, a. 2, ad 3.
113 1 Cor. 13:3.

Puritanism and Jansenism. Christians can become saints without the punishing hooks of the fakirs and without the excesses of the Flagellants. Moreover, "Solitude, like poverty, is not the essence of perfection."[114]

A quotation from St. Francis de Sales will indicate the inadequacy of particular moral virtues as the essence of perfection and will fittingly conclude our consideration of various opinions about the core of perfection.

> Everyone paints devotion according to his own love and fancy. The man who is addicted to fasting thinks himself very devout if he fasts, though his heart be at the same time filled with rancor. . . . Another considers himself devout because he recites daily a multiplicity of prayers, although immediately afterwards he utters the most disagreeable, arrogant, and injurious words in his home and among his neighbors. Another cheerfully draws an alms out of his purse to give to the poor, but he cannot draw meekness out of his heart to forgive his enemies.[115]

What, then, is the core of Christian perfection? It is charity. The charity that is here understood is not a merely natural virtue, not even a natural affection supernaturalized by a supernatural modality.[116] Infused charity — called a theological virtue because its object is God Himself — is the core of perfection. Faith, hope, and charity all have God for their object and therefore are called theological virtues. Faith, however, refers to God *as not seen;* hope refers to God *as not yet attained.* Charity tends to God in Himself as the Supreme Good and *unites us to Him.* Hence it is the greatest of the theological virtues. This charity can be defined as a virtue infused into the will by God, whereby we love God for His own sake as the Supreme Good, and for His sake love ourselves and all intellectual creatures capable of beatitude.

Thus the formal object of charity is God Himself, the Supreme Good. The formal object of charity is nothing else than God's own infinite lovableness in Himself.

The love we bear Him is not primarily a selfish, interested love ("How much is in it for us" — called *amor concupiscentiae*) but it is the love of God for His own sake because He is so good (*amor benevolentiae*); and this love rises to the heights of the love of friendship — a *mutual* love, mutually manifested.

The love which we bear our neighbor in charity is not shown to an object wholly distinct from God. Since we love our neighbor for God's sake, this love is a secondary formal object of charity; it is consequent on the primary object, the love of God.[117]

---

[114] Cf. *Summa,* II–II, q. 188, a. 8.

[115] St. Francis de Sales, *Introduction to the Devout Life,* trans. J. K. Ryan (Garden City, N. Y.: Image Books, 1955), p. 35.

[116] Garrigou-Lagrange, *P. & C.,* p. 78.

[117] *Summa,* II–II, q. 23, a. 5, ad 1; cf. also II–II, q. 184, a. 3.

The material object of charity is every intellectual creature capable of beatitude and therefore all mankind — Catholics, Protestants, and pagans; the souls in purgatory; the angels and saints in heaven; but not the devils and lost souls in hell.

The teaching of the Scripture shows clearly that perfection is found chiefly in charity.

Put ye on therefore, as the elect of God, holy and beloved, the bowels of mercy, benignity, humility, modesty, patience: bearing with one another and forgiving one another: even as the Lord hath forgiven you, so do you also. *But above all these things have charity, which is the bond of perfection.*[118]

Charity never falleth away: whether prophecies shall be made void, or tongues shall cease or knowledge shall be destroyed.[119] [Thus charity endures forever.]

And now there remain faith, hope, and charity, these three: but the *greatest of these is charity.*[120] [Thus, charity is greater than the other theological virtues.][121]

Being rooted and founded in charity, you may be able to comprehend with all the saints what is the breadth, and length, and height, and depth. To know also the charity of Christ, which surpasseth all knowledge, that you may be filled unto all the fullness of God.[122]

But *before all things* have a constant mutual charity among yourselves.[123]

Charity is inseparable from the Divine life. It cannot co-exist with mortal sin in the aversion from God. The presence of charity in the soul is the constitutive sign of our being with God.

God is charity: and he that abideth in charity abideth in God and God in him.[124]

If anyone love me . . . we will come to him and will make our abode with him.[125]

He that loveth not, knoweth not God: for God is charity.[126]

He that loveth not, abideth in death.[127]

---

[118] Col. 3:12–14.
[119] 1 Cor. 13:8.
[120] 1 Cor. 13:13.
[121] Cf. St. Paul's other words: "If I should have all faith so that I could move mountains and have not charity, I am nothing" (1 Cor. 13:2).
[122] Eph. 3:18–19.   [124] 1 Jn. 4:16.   [126] 1 Jn. 4:8.
[123] 1 Pet. 4:8.   [125] Jn. 14:23.   [127] 1 Jn. 3:14.

These words of the Scripture are simply the echo of Christ's meaning when He was asked what one had to do to possess eternal ilfe, and He said:

> Thou shalt love the Lord thy God with thy whole heart, and with thy whole soul, and with thy whole mind. This is the greatest and the first commandment. And the second is like to this: Thou shalt love thy neighbor as thyself. On these two commandments dependeth the whole law and the prophets.[128]

It should be noticed that these words give us a *precept* of charity. God gives us the ability to love Him. He reveals to us some of His infinite lovableness, He pleads with us to love Him and to make sure of our love. He gives us a positive precept of charity: "Thou shalt love . . ."

From the revelation of God in the Scriptures, then, we glean that charity is the greatest of all the virtues, greater even than faith, something to be had above all; that it is "the bond of perfection"; that its presence or absence means union or disunion with God, spiritual life or spiritual death; that it will endure eternally; that it is the means singled out by Christ as leading to the attainment of man's ultimate end; that, moreover, God has given us a positive precept of charity — we have an obligation to love Him. Therefore we say that the core of our perfection in Christ is in charity. Education that fosters charity in a child, no matter what else it may be lacking, is fostering that which is indispensable, greatest, and eternally enduring. Nothing else, no matter how useful or noble in its own order, can compensate for the mediocrity or the loss of charity. This thought must be a norm for parents, teachers, and especially school administrators in the many practical decisions that confront them — decisions about selecting a school, building new schools, organizing the curriculum and cocurriculum, molding the tone of the school, making decisions about coeducation, about the details of school retreats, the students' attendance at parochial missions, the worth of a teacher, etc.

Much could be written in explanation and analysis of this charity and its interrelations with all aspects of life. Here, however, we give five explanatory statements.

1. According to the Thomistic school, *the charity in which Christian perfection chiefly consists is formally the act of charity and antecedently the virtue of charity.*[129] The virtue is the principle whence proceed the acts of charity, and in these acts is found that actual union with God which is actual perfection (yet in varied degrees as will be explained later). "Life consists especially in the act of living."[130] Here, then, is the basis for the recommendation of the saints that our days be sprinkled

---

[128] Mt. 22:37–40.
[129] Cf. Garrigou-Lagrange, *P. & C.*, p. 144, n.
[130] *Ibid.*

with prayer and especially with acts of love. This is the theological reason behind the frequent acts of charity interspersed throughout daily prayer in Catholic schools;[131] and herein is made manifest one deficiency of the "release-time" programs or of any mere "afterhours" religious instruction — not to mention the outright secularistic schools. The most typical Catholic schools will gently but systematically form their pupils to the practice of making fervent acts of charity and will accustom them to season all their activities with this supreme act of Christian virtue.[132] This formation must be given prudently of course, keeping in mind the condition of the educands. They are neither adults nor consecrated religious; hence adult religious behavior should not be expected of them. Such pressurizing could only bring subsequent spiritual disaster.

In cultivating delicately this practice of charity the school is training the child to perform the noblest and most exalted single act it can perform on earth. At the risk of being misunderstood by those critical of Christian education we quote St. John of the Cross:

> An instant of pure love is more precious in the sight of God, and of the soul, and more profitable to the Church than all other good works put together, though it may seem as if nothing were done.[133]

No one can doubt, for example, that St. Gemma Galgani, confined to her room, lived a life more significant for others than that of some headlined philanthropist.

For the proper understanding of these words of St. John it should be noted that he says *"more profitable . . . than . . . good works"*; he does not praise these the less, but rather charity more. This truth is a principle for judging the worth of life's activities. It has a valuable application in the education and adjustment of deformed students of whatever kind, also in vocational guidance. A graduate electing to enter a contemplative order is not wasting his or her life!

2. *The charity in which perfection chiefly consists includes not only the love of God but also the love of neighbor.* We shall now expand briefly the mention already made of the secondary object of charity.

This aspect of charity is given us by Christ in the words already quoted "and thy neighbor as thyself."[134] It is not enough to attempt to love God and at the same time to bypass one's neighbor, who incidentally is all mankind. "If any man say I love God, and hateth his brother; he is a

---

[131] For example, in the "prayer of the hour" that is characteristic of the Marist Brothers' schools.

[132] It is manifest, however, that no human being, the Blessed Virgin excepted, can ever love God *actually* at every moment; the conditions of the present life do not permit it. Cf. *Summa*, II–II, q. 184, a. 2, ad 3.

[133] St. John of the Cross, *Spiritual Canticle*, S. XXVII, quoted in E. Boylan, *This Tremendous Lover* (Westminster, Md.: The Newman Bookshop, 1947), p. 267.

[134] Mt. 22:39.

liar. For he that loveth not his brother, whom he seeth, how can he love God, whom he seeth not? And this commandment we have from God: that he, who loveth God, love also his brother."[135] It is not enough to love only the more eligible and the more "important" among one's neighbors, excluding the "unimportant." "Amen I say to you, as long as you did it not to one of these least, neither did you do it to me."[136] Christ identifies Himself with the angular, poorly dressed, or moronic child over in the far corner of the classroom, who never makes the front row on special occasions, is never chosen to be flower girl or parade boy, never asked to "help teacher." He may be ungainly; algebra may bring a stony look to his eyes. But he must never be excluded from the teacher's charity, never made to feel less important than the others. Here is a motivating principle for teacher dedication and for warm teacher-pupil relations that transcends the merely natural kindness of a teacher — without in any way destroying or lessening his natural kindness. Lack of charity is a shibboleth that differentiates the hireling from the Christian teacher.

This love of neighbor has its degrees ranging all the way from the minimal to the ordinary, to the eminent, to the heroic. By the understanding and proper teaching of these degrees much confusion can be precluded.

I. There is a love of neighbor which is of precept. Without it, charity is impossible. It is necessary for salvation.
  A. This minimal love consists in having nothing in one's heart seriously contrary to charity and in positively excluding nobody from one's love.
  B. Its qualities? It must be:
    1. True, i.e., wishing good to another without selfishness.
    2. Well ordered, i.e., preferring a greater good to a lesser good.
    3. Holy, i.e., ordained to God.
    4. Efficacious, i.e., showing itself in good works, given the need.

II. There is a love of neighbor, a more perfect charity, which is of counsel. It can be considered in a threefold way.
  A. According to the *extension* of the love. There is a love which:
    1. Extends only to friends and acquaintances in a positive way; yet does not positively exclude others.
    2. Extends positively to strangers also.
    3. Extends positively and gratuitously to enemies even outside those cases when charity to them would be of precept.
  B. According to the *intensity* of the love, manifested in and measured by the things it overcomes and even despises for one's neighbor.
    1. External goods, such as giving one's money, food, clothing for others. St. Martin sharing his cloak with a beggar is an example of this degree.

---

[135] 1 Jn. 4:20–21.   [136] Mt. 25:45.

2. Bodily comfort, undergoing bodily fatigue, inconvenience, etc., for one's neighbor. There readily comes to mind the example of St. Francis Xavier, the former Spanish nobleman and rising young professor, now trotting for days as a lackey in the entourage of a Japanese nobleman in order to win permission for the Christian instruction of those pagan peoples — a sacrifice of bodily comfort indeed. But nearer home, this intense and sustained charity can be and is manifested in our hospitals, asylums, orphanages, schools.

3. Life itself. "Greater love than this no man hath, that a man lay down his life for his friends."[137]

A life of self-sacrificing service of others is in some way akin to the very renunciation of life. For life is manifested in the power of immanent activity which pre-eminently includes responsible, self-chosen activity; something which is moved only by something else is inanimate or dead. But a life of self-sacrificing service, spending oneself and being spent by prompt and generous attention to the needs of others when and how and where these are seen, is an habitual and heroic renunciation of self. It is death to self on the highest level of life. True, the life of the body remains — the heart beats, and the blood still flows; but freedom, personal preferences, and convenience are fettered and subjected to the need of the neighbor. The Curé of Ars, for the last thirty years of his life the prisoner of the pilgrims' needs and scarcely finding three hours daily for sleep, was a luminous example of this living death to self. But the Christian teacher, by generous dedication to the child's intellectual and spiritual needs, can also find scope for exalted charity. This is especially true of the religious under vow of obedience. The teacher's dedication in the classroom is a far higher fraternal charity than the benefactor's donation for the classroom; yet, so often, the benefactor receives more appreciation and consideration.

C. According to the *effect* of the love. The greater the good brought to the neighbor the greater the love, other things being equal. No one equates $1 and $100. Under this aspect, the degrees of fraternal charity follow the threefold hierarchy of goods.

1. Bodily goods. To feed the hungry, to clothe the naked, to nurse the sick, etc., are truly works of charity canonized in the Gospel.

2. Rational goods. To teach the ignorant, to counsel the confused, to recall the erring are all goods of a higher order.

---

[137] Jn. 15:13. For a discussion of these degrees of charity, cf. St. Thomas, opusculum, *De Perfectione Vitae Spiritualis*, Chaps. 13 and 14.

3. Supernatural goods. To teach the truths of faith, to lead others to God, to bring them to, or administer to them the sacraments — these are the greatest goods charity can find to give one's neighbor. The communication of such goods adds a special perfection to fraternal charity because by them the neighbor is orientated to his ultimate end wherein alone can be found true happiness, present and ultimate.

Ex officio the communication of such goods is the prerogative of the priesthood, but the dedicated Christian teacher notably shares this supreme work. He gives the child more than the wealthiest philanthropist, much more.

Everybody feels the need of some idealism. In this century many find it in guidance of youth; it is currently the fashion to eulogize teaching as a noble profession. These considerations on Christian charity put meaning and richness into what otherwise could be a vapid cliché!

In every generation some are called upon to manifest heroic charity — nor do they have to go to Molokai to do so. Hence the inculcation and example of such ideals should form part of typically Christian education. Anything less exalted would be a counterfeit.

3. *The charity in which perfection chiefly consists does not exclude the practice of all the other infused virtues.* It is important to grasp this point. Charity is a queen in the soul, not a hermit. It is not an exclusive virtue. The true Christian is resplendent with many virtues; yet always they are subordinated, co-ordinated, sublimated, bonded in charity, which under different respects is called the form, the root, the mother of all virtue.[138] It is called the form, primarily in the sense of efficient rather than of exemplary causality. Charity ordains the acts of the other virtues to the ultimate end; and in moral matters the form — species and mode — of an act is taken principally from the end, precisely because the will which produces the act has the end as its object and form.

It is called the root, not in the sense of material causality but in as far as all the virtues draw their sustenance and vigor from their ordination to the end of charity; all virtues arise from love of the immutable good which is loved in charity. For example, faith without charity is "dead." We believe someone we deeply love much more readily and efficaciously than someone we hate. Thus, charity nourishes faith to its perfect development.

It is rightly called the mother. Just as a mother conceives life from

---

138 Cf. *Summa*, II–II, q. 23, a. 8; *ibid.*, q. 4, a. 3; also I–II, q. 84, a. 1, ad 1. Cf. a lengthy discussion of this matter by A. J. Falanga, *Charity the Form of the Virtues According to St. Thomas* (Washington, D. C.: The Catholic University of America, 1948); also Gerard Gilleman, *Le Primat de la Charité en Théologie Morale* (Paris: Desclée de Brouwer et Cie, 1952).

another, charity, from the desire of the last end, conceives by commanding the act of the other virtues.

Hence St. Paul says:

Charity is *patient*, is *kind:* charity *envieth not*, dealeth not perversely: is *not puffed up;* is *not ambitious*, seeketh not her own, is not provoked to *anger*, thinketh *no evil;* rejoiceth not in iniquity, but rejoiceth with the *truth* [italics added].[139]

Charity needs *humility* as a foundation because humility expels pride which God resists, making man submissive to God and hence always susceptible (St. Thomas uses the word *patulum*, signifying something standing wide open) to the influence of God's grace.[140]

Charity needs faith,[141] which is the first step toward God who, first known *ut sic* by faith, is then loved. Hence, St. Paul elsewhere says, "He that cometh to God must believe."[142]

St. Paul elsewhere speaks of "doing the truth in charity."[143] Later we will see the implications of charity's need for truth.

The Christian life is a spiritual warfare. "The kingdom of heaven suffereth violence and the violent bear it away."[144] Growth in charity demands and effects the overcoming of laziness, selfishness, natural impulsiveness, impatience, egoism in all its forms. What a blessed school would that be where no one among teachers or administrators was egotistic or impatient, where laziness and sensuality were not found among the students — as far as it is given to fallen human nature to inhibit these lower tendencies. While a certain degree of natural control over these tendencies is possible by natural effort and natural habit, they are more powerfully combated by the supernatural means that the Christian has at his disposal; and supernatural charity provides the strongest motive and most effective means of curtailing them.

The expression of the precise relationship between charity and all the other virtues, infused and natural, is not agreed on and need not concern us here: it is a matter for theology.[145] The important point for education

---

139 1 Cor. 13:4–6.   142 Hebr. 11:6.
140 *Summa*, II–II, q. 161, a. 5, ad 2.   143 Eph. 4:15.
141 *Ibid.*   144 Mt. 11:12.

145 Cajetan considers that charity bears a relationship to the other virtues as causes of perfection similar to the relation of principal to instrumental causes. Fr. Dominic Hughes in a recent article expounds this view in "The Dynamics of Christian Perfection," *The Thomist*, XV (April, 1952), 247–288. Garrigou-Lagrange, O.P., does not like this view. He, with Passerini, O.P., considers that the other virtues, insofar as they are of precept, pertain to the essence of perfection as matter pertains to the essence of a natural composite, with charity the formal element in that essence; whereas insofar as these other virtues are of counsel they are accidents of perfection. "Passerini introduces a precision which Cajetan had forgotten, and clearly expresses the thought of St. Thomas," says Garrigou-Lagrange, *P. & C.*, p. 145, n.

is that the perfection in Christ, which is its proper and immediate end, consists chiefly but not exclusively in charity; it requires the array of all Christian virtues.

4. *The charity in which perfection chiefly consists implies the development of all man's gifts and capabilities,* both natural and supernatural.

The parable of the talents[146] with its commendations, reproofs, and punishments hinging on the use or neglect of the talents, irrespective of their number; the parable of the vine bearing fruit;[147] the parable of the barren fig tree given one more year to bear fruit;[148] Christ's cursing of the barren fig tree that produced leaves only;[149] His words: "Unto whomsoever much is given, of him much shall be required"[150] — all these things show the mind of Christ regarding the use of God's gifts. He errs hopelessly who thinks that he can protest his love for God and at the same time neglect to cultivate the operative gifts of God. The love of God the Giver and the appreciation of these operative gifts are best shown by their use and their cultivation; just as a man shows that he appreciates a gift automobile by driving it, not by cementing it down in his garage.[151] These powers will naturally be cultivated according to their respective importance. The higher the power, the more attentive the cultivation. Hence, the intellect, one of man's loftiest powers, will necessarily receive special attention in any scheme of education ordained to perfection in Christ, who called Himself the Truth. St. Thomas, the teacher, would never have reached sanctity had he neglected study and failed to cultivate his intellectual gifts. His surpassing intellect was providentially given him for the great synthesis of philosophy and Revelation. To the making of this synthesis Thomas the saint, the man of charity, applied himself with an ardor that would compel admiration from the most academically minded. Yet it was charity that motivated, sustained, and orientated to God his prodigious intellectual activity.

Christian education cannot concern itself merely with fostering charity and at the same time blithely neglect all other development of man according to his capabilities and powers.

5. *Charity absolutely requires the keeping of all the commandments and is greatly facilitated by the observance of the counsels.* This keeping of the commandments we will discuss more fully under the heading of man's co-operation with God. Here we merely note the relation of the

---

146 Mt. 25:14–30; cf. also the parable of the pounds, Lk. 19:11–27.
147 Jn. 15:1–2.
148 Lk. 13:6–9.
149 Mk. 11:13–14, 21.
150 Lk. 12:48.
151 This does not deny " 'that the best thing that one can do with the best of things is to sacrifice it' on condition, however, that we safeguard the hierarchy of the gifts of God and of the virtues, and that we do not sacrifice something superior to what is inferior" (Garrigou-Lagrange, *P. & C.*, p. 132, n.).

commandments and counsels to charity. Perfection essentially implies the observance of the commandments since these are directed to the removal of those things that are incompatible with charity. Perfection is facilitated by the observance of the counsels, which contribute to it instrumentally, says St. Thomas.[152] They remove things that hinder charity, yet are not of themselves incompatible with it, e.g., occupation with worldly business.

Of all that we do so laboriously in life, be it ever so learned or famous, that only will last which is done for love of God. Scholars therefore must love God in their learning and busy people must seek Him in their activity; otherwise the learning, the great works, will vanish like smoke.

Objections. The chief objections to Christian perfection being centered in charity are that this is too exclusive, too unreal and passive, and moreover is a deordination.

Too "exclusive" — the explanation given above under "3" and "4" disposes of this objection.

"Unreal and passive" — the explanation above under "5" and still to follow in regard to man's co-operation with God disposes of that objection in a theoretical way; it is enough to say here that love of its nature seeks to express itself and that our active co-operation with God's plan is a necessary element in our restoration. A little reading of the lives of the saints — of St. Teresa of Jesus, of St. Alphonsus de Liguori, of St. John Bosco, of the Curé of Ars working approximately a twenty-hour day — would dispose of the objection in a practical way, making it clear that charity is not inert, impotent, passive. *E contra* it provides just that dynamism which is needed to make a teacher dedicated and a student earnest. It is the unseen powerful motive behind the priests, Brothers, and Sisters who leave their homes, shorten their sleep, delimit normal social activity in order to teach in the Catholic schools of this country without any personal payment beyond their mere sustenance.

A "deordination" is a third objection, and a very old one; it is answered admirably by St. Thomas, with a distinction.

This is the problem. Taken absolutely (*simpliciter*) the intellect as a faculty is superior to the will because its object, which is "being" in all its transcendence, is simpler and more abstract and therefore nobler than the object of the will, which is the appetible good thing itself.[153] If the intellect taken absolutely is superior to the will, how can knowledge, which is the act of the intellect, be inferior to charity which is the act of man's will? How can the official acts of the President be less important

152 Cf. *Summa*, II–II, q. 184, a. 3.
153 Cf. *Summa*, I, q. 82, a. 3. It is obvious now by the same reasoning that to know earthly things is better than to love them — a man's deep knowledge of frogs entitles him to respect as a biologist, a learned man of science: his deep love of frogs would bring him fitting ridicule.

for America than the official acts of the Vice-President? (This analogy limps on both legs but it serves to indicate the point of the objection.)

The answer to the objection is contained in the very analysis of the interrelations of the two faculties, intellect and will. Absolutely (*simpliciter*) the intellect is superior to the will, for the reasons indicated above; relatively (*secundum quid*) the will may be superior to the intellect insofar as a particular act of the inferior faculty may be superior to the act of the otherwise superior faculty. In illustration of this we can say that the hearing of a beautiful symphony is of a higher artistic order than the sight of an ordinary color, although people commonly regard sight as a gift more precious than hearing.

In the same way in this life the will's love of God in charity is nobler than the intellect's knowledge of God, since the will tends to God as He is in Himself, the *Deitas ut sic,* whereas the intellect in knowing Him has only a created likeness (*species*) of God within it; and this *species* is limited by the intellect's own created condition.[154] Hence our knowledge of God confines Him within the bounds of our limited ideas; our love of God in charity tends toward Him as He is in Himself, the *Deitas ut sic,* and is therefore nobler than our knowledge.[155] It is better, then, "to love God than to know Him although love always presupposes a certain knowledge and is directed by it."[156]

Charity is the jewel of Christian perfection. If we view it in the light of faith, its beauties glisten and flash in profusion, and every ray becomes a guiding beam for conduct. We will note some of the corollaries of charity's excellence.

To receive charity from God is to become rich, to pass from oblivion to distinction, darkness to light, emptiness to fullness, poverty to wealth; these attributes are of course spiritual. "All the glory of the king's daughter is within," says Psalm 44.

In this life, to love God is greater than to know Him. Clearly then, if an absolute choice must be made, charity is preferable to knowledge. A moron's earnest love of God is more precious, more ennobling, more enduring than a scientist's knowledge of nature's most secret powers, than a theologian's profound grasp of this noblest of sciences — though there is no reason why all three should not excel in charity; indeed, knowledge stimulates charity. While we marvel at the profundities of St. Thomas expounded in the more than twenty volumes of his *Omnia Opera,* it is

---

[154] Cf. *Summa,* I, q. 27, a. 4; also I, q. 16, a. 1; also II–II, q. 27, a. 4, ad 2.

[155] But in heaven aided by the light of glory we will know God *sicuti est* by seeing Him face to face in a clear intuitive vision without the limitations of species. We will of course never adequately comprehend God, since God alone can understand Himself perfectly. Seeing Him, we will immovably love Him and will be inundated with unspeakable joy.

[156] Garrigou-Lagrange, *P. & C.,* p. 142.

well for us to recall that he referred to these works as being no more important than a little straw, when compared with the love of God.

Charity moreover attunes us to God so closely in its perfection that we have thereby a certain sympathy or connaturality with divine things, and our hearts and minds react to them in sympathetic vibration as it were.[157]

It will be apparent that the Christian teacher can bring to special education — that branch of education concerned with the exceptional child, particularly the physically and mentally handicapped — a motive and a dimension that others cannot have, however naturally earnest, well financed, and well equipped with Bulletin typewriters, talking-book machines, etc. We do not decry these material aids, so helpful to the handicapped; we do not depreciate the valiant efforts made by all devoted teachers in this field to develop the varied natural talents of afflicted children. We wholeheartedly endorse and commend them, for grace builds on nature. But the contents of this chapter in general and more specifically what has been said about the importance and efficacy of charity will indicate sufficiently the supernatural beauties which only the Christian teacher can unveil. While spastic or ataxic hands struggle weakly to use the aids that modern science provides, or perhaps are completely helpless in paralysis, the teacher can direct the discouraged eyes to the crucifix on the wall of the Christian school, show them His hands and feet also made helpless — by the nails. He can remind his pupils that those sacred limbs, nailed immovable in loving obedience to God's will for the redemption of man, were in *that very state* accomplishing their greatest good — far more so than when they moved about Palestine healing the sick and distributing food.

In analyzing some aspects of Christian perfection we have found that its core is supernatural charity. We have found that this charity necessarily includes the love of our neighbor, and implies the development of all the other virtues as well as of our talents and capabilities; hence in no sense is charity exclusive or inert. We have seen, too, that the emphasis on charity is not anti-intellectual.

B. DEGREE OF CHARITY

The importance of charity as the bond of perfection is clear. Clear, too, is our obligation to love God.

Now the question of considerable importance, ascetical and educational, arises. Does this obligation of charity prescribe for us the highest degrees of charity? Yes. There is no limit to the charity that is prescribed to us. Higher perfection is prescribed for us; we can never accept mediocrity as an ideal. St. Thomas says:

---

[157] *Summa*, II–II, q. 145, a. 2 and a. 4.

The love of God and of our neighbor is not prescribed according to a certain measure so that whatever would be over and above that measure would be of counsel. This is clear from the form of the precept which indicates the perfection required "Thou shalt love the Lord thy God with thy whole heart. . . ." Remember that "whole" is the same as "perfect" according to Aristotle (Phys. 111.64). Likewise it is said "Thou shalt love thy neighbor as thyself" and each one loves himself most. The reason of this is "the end of the commandment is charity" as the Apostle says (1 Timothy 1.5); and the end is not subject to a measure, but only the means to the end are measured, as the Philosopher says. For a doctor does not seek half a cure of the sick person. He measures the medicine, the amount of food [that is, the means] but not the health, which he seeks without measure.[158]

Pius XI expresses this authoritatively:

All men of every condition, in whatever honorable walk of life they may be, can and should imitate Christ Our Lord, the supreme Exemplar of all holiness given to men by God, and with God's help reach *the summit of Christian perfection* — as is shown abundantly by the example of the saints[159] [italics added].

The *Catechism of the Council of Trent* says: "It is the pastor's duty to seek the holiness and perfection of the faithful."[160]
Cardinal Mercier expressed the same idea:

We are all called to ascend the summits of perfection . . . to ascend . . . even to complete detachment from created things and to the spirit of union with God alone for Himself alone. In regard to this ascent, there are in the world and at times among the clergy, sad and profound prejudices, which we ought all to apply ourselves to extirpate. I repeat, everyone is called to the fullness of evangelical perfection. . . . To all it is said: Be ye therefore perfect as your heavenly Father is perfect (Matt. 5:48).[161]

Garrigou-Lagrange says:

It would therefore be a great illusion to think that only imperfect charity is prescribed and that the higher degrees of this virtue are only of counsel.[162]

---

[158] *Summa*, II–II, q. 184, a. 3. This is also the teaching of St. Augustine, St. Antoninus, Cajetan, Valentia, Passerini, Garrigou-Lagrange; Suarez, however, thought otherwise. Cf. Garrigou-Lagrange, *P. & C.*, p. 179.
[159] Pius XI, *Christian Marriage*, December 31, 1930, *AAS* (XXII), p. 548.
[160] *The Catechism of the Council of Trent*, Part II, Chap. 8, I.
[161] Cardinal Mercier, *La Vie Interieux*, 1919, p. 98, quoted in Garrigou-Lagrange, *P. & C.*, p. 187.
[162] Garrigou-Lagrange, *P. & C.*, p. 185.

Clearly we must not measure out and restrain the charity we seek for ourselves or desire for others as teachers or parents — we should not decide that children will be just so good and no more. Mediocrity in charity as an ideal can have no accepted place in Christian education, since charity is the core of the end. But we do indeed measure and restrain the *means* to the end and keep them within due bounds, that is, within a happy mean. Vocal prayers, fasting, austerities, privations, etc., as means to the end must be restrained and controlled by prudence. This is a distinction important for the balanced living of the Christian life and important as an educational attitude. God, the end, is to be loved without measure; the means by which we reach the love of God are to be measured according to prudence.

All men do not arrive, however, at an equal degree of perfection, as St. John of the Cross points out.[163] But this inequality is to be left in the hands of Providence, and not determined by a person's sloth or a director's negligence. Nor does this charity have to be achieved rapidly, let alone all at once. It will depend on the designs of Providence. Usually it will be gradual but always it will tend toward the higher degrees. What do the higher degrees of charity include? Some writers distinguish a life of perfection called "ordinary" or "ascetical" to which the many should aspire, from a life of perfection called "extraordinary" or "mystical" to which the privileged few are destined. According to this concept asceticism is not on the same continuum as mysticism.

This view is not, according to Garrigou-Lagrange, typically Catholic; it is untraditional. It may rationalize mediocrity under the guise of humility and of avoiding presumption, it may be a convenient salve for self-chosen half saints, but it is opposed to the teaching of the great Christian writers — St. Augustine, St. Albert the Great, St. Thomas Aquinas, St. Bonaventure, Denis the Mystic, Tauler, Louis de Blois, Blessed Henry Suso, Venerable Denis the Carthusian, Blessed Bartholomew of the Martyrs, St. John of the Cross, St. Teresa, Vallgornera, O.P., and the early Carmelite theologians — Thomas of Jesus, Dominic of the Blessed Trinity, Anthony of the Holy Ghost.[164] Garrigou-Lagrange, O.P.,[165] Fr. Lallement, S.J., and Fr. Gabriel, O.C.D.,[166] are notable among moderns in re-emphasizing and explaining the many points of obscurity in the traditional doctrine.

There is no double track in the *essentials* of Christian perfection — one for the average, one for the few. No artificial dichotomy is to be made between asceticism and mysticism.[167] The perfection of charity,

---

163 *The Ascent*, Bk. II, Chap. V, quoted in Garrigou-Lagrange, *op. cit.,* p. 162, n.
164 Quoted in Garrigou-Lagrange, *P. & C.,* pp. 24–25. See also pp. 368–372 where the author quotes the opinions of St. John of the Cross, St. Teresa, and others.
165 Cf. *Christian Perfection and Contemplation, passim.*
166 Fr. Gabriel, *St. John of the Cross* (Cork: The Mercier Press, 1946).
167 Cf. Garrigou-Lagrange, *P. & C.,* pp. 43 and 46.

even in its highest degrees of transforming union with God, is a continuous process and it is a perfection that all should aspire to according to the degree and mode of God's providence. It is simply the normal[168] development of the stupendous supernatural gifts given to every man in baptism. This, then, is the ordinary way of perfection even though the attainment of its highest degrees may, through the feebleness of man, be numerically infrequent.

The following exalted but logical implications of this traditional doctrine should be clearly understood.

1. The full perfection of charity presupposes the passive purification of the senses — whereby a man's passions are curbed and he leads a spiritual life detached from the domination of his senses — and the purification of the spirit — whereby he is purified from his own inmost attachments.[169] It is unfortunate that these terms have acquired a fearsome connotation; at their mention people somehow think of St. Peter of Alcantara's clanking chains and St. Rose of Lima's penitential bed. Some voluntary mortification is certainly needed; but life has many trials which people have to endure anyway — the trials of generous parenthood, of daily work and especially of teaching, of vexation and frustration. No one can successfully escape them; in eluding one we find another. People forget that the devout acceptance of these trials is very purifying. They forget, too, that these "crosses" carried for Christ rather than dragged are thereby lightened and sweetened. In this providential way the basic self-purification needed for spiritual growth can be effected; at the same time, by a divine paradox, life's load is partially lightened. Hence by the proper pursuit of Christian perfection, man is refreshed amid life's labors and burdens — as Christ has promised. Later we will see the educational implications of these truths regarding discipline and self-denial.

2. The perfection of charity excludes any affection for *deliberate* venial sin; such sins cool the fervor of charity.[170] Any educator, parent, or teacher who has not the strong desire to see his pupils eliminate *deliberate*

---

[168] According to Garrigou-Lagrange, Mintero, Lamballe, and others, "ascetical" and "mystical" are terms legitimately used to indicate degrees of perfection, but along the same continuum; just as infancy, adolescence, and adulthood are terms used to indicate the stages of one man's life. The ascetical stage is *characterized* by the human mode of the Christian virtues without by any means excluding the manifestations of the gifts of the Holy Ghost. The ascetical life is that state of the spiritual life in which the soul's chief labor consists in struggling against sin and seeking to make stable progress in virtue. The mystical life — spiritual maturity — is characterized "by the divine mode of the gifts of the Holy Ghost, intervening no longer in a latent or transitory way, but in a manner both manifest and frequent" (Garrigou-Lagrange, *P. & C.*, p. 36; cf. also pp. 29–43 for a discussion of this whole viewpoint).

[169] Garrigou-Lagrange, *P. & C.*, pp. 146–156.

[170] *Ibid.*, p. 427.

venial sin from their lives needs to study Christian truths and to examine his own conscience.

3. The true Christian seeking the perfection of charity will earnestly but prudently (and this normally requires proper guidance) strive to overcome the imperfections which beset the lives of even good people.[171]

4. All the baptized may laudably desire and should desire contemplation and the union of fruition with God in charity.[172] "This contemplation can be merited at least *de congruo,*"[173] according to many eminent theologians. This is by no means to say that all or anyone may desire visions and ecstasies, etc. In fact no one may desire these things — to do so would be pride; nor are these at all necessary for Christian perfection. Hence, no educator is asked to prepare his lisping dullards for visions!

It is important to notice that these processes belong strictly within the sanctuary of the individual soul and are under the care of the proper guides of conscience. It is not for teachers to interfere and to direct individual souls in these matters. But it is rather their sphere to encourage tactfully and generally the highest ideals of Christian perfection and to see to it that the school provides the best possible climate for the development of this marvelous spiritual potential without choking it in any way — just as the curator in the botanical gardens sees to it that the precious seedling is given the right conditions for the fullest growth, and moreover nourishes that growth.

The school can early and easily provide frequent opportunity for the practice of obedience, of self-denial, of self-detachment, of fortitude, preparing the student for the passive purification of the senses needed for the preservation and increase of charity. The balanced and sublimated discipline of school life requires student self-restraint, reverential submission to proper authority, and the renunciation of whims and impulses such as the desire to gossip in class or study period. The school's academic stimulus encourages other good character habits — habits of industry and perseverance, the conquest of laziness, envy, and sensuality. Parents, good schools, and good teachers can do so much by daily opportunities in this way; however, it needs the motivation that comes from high

---

171 An imperfection is an act morally good and ordained to the end of charity, but lacking a certain perfection suitable to spiritual progress. It would be an imperfection, e.g., to make a less fervent act of the love of God than becomes our degree of charity, or to do, for a legitimate motive, something which is less good when we could have done something which we clearly knew to be a greater good and within our competence. Imperfections are not of themselves venial sins, but many of them mar the peace and vigor of the spiritual life. *Per accidens* some of them can become venial sins. A deliberate habit of imperfections can lead on to venial sin. Cf. Garrigou-Lagrange, *P. & C.,* pp. 430–434.

172 Cf. *ibid.,* p. 197, n.

173 *Ibid.,* p. 161, n.

Christian ideals. It needs tact, too. But it is a legitimate goal and challenge for the Christian teacher. This is not the place to say in detail how he is to find such opportunities. If only he be utterly imbued with the highest Christian ideals his example, his casual remarks, his manner will be an encouragement, and he will find opportunities hourly in handling discipline cases, in making and correcting assignments, in the reading he encourages, etc.

We say then that the precept of charity is not only without limit, but that its fulfillment is a continuum extending to the summit of Christian perfection.

At once the further question arises: Does a man break this precept by not possessing the higher degrees of charity? Not necessarily. One does not break a command by not fulfilling it in the best possible way. A sufficient fulfillment avoids a transgression. And this sufficient degree is had when nothing — career, children, parents, money — is loved more than God, equally with God, or contrary to His will. This supreme love of God in charity — as likewise our love of neighbor — is to be appreciative and effective, not necessarily affective. Hence we are not obliged to feel a warmer glow of affection for God than for parents or family; this affection may or may not be present. But if perchance the choice has to be made, despite our feelings we are bound to choose God before parents and family. St. Perpetua, a young mother of twenty-two, did right then in adhering to her faith and facing execution by beasts and sword, even though it meant the orphaning of her newborn baby. It was a clear but heart-rending choice. She chose with true wisdom — and with well-placed confidence in the heavenly Father's protection over the child orphaned by a martyrdom.

Various estimates of the grades of charity have been made. St. Thomas' estimate is clear. He says that the first degree of charity, seen in beginners, consists chiefly in the overcoming of sin and the liberation from the slavery of concupiscence. The second, seen in proficients, consists chiefly in the relentless struggle for stability and progress in good; the third, seen in the perfect, consists chiefly in aiming at union with God and enjoyment of Him, even while they progress in charity. It is like the making of a journey. The first general stage is the departure, the next is chiefly one of progress and approach to the destination, the third is arrival and rest.[174]

Another question arises. Are educators who are imbued with the spirit of the precept of charity always obliged in their exterior actions to do not only what is good but also what is objectively *best,* and so to teach their students? No. A person is obliged to *desire* what is objectively the best: "Whence he who does not always wish to be better cannot

---

[174] Cf. *Summa,* II–II, q. 24, a. 9.

114   The Proximate Aim of Education

without contempt refrain from wishing it."[175] But in his acts, since the objective best is not always the prudential best for a particular person in particular circumstances, a person is not always obliged to *do* what is objectively best. Yet everyone will surely admire those saints such as St. Teresa of Jesus and St. Gerard Majella who took, under guidance, a vow to do always whatever was more perfect. This indeed was an heroic ideal.

In this context, we quote in full St. Thomas' answer to an objection. It is terse, clear, precise; it distinguishes beautifully, thereby avoiding dangerous extremes; its limpid reasoning offers a noble ideal to the generous and yet accommodates the ordinary.

> Just as all are bound to love God with their whole heart and there is a certain wholeness of perfection which cannot be neglected without sin and yet a certain wholeness which can be omitted without sin provided there be no contempt [for what is better and best] . . . so too all, both religious and seculars, are bound in a certain measure to do whatever good they can, for to all without exception it is said: "Whatsoever thy hand is able to do, do it earnestly" (Eccles. 9:10). There is, however, a way of fulfilling this precept so as to avoid sin, namely, by doing whatever one can according to his state in life, provided there be no contempt for the doing of better things, which contempt hardens the soul against spiritual progress.[176]

An educational ramification of this is the attitude toward the counsels (poverty, chastity, and obedience) that are to be cultivated in the children of our schools. Clearly all are not obliged to follow the counsels: but all should respect the way of the counsels as a mode of life and should observe the *spirit* of the counsels according to their own condition in life. Contempt for the counsels would be un-Christian.

---

[175] St. Thomas, *In Matt. 19:12.* Garrigou-Lagrange holds that the arbitrary choice of the less good in a concrete case is not, as such, a venial sin because the less good is still a true good and specifies the action as a good action. De Guibert is of the same view. Many theologians hold, however, that the arbitrary choice of the less good in a concrete case is irrational and a venial sin against prudence. They also find it hard to see how such an arbitrary choice could be a fitting tendency toward the ultimate good which is to be sought without measure. This view is held by Elter, S.J., Passerini, O.P., Prummer, O.P., Osbourne, etc.

This whole discussion is of practical consequence for high school students in many ways: e.g., the frequentation of the sacraments — "X" could easily receive Holy Communion each week at Sunday Mass but arbitrarily neglects to do so; the following of a special vocation — "Y" feels after due prayer and counsel that the consecrated life is her earthly vocation, but arbitrarily relinquishes the more perfect choice (cf. A. Motte, "The Obligation to Follow a Vocation," *Vocation* [London: Blackfriars Publications, 1952], pp. 18–36).

[176] *Summa,* II–II, q. 186, a. 2, ad 2.

In continuing our analysis of some aspects of Christian perfection, we have considered the degree of charity implied by Christian perfection. We have seen that the precept of charity is without limit — that the highest degree of charity extending even to mysticism is on a continuum with ordinary charity. We have seen that the precept of charity is sufficiently fulfilled — so as to avoid a transgression — if nothing else is loved more than or equally with God; we have also seen that it requires that we at least desire what is *best*.

Now we come to consider another aspect, namely, the variation of charity — its increase, its diminution, its loss.

C. THE VARIATION OF CHARITY

The Increase of Charity. The precept of charity is without limit. "The servant of God ought to aspire without ceasing to more perfect and holier things."[177] How is the increase to be made and its cessation avoided? What is the role of the educator in this vital growth which is the very heart of total Christian development?

The *fact* that charity increases with the other theological virtues is absolutely certain. It is certain too that this increase is not merely extrinsic, i.e., extending to more persons, and becoming as it were easier to exercise; it is also intrinsic, that is, there can be an increase in the virtue of charity itself.

A powerful *motive* for each in seeking his spiritual increase in grace and charity is the fact that one's degree of glory and happiness in heaven is proportioned to the degree of grace and charity to which he attains, by God's help, here on earth. Each child in the schoolroom is on earth to earn, not merely his heaven, but his degree of glory in heaven. Any good teacher can assist his pupils in reaching an academic standard whose professional and cultural benefits they will feel for the duration of life. But the Christian teacher or parent can do much more. He can delicately stimulate and assist children to grow in God's grace and love, thereby leading them on to heavenly treasure whose richness is immeasurable and whose benefit will be eternal. Truly, the teacher's work projects far beyond the dimensions of earth. It is fraught with eternal issues.

The *source* of the increase of charity is God. God alone is the ultimate source since this is a supernatural, infused virtue. Christ by His excelling power is the primary instrument of grace. Mary by the will of God is the Mediatrix through whose hands this and all graces are distributed to us. No teacher, no parent can give the increase of charity. No child can give himself charity or its increase. However, he should so live, with

---

[177] St. Thomas, *In Ep. ad Hebraeos,* 6:1, lect. 1.

God's help, as to receive from God this increase; and parents and teachers should enlighten and guide him to this right living.

The *mode* of the increase of charity is qualitative by way of greater intensity, not quantitative by way of addition. God does not add charity to charity as one might add stories to a house or stamps to an envelope; rather He intensifies charity within the subject — just as a stage light dimmed down may be intensified and be more luminous. Nor is this increase made with mathematical proportion to time or to the number of acts. One does not travel a quasi turnpike of charity averaging sixty degrees per year and therefore in three years totalling 180 degrees! One does not increase his charity in mathematical proportion to each act of charity. St. Thomas says:

> Charity does not actually increase by every act of charity. But each act of charity disposes to the increase of charity in so far as from one act of charity a man becomes more ready to act again according to charity and, this readiness increasing, he breaks out into more fervent acts of love and tries to advance in charity; and then his charity actually increases.[178]

The child who can mark up ten "acts" on the classroom chart (if such be still on the wall) is not thereby four degrees richer in charity than the other child with six "acts." This is by no means meant to discredit the multiplication of acts of the love of God — a practice urged by St. Mary Magdalene de Pazzi, St. Alphonsus de Liguori, and St. Therese of Lisieux, on the soundest theological basis. It is meant to discredit the egoistic misinterpretation of the mere multiplication of such acts.

Precisely how God gives and conditions this increase is shrouded in the inner activity of the Holy Trinity. We creatures must thank Him for the secrets He has given us and humble ourselves in the face of our remaining ignorance. The Council of Trent, however, associates grace and the infused virtues so as to indicate that the increase of grace means the increase of the infused virtues.[179]

The *measure* of the increase of charity is in the Divine Counsels. "To every one of us is given grace according to the measure of the giving of Christ."[180] The initial degree of charity and its increase are not proportionate to one's natural endowments, accomplishments, or natural virtues — an important point for the teacher to remember *efficaciously*. Some of the teachers and associates of St. Joseph Cupertino, St. John Vianney, and St. Bernadette forgot this point. The student with the high I.Q. or the bright clean face or the "cute" manner does not neces-

---

178 *Summa*, II–II, q. 24, a. 6. Other theologians however think differently. The basis of the differences of opinion is the different metaphysical conception of habit.
179 Cf. B.A.C., *op. cit.*, III, 723–24. Cf. *Summa*, I–II, q. 114, a. 8.
180 Eph. 4:7.

sarily have the highest degree of infused charity. Supernatural charity and its increase are not proportionate to a "sweet" and accommodating natural disposition as such. St. Clement Mary Hofbauer was, by natural endowment, a man of rugged temperament who rose to the heights of charity.

The *means* of obtaining an increase in charity are obscure as to their inner workings and relative efficacy. Our reception of the sacraments with the proper dispositions obtains for us an increase of grace and charity *ex opere operato*. Its reception with fervent dispositions can obtain for us a greater increase *ex opere operantis*. Our reception of Holy Communion is especially efficacious in gaining for us this increase. Hence it is so important for children to go to Communion frequently, even — with the right dispositions — every day. St. Pius X has urged this. A school which graduates its students with an enlightened and convinced habit of frequent Communion has done something wonderful for them.

By our supernatural merits[181] we can obtain from God this increase.

---

[181] 1. Merit in general is the right to some sort of recompense. Supernatural merit is the right or quasi right arising from some supernatural action entitling or disposing the doer, by God's arrangement, to a supernatural recompense. When we say a "supernatural action" we mean any action done under the influence of grace and therefore ordained to a supernatural end. It need not be a specifically "religious" action, such as praying in a church. Studying, eating, sleeping, typing, walking, laboring, etc., as well as praying can all be thus supernaturalized.

Merit can be condign (*de condigno*) or congruous (*de congruo*). Condign merit is had where there is a true proportion between the good act and the reward; it arises therefore from justice. Congruous merit lacks this true proportion and is not therefore based on justice but rather on the privileges of friendship, or, more broadly still, on the liberality of God (cf. Garrigou-Lagrange, *P. & C.,* p. 414, n.).

2. The conditions for condign merit are:

    a) The state of mortal life. The souls in purgatory cannot merit. Herein is the foundation of our suffrages for them.

    b) The state of sanctifying grace. This influences merit negatively, positively, and effectively — *negatively* by the absence of sin (for an enemy of God cannot have condign merit with God), *positively* by making us the sons of God, etc., *effectively* as a principle of the salutary act. There is some doubt concerning the influx of charity required for a meritorious act. It is certain, however, that all acts performed under the virtual or actual influx of charity are meritorious. Cf. Falanga, *op. cit.,* pp. 137–251.

    c) Freedom: both from external force; and from necessity, as is found in intrinsic determination to one thing — a man cannot obtain merit for the necessary circulation of his blood.

    d) The doing of some good work. This must be an act which is good from its object, its end (that is, the *finis operantis, supra,* Chap. II, p. 36), and from its circumstances. It must also be a supernaturally good act, as was mentioned earlier. An indifferent act, if such exists in a concrete case, would not be capable of merit.

    e) A divine arrangement and promise. God is the absolute Master of His rewards. Who can take from Him the key of heaven unless He first offers it?

3. Merit is increased by:

While any supernatural act can perhaps be meritorious — e.g., an act of patience, fortitude, or temperance, the same act done for an actual or virtual motive of charity certainly has a special value and merit.

Parents and teachers should encourage children to be patient, to be obedient, to deny themselves, to be industrious, not merely as acts of these respective virtues, but as acts motivated at least virtually by love of God.[182] In this way they can render an immense spiritual service to the child — and so to the home or school — and increase immensely the efficacy of their educational efforts.

---

a) The excellence of the act. Thus an act of charity is more meritorious in itself than an act of patience or humility.

b) The amount of the work, e.g., as in alms, the duration of the work, e.g., as in the case of nursing the sick, and the difficulty of the work. Behold the potential merit for the Christian teacher!

c) One's degree of sanctifying grace and greater union with Christ. That is why we ask the prayers of holy people. It should be noted that it is not required for merit that the good work be referred to God by a special actual intention — a consoling point for the busy teacher.

4. What can a person merit?

Condignly, he can merit an increase in sanctifying grace, sufficient actual graces for the Christian life, heavenly glory, and an increase in heavenly glory. Condignly, too, he can merit those temporal things that are needed for salvation — an important truth for those who, later on in marriage, may be inclined to allege poverty as an excuse for sin. Sincere prayer and virtuous effort will merit for them either the needful temporalities or the special graces needed to live a good life in the midst of temporal privations. Parents and teachers can tactfully stimulate children to an unshakable confidence in striving for such merits.

A man cannot merit for himself condignly either the first actual grace, the grace of justification, efficacious grace, or the grace of final perseverance. Neither can he merit anything condignly for others.

Congruously, a man in the state of grace can merit for himself temporal goods other than those mentioned above. In the broad sense (*de congruo fallibili* — founded on the liberality of God) he can merit for himself the all-important grace of final perseverance. Here is vital truth of which every parent and teacher and hence their children can be profitably aware. So many people think that somehow God *owes* it to them to let them die a good death in His grace; whereas no one can strictly merit this. By our best efforts, we can merit it only congruously and indeed in the broad sense. This is the theological reasoning behind the laudable practice of praying each day for perseverance, e.g., by offering up the "Hail, Holy Queen" of the Rosary "for the grace of perseverance." Such prayer gives some title to perseverance over and above its intrinsic merit as a mere good work. The parent and/or teacher who implants this truth and habit in the mind and devotion of the child has indeed rendered him a notable spiritual service. This special efficacy of impetration as such flows from Christ's special promises: "Ask, and it shall be given you" (Mt. 7:7).

Congruously a person can merit graces for others by his prayers and good works just as St. Stephen congruously merited the conversion of St. Paul, and St. Monica the conversion of the wayward Augustine. Here is an avenue of real help by which the devout teacher can assist all his students, even the apparently hopeless case. Yet, since it is not condign merit, no parent, teacher, or school can be automatically blamed for the waywardness.

182 *Supra,* Chap. II, n. 68.

Diminution of Charity. The virtue of charity does not directly diminish by venial sin as the mercury sinks in the thermometer, since venial sin is a blight affecting the means to the last end, not the last end itself; and it is the last end which is the object of charity. But venial sins and the bad habits they form affect the radiation and influence of charity just as dust and soot smeared on a lamp glass affect the radiation of the light, even though the wattage of the bulb remains constant. Moreover, venial sins lessen the supply of actual graces and dispose to mortal sin.[183]

It is not for the teacher to judge consciences. But external conduct in the daily life at school may readily reveal objective, deliberate venial sins. To a Christian teacher, these are far more than a student's failure to do the "democratic" or the "decent" thing, more than a smudge on the old school tie. They are spiritual symptoms, significant diagnostically and prognostically, and they should evoke his remedial zeal in prayer, tactful instruction, and guidance.

Loss of Charity. Charity and sanctifying grace are lost utterly by mortal sin. This is not the place to expand on the ruinous effects of mortal sin, now and later; but neither the utter spoliation now nor the dreadful punishment of hell should be forgotten. It is enough to say that by such a deliberate act the soul is completely stripped of supernatural dignity, potency, titles, and merits. It is supernaturally orphaned. It received existence as a gratuitous gift from God. It depends utterly on Him now, not merely for continuance in earthly life, health, and prosperity, but for its very existence. Yet it has freely chosen with a fixed will to insult this God. Death in that state — and death can strike with terrible suddenness — fixes forever in its perversion that will now turned away from God — just as concrete sets hard. Hence such a death necessarily means separation forever from God and God's heavenly company, namely, His Immaculate Mother, His resplendent angels, His saints. That separation is its own dreadful punishment, because forever man is rent by his self-conflict — by his innate, ontological surge toward God and his own freely chosen aversion from God. Remorse adds a gnawing bitterness to this radical conflict. The positive punishment of fire — an avenging creature of God punishing the delinquency of the damned in rejecting Him for creatures, whether greed or lust or pleasure — is beyond human power to conceive; yet it is the least part of hell.

This ultimate penalty for the loss of charity has considerable significance for Catholic education as a system and for the individual educand. It gives our education a double urgency: the attaining of the supreme good and the avoiding of an immeasurable evil.

In regard to the Catholic educational system, if hell be nothing (*sic*)

---

[183] Cf. *Summa*, II–II, q. 24, a. 10.

or only a lukewarm limbo, our costly and burdensome school efforts are
wasted. In regard to the educand, hell is significant not merely as a unit
in his "religion" course but as a powerful motive for school and life
discipline.[184] For his own eternal good he has to navigate his life so as
to avoid hell. For some, the developing delinquency that dare not now
be restrained with a clip from a policeman's billy or with the school-
master's "paddling" will be the seeds of hell.

Should hell be taught to the children? Opinions vary. There are those
outside the Catholic Church who deny openly the existence of an eternal
hell. But such denial makes Redemption a farce, Christ's Passion a
waste, His earnestness in speaking about hell[185] a hoax. Educational
writers who pay only educational lip service to the "Great Teacher"
and that "great textbook of life" (the Bible) find themselves in the
dilemma of contemning the earnest, reiterated teachings of an acknowl-
edged "Great Teacher" — or of saying that his teachings are spurious!
There are those Catholics who would gladly forget about hell and do
not wish to be reminded of it — some teachers who do not wish hell to
be the subject of retreat meditations! It is hardly likely that children
in their schools will be taught and warned of hell with true perspective.
Recently a Catholic mother objected to her child in elementary school
being taught about hell. This is a peculiar, ostrichlike attitude which
assumes that facts are changed by being ignored. Most sane people
prefer to have a high-voltage wire marked with "Danger"; then they
can go about their day in security.[186]

Against this background the question is posed: Should hell be taught
to children? Yes. Should it be taught in both elementary and high schools?
Yes. Any other viewpoint seems to this writer to be temerarious.

Christ spoke of hell often and urgently and indiscriminately. There is
no mention of his separating men from women or adults from children
when he spoke of "unquenchable fire," etc.[187]

Pope Pius XII devotes a significant paragraph, often overlooked, to
this truth. The preaching of hell "has lost nothing of its need at the
present time . . . it has even become more necessary and urgent than

---

[184] The case was reported some years ago in Australia of a young schoolboy about
to give evidence in court. He was asked by the judge what would happen, if, being
sworn to tell the truth, he lied. The boy replied that he could go to hell for it.
Allegedly, the judge publicly deplored the expression of such outmoded attitudes
and bugaboos. It would be an interesting avenue of "research" to find out whether
or not this boy's vivid belief in hell was a more powerful deterrent against perjury
than the mere implication of democratic infidelity, or the prospect of being punished
by the law if caught!
[185] Mk. 9:42–47; Lk. 16:22–26; Mt. 25:41, 46.
[186] Cf. *supra*, Chap. II, n. 92; also p. 69.
[187] The acceptance of these words of the gentle Saviour will be a stumbling block
only to those for whom religion is a matter of sentiment rather than of truth.

ver"; it must be taught "with dignity of wisdom" "just as Christ
revealed it, without any attenuation." This is an obligation "binding in
conscience on every priest," and "no condition of time can reduce the
gravity of this obligation." He notes that "the desire of heaven is a
motive more perfect than the fear of eternal punishment, but it does
not follow that this desire is for all men the motive most efficacious to
keep them from sin and to convert them to God."[188] The reason for the
Pope's insistence is that the Christian Faith, as revealed by Christ, is
a seamless garment; it is not a doctrinal cafeteria where people choose
or reject according to their fancy.

How is hell to be taught in Christian education? It should be taught
dogmatically, constructively, adequately, with dignity and wisdom. "Constructively" is important: it should be made clear that by the Christian
life we seek to gain heaven and avoid hell, that this is all conditioned
on our own free will and the lives we *freely choose to lead,* that we have
more than adequate spiritual helps in Christ and through Mary if we
choose to use them.

Should hell be taught to children with some emotional resonance? The
view here ventured is yes. Emotions properly used can reinforce and
facilitate rational choices. Hell can be taught vividly and constructively
without leading to emotional unbalance and psychological harm. Does
not a mother commendably give vivid warnings to her children about
the danger of fire? Which is worse psychologically and practically: to
have the child warned of the danger of fire or to have him receive a
shocking burn? There is no question of spiritual morbidity in these considerations. The Christian imbued with a true spirit of faith navigates
his soul safely through life with his eyes fixed on God as on a guiding
beacon; but he never forgets the rocks at the side or pretends they are
only an illusion.

We therefore submit that the educator, in fostering charity in his
charges and in solving the many problems associated with Catholic
schools, should never forget or discount the calamity, present and future,
that follows the loss of charity by mortal sin. He should have a vivid
and efficacious sense of this calamity, convinced that this deprivation is
a worse thing than a broken leg, than knowing no Greek, than not
making the athletic team, than losing the championship cup, than not
keeping up with the social or academic "Joneses." Any other attitude
would not be typically Christian; it would indicate a myopic tepidity.[189]

In continuing our analysis of some aspects of charity, the core of
perfection, we have seen that charity can and should increase quali-

[188] *AAS,* XLI (1949), 185.
[189] St. Alphonsus Rodriguez, when a merchant, prayed God that his infant son
might die rather than ever lose charity and endanger his temporal and eternal welfare
(feast, October 30).

tatively; that on its final degree depends the degree of our glory and happiness in heaven. The source of the increase is God alone, according to the mode and measure known to Him; nevertheless, we have the God-given means of obtaining this increase.

We have seen that venial sin does not directly diminish charity; but it diminishes charity's radiation and disposes to its complete loss.

We have seen that this total loss is effected by mortal sin with a dreadful spoliation now and utter ruin hereafter in hell; and we considered some of the implications of hell for parents, teachers, and administrators.

D. THE CALL TO CHRISTIAN PERFECTION

We now bring up for formal and brief treatment a question lurking close to the surface in the preceding pages. Who are called to this perfection? How are they called?

Immediately we face a semantic problem. The word "call" is used even by theological writers in the efficacious sense of being actually chosen for, raised, conducted, or predestined to the mystical life, as well as in the neutral sense of an opportunity or a general invitation. Are *all men* called to perfection in Christ even in its highest degree? Is the pagan in the kraal called to this exalted condition of Christian perfection? Is the urchin in the aldea or barrio who is baffled by the arithmetical complexity of remembering such facts as one God, three Divine Persons, seven Sacraments, and ten Commandments; is young Lucifer who is about as peaceful as a pin wheel in the classroom — squirming, talking, teasing, jabbing his neighbor with ruler or pencil or the inevitable pins and really quiet only when he is carving his name in the desk; is "the overgrown two-storied lad from Tangmalangaloo"[190] who shakes the desk and spills the ink as he lurches to his feet with a blank, red face — are all these called to Christian perfection?

This is a question of import for every teacher. And perhaps over the years bitter experience has partially hardened his thinking and dimmed his teaching ideals to the stage where he feels forced to conclude: If I can keep my young braves from breaking school windows during the week and from missing Mass on Sunday I've had a distinctly successful week. Human nature being what it is, we can readily sympathize with the teacher who feels that he may as well try to chasten the zoo as sanctify *this* class!

The answer to the question must be that all men are called to Christian perfection, but in different senses of "call." And we may as well add at once that the teacher who consciously lowers his speculative ideals will

190 John O'Brien, "Tangmalangaloo," *Around the Boree Log* (Sydney: Angus & Robertson, Ltd., 1921), p. 97.

soon find himself facing problems worse than broken windows, for in moral matters one does not guarantee the minimum by aiming only at the minimum. St. Catherine of Siena's estimate is pertinent here: 'Inasmuch as the counsels are bound up in the commandments, no one can observe the latter who does not observe the former, at least in thought, that is to say, that they possess the riches of the world humbly and without pride."[191]

This whole matter of the call to perfection in Christ is very complex. Its adequate solution is rooted in secrets of the Holy Trinity not explicitly revealed to us; it pertains to the mystery of God's pre-election of individual souls. Nearly every practical issue bifurcates and eventually becomes a labyrinth. We must simply humble ourselves in the face of our own limitations and leave the inner workings of God's providence in the safe hands of God Himself.

This much can be said here:

1. All men, by the words of Christ, are given an objective, general call to membership in the true Church. "Going therefore teach ye all nations; baptizing them."[192] "Go ye into the whole world and preach the gospel to every creature. . . ."[193] "Be ye therefore perfect. . . ."[194] As long as there are pagan souls on earth, the Church will continue her apostolate to convey to them this general call.

2. All men are given an objective, general call to justification and all individuals who reach the use of reason receive from the goodness of God remote, sufficient grace to attain it. Their co-operation will be blessed with additional and richer graces.

3. According to the Thomist and Carmelite theologians (following St. Thomas, St. Teresa, and St. John of the Cross), all souls in the state of grace are called in a general, remote, and sufficient manner to the mystical life.[195] The proximate call, which may be either sufficient or efficacious, is not given to all. Its giving is God's secret choice and is not a matter for the a priori judgment of anyone, let alone a teacher; yet Mother Vazou seems to have decided that the naïve, poorly born Sr. Marie Bernard was not proximately called to such perfection. The canonization of St. Bernadette has since proved her utterly wrong.

In this whole matter of the call to perfection and its graces, it must never be forgotten by parent, teacher, and child, that faithful adherence to the Church in her laws, teachings and sacraments, faithful prayer

---

[191] St. Catherine of Siena, *Dialogue,* Chap. 47, quoted in Garrigou-Lagrange, *P. & C.,* p. 193, n.
[192] Mt. 28:19.
[193] Mk. 16:15.
[194] Mt. 5:48.
[195] Garrigou-Lagrange, *P. & C.,* pp. 340, 343, 382. Cf. St. Teresa, *Way of Perfection,* Chaps. 19, 20.

and co-operation with the graces given us by God will obtain greater graces from our Father in heaven.

We close this consideration of the call with two authoritative statements of the Popes:

> At present there are many who neglect the supernatural life and in its place cultivate a fruitless and vague sentimentalism; hence the absolute necessity of recalling more often what the Fathers of the Church along with Sacred Scripture have taught in this matter, especially by taking St. Thomas as our master since he has so clearly set forth their doctrine on the elevation to the supernatural life. We must besides draw attention to the conditions required for progress in the *grace of the virtues* and of the *Gifts of the Holy Spirit,* the perfection of which is found in the *mystical life.* And this is exactly what you have undertaken to do in your review [*La Vie Spirituelle*] in a way that is learned and sound.[196]

> Christ constituted the Church holy, and indeed the agent [*effectrix*] of holiness. All those who take her for leader and teacher, must, by the Will of God, strive for holiness of life. "This is the will of God," says St. Paul, "your sanctification." And the sanctity meant is that which Our Lord Himself delineated when He said: "Be ye therefore perfect as also your heavenly Father is perfect." No one is to think that this is addressed to a few very select souls leaving others free to aim at a lower grade of virtue. It is clear that the law obliges *absolutely all* [*omnino omnes*], with no one excepted. Moreover, all who have reached the summit of Christian perfection — and history shows that their number is legion, drawn from every age and class — all have overcome the same weakness of nature and the same obstacles that beset the rest of men. St. Augustine puts his finger on the matter very well when he says: "God does not command the impossible; but He bids us do what we can according to our strength and to beg His help for whatever exceeds our strength."[197]

The conclusion is that all men — Catholic, Protestant, pagan — are called to perfection in Christ, but in different senses of "call." A Catholic teacher who deals with children of various religions — and none — must always respect a sincere conscience; but he should pray that all will hear and co-operate with this call, and at the same time so live and act as to be himself a witness for Christ. He can never know which day and which act of his own life will, in the dispositions of God, be a special external grace for one of his pupils.

---

196 Benedict XV, letter to Fr. Bernadot, O.P., *AAS,* XIII (1921), 528.
197 Pius XI, *Rerum Omnium Perturbationem,* encyclical to commemorate the third centenary of the death of St. Francis de Sales, *AAS,* XV (1923), p. 50.

Summary

According to the Christian view the proper and immediate end of education is to co-operate with grace in the formation of the true and perfect Christian. This is clear from the works of the Popes, who speak as scholars and pontiffs.

In considering the notion of Christian perfection we have seen the general details of God's over-all plan: (1) God's creation of man in original justice; (2) when man fell, God's restoration of man through Christ.

We have seen the principal elements of this restoration: (a) the elevation to the supernatural order, (b) sanctifying grace and its consequences, (c) the Divine Indwelling, (d) the Divine Adoption, (e) the perfect Exemplar, Jesus Christ, (f) the incorporation into the Mystical Body of Christ, (g) our co-operation with God's plan.

Who would glimpse the Taj Mahal without wanting to look closer? We looked closer at something more wonderful, the simplicity and munificence of God's supernatural arrangements for our perfection. We examined some special aspects of this perfection. We have seen that its core is charity, that the degree of this charity is without limit as far as our human seeking is concerned. We have seen that charity can and should increase, that it cannot directly diminish, but can be lost with a dreadful penalty. We have considered that all men are called, but in different senses of "call," to this perfection.

In the course of this treatment many educational reflections were made.

CHAPTER V

CATHOLIC VIEW OF THE PROPER AND IMMEDIATE END OF EDUCATION (cont.): MAN'S CO-OPERATION IN GOD'S PLAN

IN THE previous chapter we considered the elements of our restoration in Christ. For convenience we deferred the treatment of one of these elements, namely, our active co-operation with God in the pursuit of perfection. Obviously this chapter will be concerned with the educand's self-activity, a sacrosanct concept in modern education — and rightly so. As we progress it will be perceived that the Christian concept of this self-activity is wider and deeper than that proposed by others.

We will treat the necessity and the mode of man's co-operation in God's plan for his perfection, then the natural and supernatural equipment marvelously given him for that co-operation.

Necessity of Man's Co-operation

In the elements of our restoration previously considered, man has been seen as a recipient, benefiting wonderfully by the goodness and liberality of his Saviour. Is his role then purely passive, with no more self-activity than a series of heartfelt *Gloria Patri*'s? Or is his role arbitrary, a matter of personal whim? By no means. After receiving Baptism and its prerogatives man must actively co-operate with the divine largess by his good works. This co-operation is prescribed by Revelation, is philosophically required by man's nature, and fulfills a psychological need.

It is prescribed by Revelation in the clear words of Holy Scripture:

If you love me keep my commandments.[1]
If anyone love me, he will keep my word.[2]
Not everyone that saith to me, Lord, Lord, shall enter into the

---

[1] Jn. 14:15.
[2] Jn. 14:23.

kingdom of Heaven: but he that doth the will of my Father who is in Heaven, he shall enter into the kingom of Heaven.[3]

Even as the body without the spirit is dead, so also faith without works is dead.[4]

This is the charity of God, that we keep his commandments.[5]

Many other texts could be adduced to emphasize the same doctrine of active co-operation.

Moreover the Church has condemned religious Quietism.[6] No one can be quietistic and think himself on the road to Christian perfection.

This theological doctrine is perfectly in accord with what philosophy has to tell us about man's nature.

Every agent acts for an end according to its nature, as we have seen. Man as a free agent endowed with powers of operation must therefore seek his proper end by his free operations.[7] Indeed, since a thing is perfect only insofar as it is actual (what family is satisfied with an automobile in blueprint!) and operation is the last act of the agent, man's final happiness will be found in an operation — his mind will be joined to God in one continued, everlasting operation.[8]

This proper operation by which man is to reach his end is primarily immanent activity. It must not be limited to any sort of transient activity, predicamental *actio*.

It is clear philosophically that man's perfection of himself (in the supernatural order) is a strictly personal attainment. He needs the constant help of God; in varying degree he needs the guidance and encouragement of others, especially of parents, teachers, counselors. But fundamentally it is a personal attainment, a self-activity. Neither parents, teachers, nor angels can do it for him because he is an incommunicable person, and free. Nor will God force him to it because He respects His own gift of freedom.

Psychologically, the normal man likes to feel that he has accomplished his own good, done something himself or for himself. Even a toddling child has a thrill of achievement in doing something unaided — "Look, mum, no hands!" It is not given to man to be completely independent because as a contingent being he depends always on the divine *concursus*. Yet by a marvelous dispensation which preserves divine omnipotence and human dignity, man's whole perfection is to be achieved only through his own active co-operation — *totus sed non totaliter*.

---

[3] Mt. 7:21.   [4] James 2:26.   [5] 1 Jn. 5:3.

[6] Quietism was condemned in 1687 by Pope Innocent XI. Cf. Denzinger, *op. cit.*, n. 1221 et seq.

[7] *Summa*, I–II, q. 1, a. 2.   [8] *Ibid.*, I–II, q. 3, a. 2, ad 4.

In these considerations about man's personal role in his own perfection we have the theological, philosophical, and psychological bases for the emphasis on self-activity in education. It is necessarily at the heart of Christian education, which gives this activity a validity and importance it could never have in mere Progressive education.

These considerations and especially the distinction of transient and immanent activity already made in Chapter II give us also a guiding principle that will safeguard our education from mere transient activity for its own sake. In terms of classroom procedure this means a safeguard from the excessive making and building of things — as though transient activity as such had a high personal value, as though the mere quantity of paper used, books worn out, and things made denoted or at least connoted proportionate personal development. The same considerations will likewise save educational procedures from excessive emphasis on low-grade immanent activity, such as mere locomotion and noise, under the guise of high personal self-expression and self-development. Transient and lower immanent activity have a place in the classroom, especially in the junior grades. Let it be remembered, however, that an advanced student can be motionless, yet intensely active; he can be idle or sluggish as far as paste and crayons and "cutouts" and projects are concerned, yet be nobly productive in his highest faculties.

Man must respond to God's call by co-operating actively with it. In doing so, he acts freely; therefore, the individual's co-operation with God's call will be characterized by all those influences and vagaries that accompany the exercise of freedom generally. Some will fail to co-operate through ignorance, either in good or bad faith; some will stubbornly refuse, no matter what efforts teacher and school make; some will be halfhearted; some will co-operate generously to produce thirty, sixty, a hundredfold.

The Mode of Man's Co-operation

The mode of man's co-operation with God's plan has a twofold aspect, objective and subjective.

OBJECTIVE MODE

Man in his activity must fulfill the objective plan laid down by God for his perfection and salvation.

The fundamental issue in the consideration of man's objective co-operation is this: Does man deal with his Maker on the Maker's terms or on his own arbitrary terms? This question must be asked and answered honestly; from different answers will flow contradictory schemes of life and education.

The Christian answer is clear. Man is contingent; he depends absolutely on his Maker. Everything made depends in some way on its maker, the watch on the watchmaker, etc.; why not man on his Maker? Man of course has the unique power of recognizing his dependence. But the power of recognition does not give the right of repudiation; rather it gives him a higher dignity and a double debt. Hence, man must co-operate with his Maker and co-operate in the right way, his activity fulfilling his Maker's objective plan. It is not enough for him to perform just any sort of arbitrary activity. An employee does not perform just any sort of work here or there as the mood moves him, nor does a surgeon perform just any sort of operation — amputates the leg because *some* sort of surgery is needed anyway! Mere activity is not enough; it must be the right activity, the right co-operation with God, since God is the master of His own gifts and has the right to choose the key to His own heaven. "Unless the Lord build the house, they labor in vain who build it."[9]

This is an important consideration in the present age of sentimental religion, "sawdust trails," vague, insipid, revivalist "conversion" to Christ, conventional reference to God — someone has said that "God" is a word used in the last paragraph of a campaign speech! Our self-activity must be the right sort of activity. It is vitally important to find out from God the objective co-operation He wants from us and to fulfill it. Only this is the right kind of activity.

He gives us the answer. "For other foundation no one can lay but that which is laid which is Christ Jesus."[10]

Objectively, God surely requires our conformity to the plan laid down in His Revelation for our restoration in Christ. This plan entails our full and active membership in the one, visible, universal Church founded by Christ, whereby we receive its holy teachings, its means of grace, its guiding law. There is one God, and therefore one Church founded by God to guide man to the one heaven — which is God's heaven. This Church is seen in systematic Apologetics to be the Catholic Church, which alone goes back historically to Christ and the Apostles.

The will of God is manifested through all just civil laws; through the duties of one's personal state of life, for example, as a married man; through the duties of one's particular calling in life, for example, as a doctor, a teacher, a policeman; through the providential circumstances of life that happen to us by God's signified or permissive will, as soon to be explained. It will be noted that this manifestation of God's will is *humano modo*, manifested through *human authority;* there are no heavenly trumpets or angelic whisperings. Just so Christ Himself, God,

[9] Ps. 126:1.
[10] 1 Cor. 3:11.

fulfilled the will of the Father at Nazareth as manifested in the human authority of Joseph and Mary.

Clearly there is a scale of values which objectively all must recognize and to which they must conform. Such values exist independently of our recognition. The school counselor, in assisting others to this recognition, is not thereby "introjecting" arbitrary values into the client's consciousness; he is only leading the latter to a recognition and acceptance of *reality*. However tactfully and indirectly he proceeds and if need be guides, he, unlike Rogers, can never be indifferent whether the client choose for himself values which are social or antisocial, moral or immoral.[11]

In this consideration of the objective mode of our co-operation we have a lofty concept of teaching as a vocation in life leading children to what is good in itself and best for them. Its understanding and proper application will provide a rock foundation for that spirit of dedication that is so valuable in teachers. Here again we have the Christian foundation for educational discipline, respect for society and its just laws, respect for legitimate government. How many desirable attitudes does the one conviction of doing the will of Christ bring forth as corollaries!

SUBJECTIVE MODE

Man is capable of many good actions. In which of his diverse good actions does his co-operation with God primarily and essentially consist? In knowing God? In being patient? kind?

It consists in the loving adhesion of his will to the will of God — doing the will of God is only love of God in action. This is the subjective aspect of the mode of his co-operation with God's plan.

Love is a noble word that has been cheapened, rationalized, sentimentalized; but the love of God is not such base coinage. It is nothing else than the efficacious adhesion of man's will to God. "Love . . . is the fulfilling of the law."[12] The texts quoted above regarding the necessity of our co-operation reinforce the same point. Love of God and doing the will of God are two sides of the same coin.

The theological reason for the primacy of doing Christ's will is evident from what we have said about man's incorporation into the Mystical Body of Christ. Despite this incorporation man's actions are still free, still under his own control, and independent of the spirit and rule of the whole Body. They are made conformable to the whole Body by being conformed to the directions of the Head, Christ. By this free dependence on the Head, the good of the whole Body and of the

---

[11] Cf. Carl Rogers, *Client-Centered Therapy* (Boston: Houghton Mifflin Co., 1951), p. 48.
[12] Rom. 13:10.

individual member, is assured — otherwise the individual member would be as it were cancerous, something in the Body yet foreign and disorderly. Doing the will of Christ brings about *de facto* our union with Christ in the Mystical Body. It is an intimate intercommunion with Christ and the other members. It puts us in contact with the life-giving circulation of the Mystical Body.

Hence obedience is the prime law of life and leads to the fulfillment of man's restoration in Christ. Since all legitimate authority comes from God as a delegation and returns to Him bringing the obedient with it as it were, we have herein a granite foundation and powerful motive for proper discipline in our educational system. We will discuss the implications of these notions later.

In the conformity of his will to Christ, man not only has a prime law of life but he has the means of fulfilling a reverential need, and the psychological urge of love. As a contingent being, created and held in existence by God at every moment, his dependence on God cannot be sufficiently expressed by words: but doing God's will expresses this dependence in action and so fulfills the reverential need. Moreover, love is never content with mere words; deep love finds words hollow, however lyrical they be. Pleasing God by fulfilling His will, however high the mountains over which that will leads, fulfills the deep psychological urge of man's love.

Lest, in this century of personal independence and self-sufficiency, God be considered tyrannical in asking for our conformity to His will, it must be said that God is not selfish in requiring this, nor does He have any essential need of us, naturally or supernaturally. By ordaining all things to Himself — including man's free acts — He is merely preserving the ontological rectitude of creation and therefore accomplishing creation's own good. "God seeks His Glory not for His own sake but for ours."[13] There is no indignity for man, no disadvantage in conforming himself to this all-holy, all-knowing will of Christ which proved its love for him so convincingly in the gratuitous Redemption. By this conformity of his will to Christ man flies like an arrow swiftly and unerringly to the completion of his destiny and the repose of his true end.

True service of God is founded on accurate knowledge. Hence we append some explanations regarding the will of God that will assist education for prudent and fruitful living. It must not be thought that such considerations belong only to religion or asceticism, with no import either for practical living or for the education that is both a part of and a preparation for living. Religion is not just a Sunday suit; education is not just learning to count and getting a job. Education is "intimately and necessarily connected" with "the pursuit of the last

---

[13] *Summa*, II–II, q. 132, a. 1, ad 1.

end," "wholly directed to man's last end";[14] and these truths of religion
are God's revelation about this last end and the means thereto.

> Religion applies to *every moment* of our life. Christ wants to
> share every single action which we perform and what He cannot
> share is well-nigh worthless. To enable Him to share everything all
> this division and inconsistency must be removed from our life and
> everything brought under a uniform ideal. That . . . suitable ideal
> is supplied by the aim to do God's will *in all things* [italics
> added].[15]

That divine will must be rightly understood; hence these few general
observations.

God is in Himself absolutely simple and undivided, but we have to
abstract and separate His attributes in order to grasp some of their
import. Hence we distinguish God's "signified will" from His "permissive
will." Under God's "signified will" fall the things that God positively
wishes to happen and which He commands; for example, that we carry
out His plan for our perfection and salvation. Under God's "permissive
will" fall the things that God does not will directly but which He does
not prevent from happening;[16] for example, He does not prevent an
incompetent official from receiving some office in a school system, a
drunken father from breaking a child's arm, or a deformed child from
being born.

Everything in the world, the general government of the universe and
the smallest detail,[17] is completely under God's control. Nothing happens outside either His signified will or His permissive will. God does not
wish a man to do wrong; He merely does not prevent from doing wrong
that man who freely chooses to abuse his freedom; but God does will
the consequences of the abuse of freedom.[18] Thus, God does not wish
the drunken father's sin; but He does wish the child to seek his perfection and salvation by bearing the injury done him. This truth, coupled
with the other, "To them that love God all things [notice the word
'all' things] work together unto good,"[19] has significant implications.
Christian teachers have herein a basis for an unquenchable optimism
that will not only help them in their own personal and professional conduct, but will inspire and enlighten counselors in their educational
guidance, and will give proper orientation to special education — that

---

[14] Pius XI, *Christian Education of Youth*, pp. 4–5.
[15] Boylan, *op. cit.*, p. 126.
[16] Cf. J. De Guibert, *The Theology of the Spiritual Life*, trans. P. Barrett
(London: Sheed & Ward, 1954), pp. 96–97, for a further discussion of these terms.
[17] Cf. Mt. 6:26, 30.
[18] Cf. Boylan, *op. cit.*, p. 172.
[19] Rom. 8:28.

branch of education that is concerned with atypical children. Their deformities, great or small, happen *according to the will of God.* Their route to restoration in Christ is clearly indicated.

There are degrees of adhesion to the will of Christ ranging from observance to resignation, to acquiescence, to abandonment. Mere servile toleration — putting up with a situation because one has to — is unworthy of a Christian.

A brief note on this notion of abandonment will be in place because it is the very summit of the co-operative self-activity that becomes every Christian — pupil, parent, teacher.

By abandonment to God's will a man renounces his own desires, gives himself without reserve and with a deliberate cheerfulness to the accomplishing of God's will, throws himself completely into the arms of Christ as it were. This abandonment is not irrational; the virtue of prudence is never flouted. Abandonment to the will of God connotes many things, three of which can fittingly be mentioned here:

1. It means that a man *accepts* generously whatever God permits to happen to him, and does cheerfully and promptly and wholeheartedly what his duty calls him to do. There is then no hint of Quietism or passivism in true Christian abandonment.

2. It means that a man is earnest and persevering in the *effort* to accomplish God's will but is *supernaturally* indifferent about the external success of his effort, leaving it in the hands of God who alone "giveth the increase."[20] Naturally speaking, he desires and can fervently pray for this external success; yet he will recall that God sometimes writes straight with crooked lines.

"A father's [a teacher's] attempt to educate his children may be partly frustrated by the non-cooperation of the children, by mistakes on the part of the teachers [parents], by illness, or by many other misfortunes. All God asks is that one should make a reasonable attempt. *The rest is God's business.* And the outcome of it all, whatever it may be, is God's will."[21]

Here is perfect abandonment to Christ and high virtue indeed; but it is a logical, confident attitude based on the principles of Christian perfection. It is the open door to wonderful peace. It is a golden key to a teacher's personal adjustment.

3. Abandonment excludes the worry of futility, that egoistic worry that revels in its own luxury. It does not, however, exclude the worry of responsibility which exists when a man with a decision to make or consequences to count cannot decide easily but seeks whatever help or counsel is at hand and prays confidently and calmly for the divine guidance.

---

[20] 1 Cor. 3:7.
[21] Boylan, *op. cit.,* p. 193.

Having considered the necessity and mode, objective and subjective, of our co-operation in God's plan for our restoration in Christ, now we will consider the means of co-operation that He has given us.

Means of Man's Co-operation

In this section we will consider man's equipment for the active co-operation expected of him in the work of his perfection. This equipment is both natural and supernatural. Philosophy provides us with knowledge of man's natural equipment; theology, of his supernatural equipment. We now organize the pertinent truths of both at some length to indicate the varied richness of man's equipment; and again we face the dilemma that confronts us elsewhere in this book. To list is inadequate; to elaborate is digressive. Merely to list man's natural and infused virtues is meaningless except to those who have already studied them extensively. A summary can be so neat that it is cryptic for all but the periti. Hence we risk the criticism of professional philosophers and theologians, believing that some brief consideration of these habits is desirable and even necessary if Catholic educators are to realize vividly and to develop adequately the child's potentiality. Full explanations must be sought in philosophy and theology. We only hope that sufficient detail is gathered here to give teachers and, through them, parents a glimpse of the broad horizons of Christian education. A preliminary glance at the diagram which reviews this chapter may help some readers in following the matter we now discuss.

NATURAL EQUIPMENT — SUBSTANTIAL

Man is a unit. He is not just an aggregate of parts, as sugar is an aggregate of grains. He is undivided in himself and not divisible into things like himself. He is a *substantial* unit, i.e., one substance, able to exist in himself (yet not excluding his dependence on the First Cause of all things, his Creator).

He is an organism, composed of heterogeneous parts, both accidental and substantial. These parts are arranged in a determined way. He is moreover a living[22] organism endowed with the power of self-motion, which power is the sign of life; the various parts of the organism are interrelated and they operate for the general good of the whole.

This living, organized, substantial unit is a complete thing in the class of substance. He exists in and by himself, standing alone in his own right among contingent beings (yet, like them, always dependent on the First Cause). He is a whole; he is substantially unique and

---

[22] Modern writers do not necessarily identify the organic with the animate. A less elaborate degree of organization can be found in the inanimate world, e.g., in the atom, says Phillips, *Thomistic Philosophy*, I, p. 148.

incommunicable. Being also rational, he is a *person*. All true education must respect this wholeness, this uniqueness and incommunicability of the human person. Herein is the philosophical basis for the Christian view that the child in education is not expendable. In the notion of man as a living, organized, substantial, personal unit, we have his substantial equipment for his co-operation with God's designs. This is the basic principle of his co-operation, called the *principium quod —* "the principle which acts." Hence the dictum, *actiones sunt suppositorum —* "it is the supposit which acts."

What are the ontological principles of man's substantial unity? They are soul and matter. Man's soul is the active, determining, formal element of the unity. Matter is the passive, indeterminate, material element. The two are essentially united to form this substantial unit.

A word about man's soul. To combine Aristotle's two definitions:[23] A soul is the first act of a physical body; it is the principle whereby we live, perceive, move, and understand. The first part of the definition indicates the proper subject of the soul, namely, a body that has life in potency;[24] the second part indicates the primary formal effect of the soul. Man's soul is simple, not composed of essential or quantitative parts; it is incorruptible. It is immaterial insofar as it is not matter, and does not depend on matter for its existence; it does, however, depend on matter for some of its operations, intrinsically for vegetative and sensitive operation, extrinsically for the operations of intellect. It is immortal and will live forever. It came into being from God's creative hand at the beginning; it will always exist even after earthly death. Therefore its welfare must be considered above the value of all material things, which of their nature are only temporal. Hence Christ says, "What does it profit a man if he gain the whole world, and suffer the loss of his own soul?"[25] We must never allow familiarity to cloud the meaning and the source of that warning.

Yet man is not just a soul.[26] His soul is not *the* principle of his essence; it is *a* principle, albeit the formal principle. Matter is also an essential principle. This is why we speak of the souls in purgatory, and not the persons in purgatory. Hence, man's soul is an incomplete substance; it always has an aptitude to be united to the body as its co-principle.[27] Therefore, man is not just accidentally an animal, material and organic. Therefore, too, any concept of man and of education founded on a "man-is-a-soul" notion would be unreal and false. Clearly, Christian

---

[23] Aristotle, *De Anima*, Bk. II, Chap. 1.2. Cf. Richard McKeon (ed.), *The Basic Works of Aristotle* (New York: Random House, 1941), pp. 555, 557–558.

[24] Cf. Grenier, *op. cit.*, II, p. 135, for the reasons why we say "the first act of a *body*" and not "of prime matter."

[25] Mt. 16:26.

[26] Cf. *Summa*, I, q. 75, a. 5.

[27] *Ibid.*, q. 76, a. 1, ad 6.

education is by no means unconcerned about the educand's material needs.

Man's soul is wholly in the whole body and wholly in every part of the body according to the totality of its *essence*.[28] It informs the whole body and its whole essence is found in each part of the body. This is the philosophic basis for the respect shown to the human body and for the physical care given it in whole and part. We take care to protect the educand from physical mutilation in any way, apart altogether from the utility of the member which might be lost and the inconvenience of the loss.

Man's soul, however, is not wholly in the whole body and wholly in every part of it according to the totality of its *power*.[29] Thus, man has spiritual powers that are not wholly in the whole body; moreover, all his powers are not in every part, that is, he does not see, hear, and talk with his eye; but his power of sight is in the eye, his power of hearing is in the ear, etc. This is the philosophical reason why man needs the development of each of his organic powers for his full perfection and why the development of one power does not result in a perfect transfer to all the others.

These truths show us the natural dignity of man's soul, the active principle of all his activity and therefore of his co-operation with God. Our philosophical conviction of this dignity is immeasurably reinforced by the practical experience of death. However impressive or eminent the person in life, the soul's passing leaves only ashen remains that must be disposed of.

The *remote principle by which*[30] a man will co-operate with God's call is his nature, for action follows being.[31] Water acts like water because it is water. Iron acts differently because it is not water, but iron. The fact that water is water is the ultimate intrinsic principle by which it acts always in this particular way *like water* and not sometimes like iron or gold. Man's human essence is the ultimate principle by which he acts as a man, and essence considered as the basic principle by which something operates is called "nature." Therefore human nature itself is the remote principle by which man acts.

Considering man's substantial equipment, his correspondence with God's call and his educational activity will not be something superficial, painted on him as it were, having no root in his deeper self, no involvement of his inmost self. It is always the person who acts — the principle *which;* and the person's acts ultimately proceed from his nature — the remote principle *by which*. It is important to keep this in mind as we speak next of man's faculties.

---

[28] Grenier, *op. cit.*, II, p. 285.
[29] *Ibid.*
[30] *Principium quo remotum.*
[31] *Agere sequitur esse.*

NATURAL EQUIPMENT — ACCIDENTAL

We have considered man's substantial equipment for his life of activity. Now we treat his accidental equipment, namely, his faculties and the habits which perfect them. Education is necessarily concerned with the development of these faculties and their habits; hence, clear understanding is indispensable.

FACULTIES: This is not the place to expound even in capsule form the whole philosophy of man's faculties. Again the reader must be referred to formal philosophy. Here we briefly indicate such points as will contribute to the development of our central theme, namely, man's natural equipment for co-operation with God's call to perfection in Christ.

Faculties may be broadly described as powers of acting. More strictly, a faculty is a proximate principle by which[32] any operation takes place. Man's soul has certain faculties or powers which are the proximate principles of his activity and therefore of his self-development. These powers are accidents rooted in the soul. They are proper accidents, not merely contingent accidents as would be a natural pallor or redness of the face. But they are really distinct from the soul.[33] This can be seen from the fact that man's soul is always in act — otherwise he would be nothing — whereas the powers of his soul are not always actually operating — he is not always walking around, studying, singing! These faculties are also really distinct from each other, as can be seen from their distinct formal objects;[34] thus the faculty of seeing color is distinct from the faculty of hearing sound.[35] Yet they are not little independent entities in conflict with each other as it were. They are not separable from the essence of the soul — not at all detachable like the radar screen or the transistor of even the most delicate mechanical equipment. They are not parts of the soul since the soul is simple and has no parts. They are not protrusions on the periphery of the soul like pillboxes around a fort! All such imaginings are equally futile, because faculties are not quantitative but qualitative, and they are rooted in a spiritual soul.

These faculties are of several kinds:

1. There are vegetative powers which are concerned with the conservation of the living organism, either in itself or in its very species. These are the powers of nutrition, growth, and reproduction.[36]

---

[32] *Principium quo proximum.*

[33] Cf. Maquart, *op. cit.,* II, p. 199 re. the importance of this distinction. Its denial leads philosophically to Pantheism.

[34] *Supra,* p. 15.

[35] The faculty should not be confused with the organ through which the faculty operates. Thus the eye is the organ, not the faculty, of sight.

[36] Cf. *Summa,* I, q. 78, a. 1.

2. There are cognoscitive powers whereby the person is united through a similitude (*species*) to the external thing about which his activity turns. Knowledge of a sense object, such as an apple, exercises a different power from knowledge of a non-sense object, such as being or truth or justice. Hence there are distinct powers of sense and of intellectual knowledge just as different instruments are required for detecting light rays and gamma rays. Yet the two faculties can be and are perfectly co-ordinated.

3. There are powers whereby the person has contact with the external thing not merely through a likeness but through an inclination toward the thing itself. So there are the appetitive powers, sensitive and rational, which tend toward things as toward an end. There is the power of locomotion whereby the boy actually walks over and takes the apple.

The diversity, yet co-ordination, of equipment on a modern battleship is a mechanical marvel: radio for this purpose, radar for that, photo-electric for the other. Completely equipped, with each of the diverse instruments doing its special work efficiently, the whole ship becomes an efficient and almost a versatile thing, adaptable to sundry needs and emergencies. All these mechanical marvels of man's work are an imperfect resemblance of the Creator's handiwork in bestowing on man himself diverse faculties, thus making it possible for him to co-operate with God's call to a richly varied perfection. These faculties constitute the accidental equipment added as it were to his substantial equipment. Yet the whole must in no way be conceived as something quantitative; for faculties are qualities of the soul.

It is clear that there is a remarkable diversity about man's equipment. He has various distinct faculties each with its own proper formal object; they are thus capable of greatly diverse functions. To drink coffee — nutritive — is very different from studying metaphysics — intellectual. Yet there is a wonderful *unity* in this accidental diversity. Man, as we have seen, is a substantial unit — one person, James Citizen, with one soul in which these diverse faculties are intimately, properly, and inseparably rooted. It is James, one and the same person, who drinks the coffee, who listens to the Ninth Symphony, who studies metaphysics.

Here is the philosophical basis for the diversity and unity which can and should be found in the process of education.

HABITS: Habits facilitate the operation of man's faculties, and therefore facilitate his co-operation with God's plan.

For smooth human operations, something more is needed than the mere knowledge of the end sought and the faculty to attain it, just as for a smooth journey something more is needed than a known destination and an automobile to reach it. If instead of traveling well-established roads to various destinations, the traveler each time had to pioneer every journey cross-countrywise — avoiding rocks, fording streams, clearing a pathway — there would be considerably less pleasant-Sunday-afternoon driving! So if man had to pioneer all his human activity on each occasion, activity would be a heavy burden.

Did you ever observe carefully a child's effort to be generous? How reluctantly he shares his toys or candy with someone else. . . . His internal struggle with selfishness shows itself in the slowness of his actions as he transfers a treasured possession to someone else. His hands move slowly and hesitantly. His eyes roam anxiously from his toy to the other child, to his mother and back again. As often as not he snatches the toy back or begins to cry. If every free decision in human life required as much effort, life would be an intolerable burden.[37]

Habits then facilitate human activity.

Notion of Habit: A habit is a quasi-permanent quality whereby man is disposed well or poorly in his nature or operations.

"Quality." A habit is a quality, that class of philosophic accident which modifies a subject in some way. A habit is not something quantitative. It does not grow out like a finger, or put phrenological bumps in one's skull.

"Quasi-permanent." This implies that, once established, it is not easily moved. It distinguishes habits from "dispositions," those transient modifications of the subject that are easily eradicated and therefore lack permanence.[38] These dispositions are transient. Either they are merely incipient habits developing perhaps into true habits as the boy becomes the man; or they are modifications founded on changeable causes and are incapable of developing into true habits. A true habit has a certain permanence.

"Man." Three conditions must be verified in the subject of a habit:[39]

a) The subject must have a potentiality not yet realized, for only potency is capable of further determination. Since God has no potency, He cannot have habits.

b) This potentiality must not be determined fixedly to one particular object. The nose needs no habit to detect perfume or H_2S.

[37] W. Farrell and M. Healy, *My Way of Life* (Brooklyn, N. Y.: Confraternity of the Precious Blood, 1952), p. 214.
[38] *Summa*, I–II, q. 49, a. 2, ad 3. These dispositions are described as *qualitates facile mobiles*.
[39] *Ibid.*, q. 49, a. 4.

c) This potentiality is capable of being realized in different ways. It should be noted that "b" and "c" eliminate the possibility of true habits in animals. Even in man there will be some limitation of habits.

"Well or poorly." Man can acquire habits of good as well as of evil. We must recognize even the philosophical fact that the educand can acquire habits of evil.

"In his nature." There is a type of habit, such as beauty or health, which pertains to the perfection of nature itself; it disposes man's body more perfectly in its relation to the soul, as a subject to its form. These are called entitative habits; but they are not perfect habits since the changeable causes on which they depend rob them of that permanence found in true habits.[40] The healthiest man may be stricken overnight.

"In his operations." These are called operative habits since they perfect man's operations by giving him a facility in his operations. Such operative habits belong entirely or principally to the soul. "Principally" is added to include those habits which are secondarily in the body, namely, insofar as the body is made a ready instrument for the soul's operations. Thus the habit found in the accomplished pianist or violinist is not just a mechanical reflex; it is referred principally to the soul through the control of reason and secondarily to the body. In this way man can have habits in his sense appetite and in his internal senses.[41] Operative habits are said then to belong to the soul.

Operations proceeding from the natural powers of the body are not capable of habits since they are already determined to their act. If I cut my finger I need no habit to start the body's healing process. Therefore man's vegetative powers of nutrition, growth, and reproduction, his sensitive powers of sight, hearing, touch, etc., insofar as they operate from natural instinct and not under the control of reason, are not capable of habits. His eyes need no habit in order to see color when they look at something. However, we know that a man may develop a habit of not looking at anything and everything.

These operative habits will be found in the faculties of the soul, but not in the soul itself since it is already and always in its essential act.

From its very notion, "every habit has a relation to an act."[42] An entitative habit perfects the nature of the thing, which is the *remote*

---

[40] *Ibid.*, q. 50, a. 1.
[41] Maquart, *op. cit.*, III, 2, p. 175.
[42] *Summa*, I–II, q. 49, a. 3.

principle by which some operation takes place. An operative habit perfects some faculty, which is the *proximate principle by which some operation takes place.*

It will now be understood that operative habits come between the faculty and its act, facilitating the act. Relative to the faculty, a habit is a perfection bringing it so much nearer to action; just as a piece of mechanism might be rust-cleansed, lubricated, ready for swift, silent action. Relative to the faculty's operation, the habit is in potency. Habit is also called second nature. Since the control of reason is a vital condition for the very possibility of habit, the influx of reason through enlightened motivation and deliberate choice will be an all-important factor in the acquisition of habits, much more important than the mere mechanical repetition of acts — as is well known to modern educational psychologists.

Regarding the multiplication of habits, it is possible to have several habits in one faculty, but not possible to have one habit equally and in the same degree in several faculties.[43] One habit can be in several powers from different points of view and in various degrees. Thus walking proceeds from the reason as guiding, the will as moving, and the power of locomotion as exercising.[44]

Considering habits dynamically we comment briefly on their origin, increase, diminution, and loss.

Origin. How do habits arise? Some habits arise from nature, some from one's own activity, some come directly from God.

1. From nature. There should be no oversimplification in considering nature as a source of habits. These generalizations can be made:

   a) Some entitative habits can proceed entirely from nature.[45] Some proceed partly from nature and partly from an extrinsic principle.

   b) True operative habits in man never come entirely from nature as their source.[46]

---

[43] Cf. q. 54, a. 1.

[44] Cf. q. 56, a. 2.

[45] Cf. *Summa,* I–II, q. 50, a. 1. A man's nature can be considered according to the species, that is, insofar as he is a man. In this regard there can be entitative habits proceeding entirely from nature, for example, the health of body demanded by the human species, so that no man can be without it.

There can also be entitative habits proceeding partly from nature and partly from an extrinsic principle as, for example, health of the body aided by surgery or medicine.

Man's nature can also be considered individually insofar as he is Socrates or Cicero or Jim. In this regard there can be entitative habits proceeding entirely from nature, for example, the sturdiness of health that becomes Hercules (compared with the delicate health of an invalid). It will be apparent that here, too, some habits can proceed partly from the individual nature and partly from an extrinsic principle, e.g., the health of a particular patient aided by the doctor's treatment.

[46] Cf. *Summa,* I–II, q. 50, a. 1. True operative habits in man never come entirely

c) Some habits in man's cognoscitive powers have their origin in nature inchoately. Such are, for example, the habit of understanding in all men (that is, the habit of first principles); and also the habits of knowledge in particular men arising from the apt disposition of the sense faculties of memory, imagination, etc.[47]

d) Some habits in the appetitive powers of particular men have their origin in nature inchoately insofar as one man's constitutional endowment disposes him more to one than the other, e.g., more to self-effacement than to aggression. This must not be exaggerated, however.[48]

2. Habits also have their origin in one's own activity. This is possible only in those activities where there is both an active and a passive principle of the act. Thus, in the operation of man's appetitive powers

---

from nature as their source, whether nature be considered in its species or as individualized. Nature can only have a part in their existence along with some extrinsic principle.

[47] In the case of the cognoscitive powers, operative habits can be natural as regards their beginning.

1. Considering nature in its specific aspect, "it is owing to the very nature of the intellectual soul that a man, once he has grasped what is a whole and what is a part, should at once perceive that every whole is larger than its part" (*Summa,* I–II, q. 51, a. 1). Knowledge of what is a whole and what is part is had through intelligible species that are derived from phantasms gained in sense knowledge. This habit, called the habit of understanding, is then natural inchoately (*secundum inchoationem*).

2. Considering individualized nature, there can also be inchoate habits of knowledge insofar as one man whose sense faculties — memory, imagination, etc. — are naturally more perfect than those of another is more apt for intellectual activity than the other, since the intellect necessarily relies on the data presented to it by the sense faculties.

[48] Cf. *Summa,* I–II, q. 51, a. 1. In the case of appetitive powers a distinction must be made.

With regard to nature in its species, appetitive habits do not have their origin in nature even inchoately as far as the habit itself is concerned; but it is of the very nature of the appetitive power to incline toward its object without need of a habit.

With regard to individualized nature, some appetitive habits have their origin in nature, inchoately. For example, Jim may be disposed inchoately to meekness more than to aggressiveness by his very constitutional endowment. In the adult, of course, this inchoate habit "is inextricably interwoven with the other determinants of personality" (James H. VanderVeldt and Robert P. Odenwald, *Psychiatry and Catholicism* [New York: McGraw-Hill Book Co., Inc., 1952], p. 6). This inchoate natural disposition is a minor factor in his adult conduct when one considers the power of his free will and the influence of grace. It can in no way be interpreted in a deterministic sense, nor used as a comfort for one's own sloth or negligence. To say that a person is a "born worker" or is just "naturally kind" is to utter clichés and to be under suspicion of rationalizing one's own inadequacy. Teachers need feel no pessimism, then, in the face of a pupil's "born obstinacy." More than likely, the obstinacy is 95 per cent explained by factors here and now changeable. Fenelon's softening of the Duke of Burgundy, Louis XIV's grandson, is a classic case of what enlightened Christian tutelage can do to mellow "born malice."

the apprehensive power presenting the object is the active principle, the appetitive power moved thereby is the passive principle. The multiplication of acts induces a certain quality, not in the first active principle but in the power which is passive and moved to perform the action: this we call a habit. For example, habits of science are caused in the intellect insofar as it is moved to acts by first principles.[49] In those who have not yet attained the full use of reason, the immature and the feebleminded, the active principle of virtue is weak. Whatever virtues these people are capable of will be fostered by an extrinsic active principle, namely, by some other rational being directing and supporting them, as the horticulturist's stake supports the growth of the seedling; and they can be fostered only to the degree of a disposition, never to the stability and permanence of true habits whose formation requires an intensive, active principle. In the case of these immature and feebleminded persons, the lack or the removal of this external direction — which, incidentally, should always be tactful and enlightened — will mean a reversion to unregulated behavior.[50] This is a philosophical reason for the need of parental and teacher vigilance, of sanctions, and for the failure of any pedagogical system that would permit to even the youngest child exclusive self-direction. Integrated virtues cannot be presupposed in the young student.[51] As reason awakens, the child should be given proportionate opportunity for that self-reliant exercise of his inherent powers which will solidify these transient dispositions and the external routine of acts into true habits. Gradually, external control and support must be removed just as the supporting stake is removed from a thriving plant.

Hence in home and school, there should be a graded regime — a program and a discipline proportioned as closely as possible to maturity. As well as fostering a healthy self-reliance, this will facilitate the transition from school life to work life. Yet at times one finds, especially in boarding high schools, an excessive uniformity strictly imposed on seniors and freshmen alike, even though there be years between their age, knowledge, and maturity. Sometimes the only real difference is a later retiring hour to provide the seniors with more study time! Naturally such a graded regime would mean additional problems for an already harassed administration — but only in the beginning. Ideals as such, however, should never be lowered for the sake of tactical difficulties. Very often the phrase "can't be done" means only "has not yet been

---

[49] Cf. *Summa,* I–II, q. 51, a. 2.
[50] Cf. Thomas C. Donlan, *Theology and Education* (Dubuque, Iowa: Wm. C. Brown Co., 1952), p. 29.
[51] Cf. Timothy F. O'Leary, "Philosophical Concepts of the Moral Virtues as Means to an End in Education," *American Catholic Philosophical Association Proceedings,* 1949, p. 123.

done"; perhaps it even means "is outside my thinking." Modern schools are laudably and capably doing things that, fifty years ago, administrators would have said "could not be done." In some of these schools a complete uniform is worn by all. Perhaps the wisdom of having all the students from the youngest to the oldest wear the same uniform is open to question. A modification of that uniform for seniors in favor of conventional wear may be found to have some psychological contribution to the development of a sense of personal responsibility.

The fact that the very young are unable to develop true habits by no means lessens the importance of their rudimentary habits; there can be no tree without the seedling. So children from their earliest years should be trained according to their maturity in the external sequence of appropriate habitual acts.

No one can say numerically how many acts must be repeated to form any or all habits. It varies with the habit being acquired and the faculty being perfected. Moral habits are not caused by one act because man's appetitive power is variously inclined to many diverse singulars and cannot be channeled to one in a single act. Yet even one act is a beginning.

Therefore it is not enough for parents or teachers to encourage children to tell the truth once and to leave it at that. A fortiori, it is not enough to teach them the notion of truth, the notion of Holy Communion, and then to pass on to other matter, blithely expecting that from now on all will acquire habits of telling the truth and of frequent Communion!

Habits in the intellect can be caused by one act, when a truth is so clearly presented and is so evidently true that the intellect at once grasps it and gives it a firm and unshakable assent. A habit can be acquired in this way about self-evident propositions, such as a whole is greater than a part. A merely probable proposition lacks the self-evident power to do this. Nor can habits be so easily acquired in those areas of knowledge that require the contribution of memory and imagination. Hence judicious repetition and review will always be necessary in teaching.

3. Habits can also have their origin directly in God, since He is the Creator and can, if He pleases, infuse directly into man qualities similar to those induced by the secondary causes that He has created. God could, and sometimes does, infuse natural habits into a particular person, for example, the habit of some foreign language never learned by the person. This rarely happens but such instances do occur in the lives of the saints. Later we shall discuss in their proper place the infused supernatural habits by which God adds to and perfects man's equipment for co-operating in the attainment of Christian perfection.

Increase of Habits: Philosophically speaking, habits are qualities.

Their mode of increase, considered strictly, will be typical of such qualities. Hence, they are not developed intrinsically by addition. One form does not add to another to make one big habit. In a limited sense a habit can be said to increase extensively (*extensive*) insofar as its application is widened. Thus a juggler who extends his balancing act from five "props" to ten can be said to have increased his habit of balance. This sort of growth, however, is not found in the moral virtues. If one really possesses the virtue it extends to all the objects in which is found the proper object of the virtue. We would rightly be nonplused to hear someone say in daily life that he has the virtue of temperance for everything but "Scotch" whisky!

More strictly, habits, as philosophical qualities, are increased by being more deeply intensified in their subject. This intensification is sometimes referred to as "becoming more deeply rooted in the subject"; and this metaphor is legitimately used provided a habit be not imagined as some sort of mistletoe striking deeper into the tree! Merely repeated acts will sustain the habit and perhaps dispose the subject for an increase but will not necessarily effect the increase. The high school student who reads only comics or the yellow press, or who merely repeats problems already solved, will not thereby increase his intellectual habits. But the increase will be effected by more intense acts.

The importance of proper motivation for the increase of habits will again be realized: it will be realized too that maximum repetition of the act is not necessarily the optimum repetition. The maximum repetition of remiss acts does not build the best habits — something to be remembered efficaciously in regard to drill and practice lessons.

Loss of Habits: This is a complex point. It hinges wholly on the understanding of the nature of a habit as a *form* inhering in a *subject*. These principles can be laid down as governing the loss and diminution of habits.

1. Since the generation of one form necessitates the corruption of its contrary, one habit can be destroyed by generating its contrary. For example, a habit of lying will be formally destroyed by developing a habit of truthfulness. This destruction will be *effected* by the placing of contrary acts.

2. Since an accidental form necessarily adheres in a subject, the corruption of the subject necessarily involves the corruption of the form. You cannot have a mural without a wall!

3. Any act which can be corrupted can in the same way be diminished.

4. Habits are diminished and even destroyed by the cessation of their acts, wherever these acts are of such a nature that their cessation would allow the exercise of contrary acts which would in turn induce a contrary form. Some habits of their nature overcome, or at least impede,

certain contrary acts. If these contrary acts be not impeded a contrary habit will be induced. Daily life presents some broad illustrations of this truth. While the aero-engines run well, their power impedes the downward drag of gravity and keeps the airplane on its lofty altitude; if they stop, gravity is unimpeded and the routine altitude changes. If the air-conditioning unit ceases to function, the room temperature soon changes even though it has been a constant 70 degrees; the steady running of the cooling apparatus is needed to counteract the air-heat.

We will now apply these principles to various habits.

Bodily habits can be corrupted directly by a contrary form and indirectly by the corruption of their subject.[52]

The habit of first principles cannot be destroyed because intelligible species caused by the active intellect and residing in the possible intellect have no contrary.[53] Nor is the intellect a corruptible subject. We cannot ever forget or deceive ourselves regarding the fact that a whole is greater than its part, and other self-evident principles.

The habit of science can be destroyed because both the premises whence its reasonings begin have their contraries, and the process by which the reasoning develops has its contrary in sophistical reasoning. The same must be said of the other intellectual virtues whether speculative or practical — wisdom, prudence, and art. "All these may be destroyed by false reasoning."[54]

All moral habits can be corrupted because each virtue has its contrary vice. These moral habits are induced in the appetitive faculties by a motion of reason insofar as those faculties are directed by reason. Their corruption will take place through a contrary judgment of reason whether this contrary judgment be made through ignorance, passion, or deliberate choice.

It is clear that to cease exercising morally good habits is to suffer the loss of these habits, since man continually needs these good acts to overcome his passions and wayward tendencies. Failure to use the mower means overgrown grass and the spoiling of a trim lawn.

St. Thomas says also that intellectual good habits, excepting the habit of first principles, will be diminished and even destroyed by the cessation of their acts.[55] "The man who continually moves in a circle far beneath him intellectually is rapidly retrogressing: the man who spends his time daydreaming is decreasing his powers of thought and concentration; the man who spends his time reading trash is rendering himself less and less capable of reading anything but trash."[56]

[52] Cf. *Summa,* I–II, q. 53, a. 1.   [53] *Ibid.*

[54] H. Renard, *Philosophy of Man* (Milwaukee: The Bruce Publishing Co., 1951), p. 220.

[55] *Summa,* I–II, q. 53, a. 3.

[56] Walter Farrell, *Companion to the Summa,* II, 169.

A number of educational corollaries flow from this consideration of habits. How can an educand with bad habits get rid of these? Not by a negative approach — "don't do this, don't do that" — but simply by the practice of the contrary good act. The elimination of vices is not therefore something negative but is best done positively by the formation of virtues.

Children and adults should continually exercise themselves in the practice of the moral virtues. Failure to do so means the diminution and finally the loss of these habits. Hence the education of the child should take positive care of this exercise. Daily living affords many opportunities for this exercise which the child can be taught to recognize as such, e.g., coming to school in the inconvenience of the rain or the heat, etc. Even the aged teacher should be interiorly consoled as the opportunity for practising patience presents itself day by day.

This doctrine of intellectual habits provides a philosophic reason for the accepted necessity of providing the student with stimulating educational experiences in order to secure not merely a continuance but an increased intensity of activity.

Division of Habits: Various divisions of habits can be made.
I. Habits are specifically distinct in respect of three things:
  1. In respect of their active principles. Habits are forms and like any form are diversified by their active principles.[57]
  2. In respect of nature:
    a) Some habits dispose to an act which is suitable to the agent's nature and therefore according to reason. These are virtues.[58]
    b) Some habits dispose to an act which is not suitable to the agent's nature and is therefore not according to reason. These are vices.[59]
  3. In respect of different objects. Since habits imply order to something, they can be distinguished by the things to which they are ordained.[60] Thus habits in the same faculty can be differentiated, just as trains that look alike and are stationed at adjoining platforms can be distinguished by a cautious inquiry about their destination. We have previously discussed this notion of "object" in Chapter II.
II. According to their origin, habits will be:
  1. Natural, from nature; but recall the limitations explained earlier.
  2. Acquired, from one's activity.
  3. Infused, directly from God.
III. According as they perfect the subject directly in its nature or in its operation, habits are:

---

[57] *Summa*, I–II, q. 54, a. 2.
[58] *Ibid.*, a. 3.
[59] *Ibid.*
[60] *Ibid.*, a. 2.

1. Entitative.
2. Operative. According as these operative habits perfect the intellect or the will — including the sense appetite insofar as it is under the control of the will — they are called:
    a) Intellectual. According as these intellectual habits rest in the knowledge of the truth or are ordained to action, they are:
       1) Speculative.
       2) Practical.
    b) Appetitive. According as the objects of the appetitive habits are good or evil, these habits are:
       1) Moral virtues.
       2) Vices.

VIRTUES: Good habits are called virtues and naturally it is with these that we are concerned in the whole matter of man's co-operation with God's plan for his restoration in Christ. Bad habits are not in accord with the agent's nature and do not perfect that nature. Our only concern with these is to avoid them.

We cannot here treat the whole matter of the virtues even in summary form. Even a digest would be too voluminous. Yet the virtues are indispensable in man's attainment of Christian perfection, and sound education must be built on a sound knowledge of these virtues. Here then we merely touch the main points to complete the picture of man's equipment. More intensive reading is available elsewhere.[61]

A virtue is defined as a "good, operative habit"[62] perfecting a faculty in man. We shall explain this definition.

1. "Habit," i.e., having all the notes of habits as explained above. Recall that virtues will then be qualities that are quasi permanent.
2. "Operative," i.e., destined directly for activity; and so it completes in some way the faculty which is the *proximate principle by which* an action takes place.
3. "Good," i.e., disposing to acts which are suitable to nature. Thus goodness is here used in a sense broader than moral goodness.[63]
4. "Faculty." Since virtues are operative habits their subjects will be the powers of operation, i.e., the faculties.
5. "Man." Only man can have true virtues.

---

[61] *Ibid.*, qq. 55–67; St. Thomas, *Quaestiones Disputatae* (Turin: Marietti, 1949). One of these, *Quaestiones Disputatae — De Virtutibus in Communi* — has been translated. Cf. John Patrick Reid, *St. Thomas Aquinas on The Virtues* (Providence, R. I.: Providence College Press, 1951). A philosophical digest of the virtues can be found in Grenier-O'Hanlon, *op. cit.*, Vol. IV, pp. 150–270. Brief, readable treatments may be found in Walter Farrell, *A Companion to the Summa*, Chap. IX, pp. 177–193; also in Walter Farrell and Martin Healy, *My Way of Life.*
[62] Cf. *Summa*, I–II, q. 55, a. 3.
[63] Cf. *ibid.*, q. 54, a. 3, c. and ad 1.

Division of Virtues: Since the virtues are good operative habits, the division of these habits as given above will be the groundwork for the division of the virtues, namely, intellectual and appetitive. These virtues are at the heart of education. Yet we cannot enter into a diffuse treatment. Rather than merely list them — which would be meaningless to all but a few — we will give a condensed comment on each in stop-press style. The philosophical reader will find this unnecessary and tedious; but others will receive at least a notion of these virtues that can be expanded by further reading.

It is clear that virtues perfecting the intellect will be ordained to truth; they are divided into *speculative* and *practical* according to the different objects which comprise the true.[64]

1. The speculative virtues of the intellect are ordained to universal, necessary truths, and are divided into:

    a) The virtue of *understanding.* This is a virtue whereby habitually man knows certain speculative, self-evident truths in themselves, and not through other truths; for example, a whole is greater than any of its parts. This virtue is called the habit of first principles; for its acquisition, no teaching is required.

    b) The virtue of *wisdom.* This is a virtue whereby truth is known through its ultimate principles. It is habitual knowledge about the ultimate "why" of things. Through this wisdom, we see the relation of one truth to another, of one science to another, and the relation of all truths and sciences to the Ultimate Truth, which is God. Wisdom is knowledge from the ultimate causes of things.

    c) The virtue of *science.* This is a virtue whereby truth is known through its proximate principles, i.e., not in itself, but through some other truth. In all sciences we either deduce truths from other proximate truths or we interpret facts in the light of higher principles. Thus, science pertains to the conclusions of reasoning from proximate causes; its truths are universal and necessary, but of a lower order than the knowledge had in wisdom.

2. The practical virtues of the intellect are ordained to contingent, and hence particular truths here and now operable.

    a) Prudence is an intellectual virtue perfecting man's practical intellect about the right way to do his truly human acts. It therefore concerns contingent truth about things to be done, *recta ratio agibilium.* Prudence gives true knowledge about the things that man does as man; these are his free acts.

    b) Art is an intellectual virtue perfecting man's practical intellect

---

[64] Cf. *ibid.*, q. 57. Also H. Renard, *Philosophy of Man, op. cit.*, pp. 222–224.

about the right way to make things. It therefore concerns contingent truth about the proper ordering of things to be made — *recta ratio factibilium.* Unlike a bee building its hive, man can make things in endless variety. The virtue of art perfects and directs his intellect for the making of usable and aesthetic things in the best way.

The order of excellence among the speculative intellectual virtues is wisdom, understanding, science.[65] How lamentable then for so-called higher education to eschew metaphysics! One might as well take the dome off the Capitol. In human development, however, the order is understanding, science, wisdom. We do not teach metaphysics in grade school!

The subject of all these intellectual virtues, speculative and practical, is of course the human intellect. The speculative and practical intellects are two aspects of the one intellect; being rooted in the one faculty, these virtues are interconnected. They interact on each other. The development of wisdom increases the potentiality for the development of the other virtues and vice versa. Here then is an ontological basis for unity and harmony in man's intellectual development. Attention to metaphysics perfects the habit of wisdom, but is not inimical to science and vice versa.

Man's intellect diversely perfected through these habits is his natural guide to holiness.[66] He does not have to grope in blindness through life. By the development of his endowment he is equipped with the faculty and the facility of directing himself toward his perfection.

The moral virtues pertain to the good of man as defined by reason. They perfect man's attainment of this good and will therefore be divided according to the diverse way that this good is attained. We list them in the order of their perfection: prudence, justice, fortitude, temperance.[67]

Prudence[68] is the virtue that puts goodness into the very act of

---

[65] Cf. L. P Everett, "The Primacy of the Virtue of Wisdom" (unpublished master's thesis, Catholic University of America, 1942). "Wisdom contains both science and understanding not indeed as a genus contains its parts, but as a potential whole is said to contain its parts, since it has in a more perfect manner whatever science and understanding embrace" (*op. cit.*, pp. 43–44). Wisdom includes science and understanding *eminenter,* not formally; formally these are distinct virtues (cf. *ibid.,* p. 44). Hence, Catholic education never pretends that metaphysics can *replace* science.

[66] Cf. Pius X, *Acerbo Nimis* (April 15, 1905), trans. in Vincent A. Yzermans, *All Things in Christ* (Westminster, Md.: Newman Press, 1954), p. 48.

[67] Grenier, *op. cit.,* IV, p. 163.

[68] Cf. W. Farrell and M. Healy, *My Way of Life,* pp. 365–374. Cf. Grenier, *op. cit.,* IV, pp. 166–177. Cf. also Walter Farrell, *Companion to the Summa,* Vol. III. This should be read in conjunction with the *Summa,* II–II, qq. 47–56. Cf. also Walter J. Buehler, *The Role of Prudence in Education* (Washington, D. C.: The Catholic University of America Press, 1950).

How does prudence the cardinal virtue differ from prudence the intellectual

reason itself. We have already defined it above. Its acts are to take counsel, to judge rightly, and especially to command one's own operation of the things counseled and judged; this command is its characteristic act. The virtues which are potential parts of prudence are:[69]

Eubulia, whose object is good counsel.

Synesis, which enables man to judge well of things to be done according to law.

Gnome, which enables a man to judge well when things are to be done which are outside and above the prescriptions of ordinary laws.

St. Thomas notes that the vices opposed to prudence by deficiency — precipitation, lack of consideration, inconstancy, negligence — arise chiefly from lust;[70] vices opposed to prudence by excess — prudence of the flesh, craftiness, guile, fraud, oversolicitude — arise chiefly from covetousness.[71]

Justice[72] is the virtue that puts goodness into our human acts concerning external things. It is defined as a firm and perpetual determination to give each one his due. Its subject is the will. Its acts are twofold — to judge justly and to execute justice by actually giving each one his due.[73] There are nine potential parts of justice, namely, religion, piety, observance, truth, gratitude, retribution, liberality, affability, and equity. Justice finds its mean, not through prudence but from the very nature of its object. The man who owes five dollars must in justice pay five dollars.

Fortitude is the virtue that regulates according to goodness the

---

virtue, or, better, what is the relationship? By its subject it is an intellectual virtue, since it resides in the intellect; by its object it is a moral virtue, since it directs man's actions to what is morally good. Hence prudence is *essentialiter* an intellectual virtue, *naturaliter* a moral virtue.

[69] In all of these cardinal virtues we have to consider integral, subjective, and potential parts. The integral parts of a virtue are those conditions which are required for a perfect act of the virtue. For example, memory of the past and the way events proceeded is obviously required for a perfect act of prudence; caution is another integral part of prudence.

The subjective parts are the species into which the virtue is divided: for example, personal prudence and prudence in government; or, in the case of justice, commutative justice, general justice, and distributive justice.

The potential parts are virtues annexed to the cardinal virtues; in them, however, the essence of this cardinal virtue is not perfectly realized; for example, *eubulia* (taking counsel) is a virtue that is surely related to prudence. Yet, it does not reach the stature of prudence whose chief act is to *command* the prudential action. *Eubulia* is, therefore, a virtue in its own right distinct from prudence, yet related closely to it; hence eubulia is a potential part of prudence.

[70] *Summa*, II–II, q. 53, a. 6.

[71] *Ibid.*, q. 55, a. 8.

[72] Cf. *ibid.*, qq. 57–79. Also cf. Grenier, *op. cit.*, IV, pp. 178–214.

[73] Cf. Grenier, *op. cit.*, IV, p. 196.

activity of the irascible appetite when this would so hinder and discourage us from attaining the good of reason that we might relinquish the effort. It is defined as a virtue which, despite difficulties and even danger of death, moderates the movements of the irascible appetite and strengthens the will lest man desist in pursuing good. The subject of fortitude is the irascible appetite insofar as it is under the control of reason. The acts of fortitude are the curbing of fear and the moderation of daring.[74] The curbing of fear is its principal act. When fortitude is not concerned with danger of death, its potential parts are magnanimity, the accomplishment of great and honorable deeds; magnificence, the production of great things at proportionate cost; patience; and perseverance. In danger of death these potential parts become integral parts.[75] Fortitude finds its mean between excess and defect through the practical judgment of the intellect according to the principles of the virtue of prudence. A man's prudence decides what is fortitude and what would be rashness or timidity for him.

Temperance is the virtue that puts goodness into the activity of the concupiscible appetite by controlling the allurements of our passions when these would thwart the good of reason by diverting us toward something else. This virtue prevents man from being enticed off the right road to God. It is clear that temperance means more than mere sobriety. It is defined as a virtue which moderates the sense appetite in regard to the pleasures of touch and taste. Taken strictly, it moderates the tactile pleasures concerned with the preservation of the individual and of the race. The subject of temperance is the concupiscible appetite insofar as this is subject to the will. The potential parts of temperance are continence, meekness, clemency, and modesty. Temperance finds its mean between excess and defect through the practical judgment of the intellect according to the virtue of prudence — a judgment of what is necessary and suitable for the good of body and mind. A man's prudence decides what is temperate for him.

These four moral virtues are called the cardinal or principal virtues. Even this brief treatment and the mere listing of their potential parts gives some idea of their comprehensive coverage of man's moral life. They perfect every aspect of his moral life. They concentrate all his natural moral effort and focus it on his ultimate end. Each virtue, with its potential parts, is like a bejeweled crown or, to make the metaphor dynamic rather than static, each is like a modern army with its varied and specialized divisions so perfected, marshaled, and co-ordinated as to form an irresistible unit for the attainment of its objective.

There is an intimate connection between these four cardinal virtues and man's last end. Justice, fortitude, and temperance concern some

---

[74] *Summa*, II–II, q. 123, a. 3.   [75] Grenier, *op. cit.*, IV, p. 219.

good to be done; and the seeking of every good is ordained to the ultimate good.[76] Although prudence is concerned with the means to the end, the practical judgment about these means proceeds from the right desire and love of the last end as from a principle.[77] It is clearly requisite for prudence, which is right reason about means to an end, that man be well disposed toward ends. This disposition depends on the rectitude of his appetite, and this rectitude of the appetite depends on moral virtue.[78]

These moral virtues are also intimately connected among themselves, so much so that if one be lacking, not one of the others can be had perfectly.[79] He who lacked fortitude could not have the stomach to acquire any of the other virtues in an advanced degree. He who lacked temperance could not render everyone his due in all things as justice requires. He who lacked prudence could have no moral virtue. Moral virtue is a habit of choosing well the end of the activity; but this involves also the right choice of means pertaining to the end, which choice is the function of prudence.[80] Yet in a different respect there can be no prudence without moral virtue[81] since one cannot choose *rightly* the means to a bad end; moral virtue inclines man to a good end for which prudence directs the means. This is no more perplexing than to say that the automobile cannot drive to New York without the driver, nor can the driver motor there without the automobile. Educators cannot therefore merely pick and choose among the moral virtues and yet hope to produce "all-round" citizens. However, imperfect moral virtues not yet fully developed and stabilized can exist separately.

These moral virtues are not merely interconnected. They are subordinated to and united in prudence.[82]

The description of moral virtue as will power, commonly understood, is hardly adequate. It is not enough that man has a certain strength and stability of will by which he acts well in trying circumstances, perhaps with considerable difficulty. The man who just manages to drag himself each time past a barroom may evince considerable will power each time, but meager evidence of the developed virtue of temperance! Only when he acts easily, agreeably, and readily, without casting around and analyzing this and that to find the mean of virtue, can he be truly considered to have acquired the developed virtue of temperance. Likewise, if a student has to force himself to open his books, his reading may be a triumph

---

[76] *Supra*, p. 39.
[77] Cf. Gredt, *op. cit.*, II, pp. 373–374.
[78] *Summa*, I–II, q. 57, a. 4.
[79] *Ibid.*, q. 65, a. 1; also cf. Gredt, *op. cit.*, II, p. 373; also Grenier, *op. cit.*, IV, pp. 161–162.
[80] *Summa*, I–II, q. 58, a. 4.
[81] *Ibid.*, a. 5.
[82] *Ibid.*, q. 68, a. 5.

of what is called his will power, but is marked a failure for the effort to develop his *habits*. Will power is, of course, always needed in the formation of the virtues and never loses complete control over them, but it is modally distinct from virtue. Hence it is inadequate to say that moral formation in education is concerned with developing will power, if this term be taken literally.

The intellectual virtues are called virtues *secundum quid*, or relatively, whereas the moral virtues are virtues *simpliciter*, simply speaking and absolutely; because the nature of virtue is more perfectly realized in the moral than in the intellectual virtues.[83] This will be clear from the following considerations. Virtue is a good habit. But something is good *simpliciter* when it is good in every respect, and actually. The moral virtues make a man good simply and actually, because they confer not merely an aptness for smooth action but the *right use* of that aptness, so that a man now is actually just and temperate. We say legitimately that such a man is good and does good.

Intellectual virtues, however, confer on a man only an aptness to act, not the right use of the aptness: a skilled surgeon, locksmith, or an attorney can use his skill immorally. Therefore, they cannot be called good simply but only relatively. The subject of a virtue *simpliciter* good can only be the will, or some power insofar as it is moved by the will.[84] It is the virtues inhering in the will that make a man good *simpliciter*. It is then more important to be good than to be learned.[85] Actually the choice, as an either-or choice, should never have to be made; but the speculative truth shows clearly where the educator's first emphasis should be.

In these habits and virtues we have an important element in man's natural equipment for the attainment of his own perfection.

They give uniformity of operation, and facility and promptitude in operation. They enable man to delight in his operations since these are "second nature" to him, proceeding smoothly and easily.

The virtues, then, are the key to efficient and successful living. They are also the road of man's progress. Never must virtue be considered a repression — as often is ignorantly the case. How could it be when it gives the facility and the perfection for action! A road is not a prison, something repressive, for those who wish to reach their destination: the

---

[83] *Ibid.*, q. 56, a. 3.

[84] *Ibid.*

[85] The object of the intellectual virtues is more excellent, since it is more universal than the object of the virtues which perfect the appetite. In this respect the intellectual virtues are nobler than the appetitive virtues. But in relation to action, since the moral virtues move a man toward the good and therefore toward the ultimate good — his last end, they make a man good and their development is indispensable for his final happiness.

smoother the road the better the traveling. Virtue, like a road, is only inconvenient for those who want to wander off arbitrarily and stray.

Clearly, the importance of developing the natural virtues in the process of education is paramount; otherwise man, whose whole conscious life is a tissue of operations, would operate only with difficulty. It would be incongruous, too, if a Catholic, after years of Christian education, was inferior to others without such benefit in the possession of the ordinary natural virtues.

There must be no dichotomy in the development of the virtues, because they are related to each other.

No dichotomy can be established between moral virtues and prudence which is an intellectual virtue. By this I do not mean that every command or advice must be rationalized, explained, or rendered acceptable: but I mean that there should be a simultaneous development of moral virtue and prudence.[86]

According to Donlan this relationship between the virtues, intellectual and moral, is not one of causality but of condition. One virtue will not cause the other but it will be a condition of the other's development, for example, moral science will not give moral rectitude but is a condition for true moral rectitude.[87]

The natural virtues have a definite, if inferior, place in Christian education. They are a practical but very distant help in the exercise of supernatural virtue. They are not to be despised just because they are inferior in comparison with the supernatural. Their good is not vitiated by the better.

Virtue is personal. Hence temperance, patience, justice in the teacher cannot be transferred to the student. These and all virtues can only be fostered in the student by enlightening him and inducing him to perform the virtuous acts. Merely teaching the student about virtue is generally not sufficient for this acquisition of virtue, either because of the immaturity of his mind or because of his proneness to evil. This proneness to evil tends to lead his intellect away from truth and his will away from goodness; it tends to warp his practical judgment.

We summarize this treatment of habits and virtues schematically.

---

[86] Timothy O'Leary, *American Catholic Philosophical Association Proceedings,* *op. cit.,* p. 124.

[87] Donlan, *op. cit.,* p. 36.

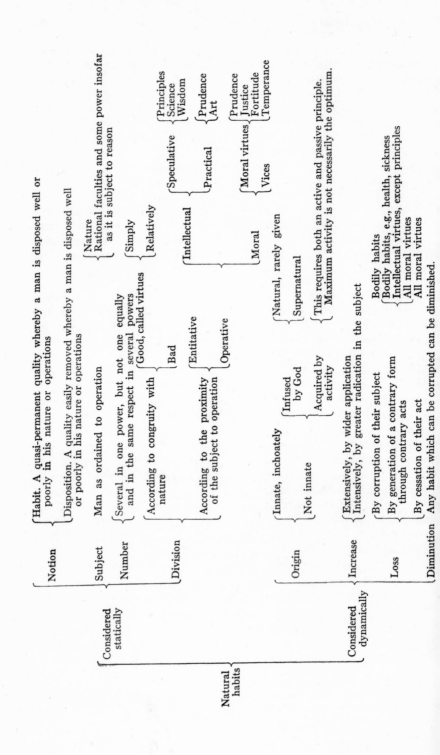

Natural habits

Considered statically

- **Notion**
  - Habit. A quasi-permanent quality whereby a man is disposed well or poorly in his nature or operations
  - Disposition. A quality easily removed whereby a man is disposed well or poorly in his nature or operations
- **Subject**
  - Man as ordained to operation
  - Nature — Rational faculties and some power insofar as it is subject to reason
- **Number**
  - Several in one power, but not one equally and in the same respect in several powers
    - Simply
    - Relatively — Good, called virtues
- **Division**
  - According to congruity with nature
    - Good, called virtues
    - Bad
  - According to the proximity of the subject to operation
    - Entitative
    - Operative
      - Intellectual
        - Speculative { Principles, Science, Wisdom }
        - Practical { Prudence, Art }
      - Moral
        - Moral virtues { Prudence, Justice, Fortitude, Temperance }
        - Vices

Considered dynamically

- **Origin**
  - Innate, inchoately — Natural, rarely given
  - Not innate
    - Infused by God — Supernatural
    - Acquired by activity — This requires both an active and passive principle. Maximum activity is not necessarily the optimum.
- **Increase**
  - Extensively, by wider application
  - Intensively, by greater radication in the subject
- **Loss**
  - By corruption of their subject — Bodily habits
  - By generation of a contrary form through contrary acts — Bodily habits, e.g., health, sickness; Intellectual virtues, except principles; All moral virtues
  - By cessation of their act — All moral virtues
- **Diminution** — Any habit which can be corrupted can be diminished.

SUPERNATURAL EQUIPMENT

We have seen that man has been given varied natural equipment, substantial and accidental, which he is to use in his co-operation with God's plan for his perfection. The extent of this natural equipment we can glean from natural knowledge, especially from philosophy. But to stop here would be sadly incomplete.

From Revelation we know that man has also been given marvelous supernatural equipment — in fact, a whole supernatural organism that makes him capable of operating on a supernatural level and of deserving a supernatural reward in heaven. This is a vital consideration for all education, which is intimately and necessarily concerned with man's last end,[88] for, by the free gift of God, this is a supernatural end. "Christian" education which ignores, vitiates, or hinders man's supernatural life is counterfeit.

St. Pius X says:[89]

The advocates of false reform, imitating the fickleness of the foolish, generally rush into extremes. They either emphasize faith to such an extent that they neglect good works or they canonize nature with an excellence of virtue while overlooking the assistance of faith and divine grace. As a matter of fact, however, merely naturally good acts are only a counterfeit of virtue, since they are neither permanent nor sufficient for salvation. The work of this kind of a reformer cannot restore discipline. On the contrary, it ruins faith and morals.

It is important for sound education to preserve the proper balance between the natural and supernatural in man, by understanding each element accurately, without exaggeration or mutilation. Having considered the natural, we now examine the supernatural equipment given him. Again the mere listing of such equipment — meaningful for the periti perhaps — is inadequate for the nontheologian. Hence, we risk the boredom of the theologian to synthesize from theology pertinent details of this supernatural endowment, so that Christian teachers may perceive something of the divine potentiality they are asked to develop in the child who now squirms noisily in the desk before them.

Two things must be recalled as a prelude to this consideration. First, this supernatural order is entirely above man's own natural powers, as we have already seen. Modern man feels competent and successful in the world of nature. But he cannot merit the supernatural order, cannot dispose himself positively for it by giving himself a real capacity or positive suitability for it. (Theologians, nevertheless, disagree as to whether it can

---

[88] Cf. Pius XI, *Christian Education of Youth*, p. 4.
[89] Pius X, encyclical, *Editae Saepe* for the tercentenary of St. Charles Borromeo, May 26, 1910. Translated in Yzermans, *op. cit.*, pp. 167–168.

be said that man can dispose himself merely negatively.) In this regard, however, there is a good deal of unwitting Pelagianism and especially semi-Pelagianism in popular Catholic thinking. Some seem to believe that with an "extra-big" natural effort they can perform supernatural acts; or that purely natural acts, e.g., natural kindness, generosity, etc., deserve a supernatural reward from God!

Second, man's elevation to the supernatural order is entirely gratuitous. God was under no obligation whatever to bestow it on him; yet some have the impression that they can callously reject the grace of God by mortal sin as often as they please and get it back when and as they please.

We now consider the notion and educational significance of sanctifying grace, actual grace, the infused virtues, and the gifts of the Holy Ghost.

SANCTIFYING GRACE. The basic element in man's supernatural equipment is habitual grace, called sanctifying grace. We have already seen that grace is a gratuitous gift infused by God into the rational creature with reference to eternal life.

Sanctifying grace is a created, supernatural quality intrinsically and permanently inhering in the essence of the soul, conferring on it wonderful supernatural prerogatives. It is:

1. "Supernatural." Entirely above nature, and therefore quite gratuitous on the part of God. It is infused by God. It is to be noticed that grace is supernatural entitatively, not just modally. Grace is not a natural quality produced in a supernatural way nor some natural act accepted by God for a supernatural end.[90] It will be already clear that no teacher can *give* or directly cause grace in a student.

2. "A quality . . . permanently inhering." After the manner of habit as explained earlier. Sanctifying grace and the infused virtues are called habits reductively. Grace is reduced to the first species of quality, which is that of a habit. "Intrinsically" inhering: It is not merely a sort of pardon or acceptance imputed to man by God.

3. "A created quality." This distinguishes it from the supernatural indwelling of the Holy Trinity in the soul, which is called uncreated grace. This created gift, however, can only come from God as its source since it is a share in His own nature.

4. "In the essence of the soul." Sanctifying grace is an entitative habit. It perfects the essence of the soul immediately and the soul's operation mediately.[91] It confers on man wonderful, supernatural prerogatives.

    a) Man is made a sharer in the divine nature itself[92] as a formal

---

[90] B.A.C., *op. cit.*, Vol. III, p. 553.   [91] *Summa*, I–II, q. 110, a. 4.

[92] "By whom [Christ] he hath given us most great and precious promises: that by these you may be made partakers of the divine nature" (2 Pet. 1:4).

effect of sanctifying grace. This is a physical, formal, accidental, analogical participation in the divine nature. It is physical, real — not merely something to be imputed. It is a formal participation whereby man precisely, and not just virtually, shares the divine nature as it is. It is an accidental sharing, as a quality perfecting us; God has His own nature substantially. Therefore it is an analogous participation. We have previously expanded this concept of analogy.

b) Man by sanctifying grace is made an adopted son of God. This effect is produced formally and adequately by grace — adequately in the sense that it follows from the very notion of grace. We have previously expanded this notion of adoption.[93]

c) Annexed to the gift of grace are the infused virtues and the gifts of the Holy Ghost. We shall consider these in the next section.

This supernatural grace is a new nature superadded to man to become the *remote principle by which* supernatural operations are performed. These acts, we re-emphasize, are not merely natural acts supercharged as it were to produce just a little more speed and efficiency! Acts that proceed from grace as a principle are truly supernatural, entitatively different from merely natural acts even though the two might outwardly appear identical, for example, an act of courtesy toward someone. It is clear, then, that Christian education must be concerned with more than the mere observable phenomena of the student's act, more than even its deepest psychological recesses.

Since grace is entirely gratuitous, the measure of its giving by God is not to be computed from the person's natural qualities. The handsome or the athletic boy is not necessarily given a greater measure of grace than the cross-eyed boy or the boy who is slow at algebra. Often the providential bestowing of graces counterbalances marvelously the inequality of natural gifts. The zealous Lacordaire was a man of great natural eloquence who drew crowds to Notre Dame Cathedral and stirred Paris. The Curé of Ars, a contemporary, was a man with meager natural gifts of oratory. But his lofty sanctity gave his simple words and his faint, raspy voice an oratorical cogency that naturally they lacked. It drew throngs to him from all over France, fascinated and moved them, even when he was repetitious and barely audible.

The glories of grace are like a litany. Grace brings us God's very special protection and the special solicitude of the angels. Without it there can be no true happiness in this world and none at all in the next, for grace is the seed of heaven's glory. In grace and its train of heavenly gifts we find our highest possible enlightenment on earth, for it brings us a share in God's own knowledge; we find truest liberty, the liberty of the

---

[93] *Supra,* p. 84 f.

sons of God. It makes us sharers in the spiritual goods of Christ and of the saints. Dependent on our co-operation, grace repairs the weakness of nature; that is why men like St. John Vianney and St. Peter Claver led remarkable lives of extraordinary energy and consistency. Grace is in a certain sense infinite in that it is limited only by the infinity of God.[94] It fills our souls with an ineffable beauty, the heavenly beauty of God Himself, who drew from His resplendence the varied beauty of earth as His created reflection.

Grace, then, is heavenly treasure; it is immeasurably superior to nature. Considering the terminus of the work, the justification of one sinner now receiving sanctifying grace is a greater and more important work than the creation of heaven and earth[95] — earth with its incalculable rubies and sapphires and pearls, chemicals and wonder drugs, sea and land life, landscapes and starry heavens that fill one with awe and somehow shrink the ego. We all admire the miracles of the saints; and anyone with human feeling in his heart would wish to extend a miraculous touch and release the paralyzed, the incurable, the insane. Yet a man co-operating with God to recover or to increase grace is doing something nobler, more beneficial, more far-reaching than the multiplied miracles which would be needed to empty the world's hospitals.[96]

Educators who assist souls to grace and to its increase are co-operating with God in something immeasurably and eternally significant. The parent laboring to form a Christian home and finance a Christian education, the teacher spending himself in the classroom, the administrator grappling with problems — expansion, staff, finances, activities — must never lose this Christian perspective. The educator should not just take it for granted as an indifferent fact that some children will lose the grace of God. Whatever be the point-of-fact outcome, his outlook and corresponding effort must never be clouded, never be lost if he is to merit the name of Christian educator.

Man's nature is not warped or destroyed by this grace. His natural equipment for co-operation with God's plan is not vitiated, nor even mutilated. The filament in the bulb, turned dazzling white by the electric power and lighting the area brilliantly, does not cease to be what it is; neither does nature, divinized accidentally by grace, cease to be what it is in itself. Not merely does nature remain unspoiled under the influence of grace; it is moreover perfected, directly and indirectly. For grace confers marvelous powers, privileges, benefits on man's soul; and man is

---

[94] Cf. Matthias Scheeben, *The Glories of Divine Grace,* trans. by Patrick Shaughnessy (St. Meinrad, Ind.: Grail Press, 1952), pp. 69–74. This is a beautiful book in untechnical language by a great theologian. It is a book that every educated Catholic should read. Francis P. Le Buffe, *Let's Look at Sanctifying Grace* (St. Louis: The Queen's Work Publication, 1944, 47 pp.) is a diagrammatical outline treatment very useful for didactic purposes.

[95] *Summa,* I–II, q. 113, a. 9, c, and ad 2.   [96] Cf. Scheeben, *op. cit.,* I, Chap. III.

one — one, substantial person. Because of this unity of the person, man's nature is perfected indirectly by the redundance of grace. A sign of this perfection can be seen in the human sense organs. Human eyes are organs of sense faculties that are distinct from reason; yet from the operation of reason they acquire a perfection not found in the animal eye. No one could mistake the crass animal eye, for the meaningful human eye — the soul's limpid window. Only the eye of the inebriate who has temporarily inhibited his reason approximates the bovine eye.

But nature also benefits directly from grace. For grace is not merely *elevans:* it is *sanans,* medicinal. One of the functions of grace is to heal, with man's co-operation, the wounds of nature received from original sin. Hence the Church in the Offertory prayer praises "God who has established human nature with marvelous dignity and more marvelously renewed it."[97]

Fallen nature is perfected directly by grace in the doing of its own natural works according to the natural law. It is certainly true that fallen man can perform each of the precepts of the natural law without the help of grace. (He always, of course, needs God's natural concursus.) But it is also certain — notwithstanding the views of the Pelagians and Rationalists — that without the help of healing grace he cannot for a long time keep the whole natural law and successfully overcome the serious temptations that will beset him.[98] Precisely what kind of healing grace may be needed is irrelevant here.[99]

It is clear that every child in every school — and every teacher too — is in need of God's grace.

The incalculable value of grace and its perfecting power does not justify sloth in man's development of his natural faculties and habits, any more than the electric power which is meant to surge into the incandescent bulb justifies the use of base material for the filament. Just as great care must be exercised to produce purified filaments of the right material rightly arranged for the best lighting effect, so man must take great care to develop all his natural talents to the full if the grace of God in his soul is to be unhindered in its activity.

This is a glimpse of the supernature given to man's nature as a principle of his supernatural activity. By it, man inaugurates a continuous series of immanent acts — a new and supernatural career, as it were — that will merit for him dividends in heaven. This is the precious supernatural reality shrouded in the children whose freckled faces, tousled hair, clumsy fingers, and noisy feet are all we now see and hear. Death will unveil it and will reveal also the increase that Christian education has helped to foster.

---

[97] Cf. *supra*, p. 92.

[98] Cf. B.A.C., *op. cit.*, III, pp. 514–521; cf. *Summa*, I–II, q. 109, a. 4.

[99] Cf. B.A.C., *op. cit.*, III, p. 521, Scholion 2.

ACTUAL GRACE. God not merely confers habitual sanctifying grace as man's new, permanent principle of salutary activity, but He gives special passing assistance to help man with individual acts. This we call actual grace, defined as a supernatural and transient help by which God enlightens the intellect and strengthens the will for the performance of supernatural acts.[100]

Man physically needs internal actual graces for all those salutary acts required for justification. When one remembers that this first actual grace is quite gratuitous, in no way able to be merited but freely given by the merciful love of God, one realizes the ignorant un-Christian folly of the view more or less expressed that people, for example, high school adolescents, can casually multiply serious sins and as it were automatically climb back to the grace of God. True, the mercy of God usually overlooks such mockery and continues to offer the actual graces needed; *but not always.* And Catholic teachers should be deeply convinced of this. It is *de fide* from the Council of Trent.[101]

Actual grace is needed for the performance of any salutary act that follows justification, that is, for any meritorious act of any virtue — according to the general opinion of theologians.[102]

Special actual grace is needed in order that anyone may persevere for a long time in the state of sanctifying grace. This too is quite certain.[103]

A *very special* actual grace is needed for final perseverance. The Council of Trent calls this the "great gift." It cannot be strictly merited.[104]

We have already seen that fallen man cannot without the help of grace keep all the natural law all the time.

The extent and the completeness of man's reliance on grace, and the way it should permeate his whole life, and therefore his education, will be apparent. Also apparent is the spiritual strangulation gradually effected by deliberate venial sins, since these restrict the flow of actual graces so vitally needed. Catholic teachers should be vividly conscious of the unseen supernatural realities that operate in the lives of their students, more necessary for them than the food which we go to *great* trouble and expense to serve clean, wholesome, and hot in the school cafeteria. Students need nourishing food; no one denies it and no sane teacher would think of refusing a student his lunch. But students need the grace of God with a need that is more fundamental and more consequential; its effects are eternal. In this whole matter of the supernatural order let educators and students simply remember and apply the words of Christ: "Without me you can do nothing" (Jn. 15:5).

It is certain that God gives actual graces to all men both just and sinners; but the degree, the time, the occasion, the efficacy of the graces

[100] Tanquerey, *op. cit.*, pp. 518–519. [103] Denzinger, *op. cit.*, nn. 183, 832.
[101] M. Denzinger, *op. cit.*, n. 813. [104] *Ibid.*, n. 826.
[102] Tanquerey, *op. cit.*, p. 525.

distributed is His own secret. It is absolutely certain too that salutary,[105] humble prayer will obtain from God the further actual graces necessary for salvation. Hence St. Alphonsus' famous conclusion to which extends the *nil dignum censura:* "He who prays will infallibly be saved; he who does not pray will infallibly be lost. All the Blessed (except infants) reached salvation by praying. All the Damned were lost because they did not pray; they would not have been lost had they prayed."[106] Moreover, as a direct correlative of Scripture's clear, oft-repeated, unqualified directives: "Ask and it shall be given to you . . ."[107] he lays down that every man has the grace of prayer at any time he wishes. Prayer is like the communication cord in a train, the thing that one grasps first and most easily in need or danger. By praying sincerely man can obtain for himself the graces he vitally needs. For one reason or another he may not here and now have all the actual grace he needs in a given situation; but by his prayer, especially prayer through our Lady's intercession, he can gain an increase in grace. To sum up: actual graces are necessary for salutary acts; in the present order of Providence some of these actual graces can only be obtained by prayer of petition. Here, then, is the importance of the prayer of petition in the attaining of Christian perfection.

Several educational conclusions appear.

The public recitation of the Our Father made each morning in some public schools is, consciously or unconsciously, the fulfilling of a vital spiritual need. Catholic teachers in public schools should try in any tactful way within their scope to encourage, not merely prayer of adoration, praise, and thanksgiving, but also some prayer of petition. To do so is a great spiritual charity.

Counselors faced with a student's personal problem, especially a moral problem, should be convinced that along with all the other means used

---

[105] Man in his present state of fallen nature cannot by his unaided natural prayer impetrate in the strict sense the grace of God, that is, by appealing to God's justice or equity; this *de fide.* Cf. Denzinger, *op. cit.,* nn. 176, 179 from the Council of Orange (529). From pure mercy God will hear such prayers provided they be sincere, persevering, asking for oneself the things needed for salvation. Cf. *Summa,* II–II, q. 83, a. 16. This is the reason for saying that everyone should pray, including every child in *any school.* Christ who responded mercifully to the adulterous woman and to the repentant thief will not spurn such sincere prayer.

[106] St. Alphonsus De Liguori, "The Great Means of Prayer," *Opera Dogmatica,* 2 vols. (Rome: Philippi Cuggiani, 1903), II, p. 646. This treatise on prayer was written by the saint to counteract the despair fostered by Jansenism. It has been published in numerous editions and translations.

In a decree of May 18, 1803, Pius VII declared that there was "nothing worthy of censure," that is, contrary to faith and morals, in the writings of Alphonsus de Liguori. A response of the Sacred Penitentiary, July 5, 1831, made it clear that this earlier decree was not a mere toleration but was a positive guarantee that the doctrine of St. Alphonsus can be safely followed by all. This is a unique encomium. Cf. Aertnys-Damen, *Theologica Moralis* (Rome: Marietti, 1950), n. 95.

[107] Mt. 7:7. Cf. also Mt. 26:41; Phil. 4:6; 1 Tim. 2:8; Hebr. 4:16.

to reach a solution it is important for the student to pray to God for the grace needed to overcome his difficulty. Tactfully they should lead him to this conviction very early in the counseling situation. They can be as nondirective and as psychological as they wish in effecting this; but it should be effected. Why would a Catholic counselor overlook the supernatural realities affecting a baptized client and work just on the natural level? One might as well furnish the room but neglect the roof!

Finally, habits of prayer as well as habits of the sacraments and habits of knowledge must be fostered in students if they are to live the life of virtue that leads to Christian perfection; "We ought always to pray."[108] Man needs prayer as a plane needs fuel. It is not enough to teach students how wonderful is Holy Communion and how beneficial is Its frequent reception; they need to pray for the grace to appreciate Holy Communion more. This teaching and praying can be smoothly coordinated in those Catholic schools where the Rosary is said daily and the decades are offered by the students for specific intentions. In these days of moral turpitude when, despite Mt. 5:28, lust is socially acceptable — a device in advertising, an ingredient in "hit" theater, a theme for some columnist — when some educational writers take certain immoral acts for granted as unavoidable and universal, or at least normal,[109] when moral lapses are commonly equated with overt acts and such acts are considered breaches of social convention rather than sins against God, it is difficult for students not to be spiritually asphyxiated. Teaching the truth about virtue and vice is altogether necessary; but it is not enough. As well as the sacraments the students need habits of daily prayer, for example, the three Hail Marys to Mary Immaculate morning and night to obtain the virtue of purity — as is recommended earnestly by St. Leonard of Port Maurice, St. Alphonsus, and others.

Somewhere, somehow, but effectively, Christian education must foster enlightened habits of prayer; otherwise there will be no growth to perfection in Christ.

INFUSED VIRTUES. Annexed to man's supernature are the infused virtues. These are supernatural habits infused by God into man's faculties giving him the proximate power to operate supernaturally. They are infused in the instant of justification. These infused virtues are not just natural virtues gold-plated as it were; nor are they merely supernatural in their mode.[110] They are entitatively supernatural and are specifically distinct from natural virtues;[111] they are, however, analogous to the

---

[108] Lk. 18:1.

[109] Cf. Luella Cole, *Psychology of Adolescence* (New York: Rinehart and Co., Inc., 1954), p. 75.

[110] Cf. Garrigou-Lagrange, *P. & C.*, pp. 37–38; also cf. B.A.C., *op. cit.*, III, pp. 772, 828.

[111] Cf. *Summa*, I–II, q. 63, a. 4; also II–II, q. 6, a. 1.

natural virtues. Here is another element in man's supernatural equipment.

The infused virtues are divided into the theological and the moral virtues.

We have previously explained the notion of *theological* virtues; these are faith, hope, and charity.

Faith is a gratuitous, supernatural, and theological virtue disposing man's mind to assent firmly, *on the authority of God the Revealer,* to all the truths so revealed by God. The act of faith assenting to these truths is an *intellectual* act. It is *obscure* since we assent on the authority of God, not from the perception of the intrinsic evidence of the truth itself. It is, nevertheless, absolutely, infallibly *certain* because God knows all things and cannot deceive. It is a *free* assent. It is an *ennobling* assent, for it lifts a man up to a share in God's own knowledge. Faith is no more an insult to man's intelligence than a telescope is an insult to his eye. As we mentioned in the first chapter, scientists would consider themselves fortunate if, *per impossibile,* some being could come to earth with an inhabitant's knowledge of outer space, of the planets, of the sun; they could share his knowledge, and the United States Government could be saved the expenditure of some of its research millions. Because faith is a sharing in some of God's own knowledge of Himself and His works, its truths are immeasurably superior to the natural intuitions of genius and the vast accumulations of scientific knowledge. Parents and teachers should never forget that a boy of twelve with a knowledge of the essential truths of faith is on a loftier pinnacle than a Steinmetz, an Edison, an Einstein without faith — loftier even than the highest angel with his merely natural knowledge. It is more important that children be taught the truths of faith than that they be taught the loftiest sciences; it is more ennobling, too. The General Judgment at the passing of the world along with its electricity and inventions and mathematics will make this very clear. It is not that human knowledge is less, but that faith is incalculably greater.

Since faith is a gratuitous gift and a free assent, the teacher must never think that he can somehow "give" a non-Catholic student the faith just by teaching or arguing religion, or that a student eventually is "sure" to become a Catholic merely from being in a Catholic environment. Nevertheless, non-Catholics can and, as well-read people, should study the faith descriptively in order to be well informed about such a widely spread and dynamic belief. It is, moreover, a great charity to pray for them that they will be given the divine light and the courage to accept the faith.

Hope is a gratuitous, supernatural, and theological virtue disposing man's will to rely on the goodness of God and to expect from Him eternal life and the means to obtain it. Thus, hope looks to the goodness of God as being good to us; by hope we show Him a love of gain, *amor concupiscentiae.* It will be recalled from the previous treatment that by *charity* we look to the goodness of God as good in Himself; we show Him a love of benevolence and of friendship.

From the viewpoint of their object, these theological virtues have no mean. The teacher need never fear that his students will love God too much or will believe in Him too firmly! There is absolutely no theological ground for rationalizing mediocrity or tepidity as a moderation of faith, hope, or charity![112]

The *infused moral* virtues are commonly listed as prudence, justice, fortitude, and temperance. These moral virtues moderate man's appetite regarding things that are means to his supernatural ultimate end. There is some dispute among theologians in regard to these infused moral virtues.[113]

The mean of these infused moral virtues is found, not in the rule of human reason, but in the rule of the Divine Mind. The infused moral virtue of temperance will lead a man to do things that his natural reason would not dictate. For example, the natural virtue of temperance will lead a man to preserve a mean of reason between starvation and gluttony for the good of human nature. The infused virtue of temperance will lead a man to mortify and deny himself for the sake of an incorruptible crown not visible or otherwise knowable to natural cognition.

The infused moral virtue of fortitude led Roman patricians to accept confiscation of properties, to die brutally with slaves as a public spectacle yet with manifest peace and happiness — to the bewilderment of Roman practicality. Another example is the history of St. Perpetua already quoted. Leaving her newborn baby, she went to execution rather than say a word that would offend the invisible God; and she did so with spiritual joy — no doubt a shocking course of action in the eyes of some modern social workers.

The acts of all these infused virtues are directed toward the act of charity as to their end.[114] All the works of life should be directed to this end of charity.

---

[112] However, on the part of man, not of God, there is a mean of faith, hope, and charity. "For although we cannot be borne towards God as much as we should be, yet we ought to approach Him by believing, hoping, and loving Him according to the measure of our condition" (*Summa,* I–II, q. 64, a. 4). For example, the credulous man does not believe too much in God! Rather, he believes his own or somebody's imaginings as if they were revealed by God. The presumptuous man does not hope too much in God, but he hopes for a good from God which exceeds his own condition, for example, pardon without true contrition.

[113] The Scotists deny the infusion of moral virtues. The clear Thomistic teaching, however, is that man has, over and above natural moral virtues, infused moral virtues which are intrinsically supernatural, not merely extrinsically supernaturalized. Cf. R. F. Coerver, *The Quality of Facility in the Moral Virtues* (Washington, D. C.: The Catholic University of America Press, 1946), pp. 5–18.

[114] St. Thomas, *III Sent.*, d. 27, q. 2, a, 4, ad 3.

These infused virtues are increased with the increase of grace and charity as already discussed. Though one virtue may be greater than another in a man, all these infused virtues grow simultaneously with an equality of proportion, just as a man's fingers, though of uneven length, grow equally in proportion.[115]

The fervent practice of the individual infused moral virtues, for example, of patience, brings about the increase of that virtue and of sanctifying grace, and, since all the infused virtues are rooted in sanctifying grace, the general betterment of the whole supernatural organism. But when these virtues are practiced under the actual or virtual influence of charity, that particular moral virtue is elevated to a higher perfection of act and contributes much more to the betterment of the supernatural organism. This is again the primacy of charity seen in action. Children should be taught thus to do all for the love of God in the proper theological sense of that dedication: to show fortitude in their studies for the love of God, to render justice to others in the sundry ways of youth for the love of God, to practice temperance for the love of God, especially through the motive of a personal love for Christ and to be like Him. Thus is every virtue enhanced, becoming a jewel in the queenly crown of charity. Fortunately the practice of no virtue is sweeter and easier than the practice of love. Charity therefore is the supreme motivation. Counselors can delicately evoke this form of motivation in educational guidance. It is the best. It is surely safe to say that for the sake of the virtue of justice alone the dissipated John Gualbert, Florentine nobleman, would never have forgiven his brother's murderer when he met him, defenseless, in a defile on that Good Friday. But for the love and imitation of Christ on the cross, John sheathed his drawn sword, extinguished his hate and private plans for revenge, and went on to become St. John Gualbert.

The benefit accruing to the individual moral virtues from the rule of charity certainly does not mean that these individual virtues can be neglected provided only charity be perfected. These virtues are specifically distinct and each must do its own work regarding its own proper object and increase.

The infused moral virtues are lost with grace and charity by any mortal sin. By mortal sin a man freely turns away from his supernatural end, God.

Like grace and charity, these virtues do not diminish directly with each venial sin as water is removed cup by cup from a tank. Rather they are affected indirectly, extrinsically; they remain as they are, but their effectiveness is hampered.

---

[115] Cf. *Summa,* I–II, q. 66, a. 2.

What is the relationship between the infused and the natural moral virtues?

1. Their origin is different. The infused virtues come directly from God as the author of the supernatural order; the natural moral virtues are acquired by our natural activity.
2. Their end is different. The infused moral virtues perfect man in regard to the attaining of a supernatural end, God as He is in Himself. The natural virtues perfect man for the attaining of a natural good.
3. Their functional benefit is different.
    a) Regarding the facility of operation: The infused moral virtues give man immediately the proximate power, *posse,* of eliciting supernatural acts along with a certain inclination toward the good which is the object of the act, since nature always has a propensity toward its end. This inclination can be called an intrinsic facility of operation.

    The natural moral virtues (not the infused) give man an easy promptitude and a certain natural satisfaction in the performance of the acts that lead to this object toward which he has the inclination. This easy promptitude has been called the extrinsic facility of virtue. It is brought about by the removal of impediments to the acts and by the discipline of the faculty through repeated acts.

    An example will clarify the contrast. One patient in the hospital earnestly wishes to get well; yet he balks at the very distasteful medicine and loathes having to take it three times a day before his meals; he has the inclination toward the end, health, but has no extrinsic facility in regard to the consumption of the medicine, which here is the means to the end. Another patient finds no difficulty in taking his medicine, but is tired of life and wants to die.[116] Again, a man may be given his passport and visa to Kenya, but that does not make his jungle journeying easy and rapid.

    However, all theologians admit and hagiography confirms the fact that the continual exercise of the infused virtues leads gradually to very great facility and promptitude in their exercise.[117]

---

[116] For a discussion of the various opinions regarding this intrinsic and extrinsic facility, cf. Coerver, *op. cit.,* p. 26 ff. The example of the two sick men is based on Louis Billot, *De virtutibus Infusis* (Rome: Gregorian University, 1921), Prolegomenon, Part 2, n. 2.

[117] B.A.C., *op. cit.,* III, pp. 718–719. Just how this facility is caused is disputed. However, the best opinion held by Molina, Ripalda, Billot, Merkelbach, John of St. Thomas, Billuart, and Schiffini contends that the repeated acts of the super-

b) Regarding the consistency of operation. The infused moral virtues confer on man the consistency of operation. The natural virtues do not necessarily produce consistency. One contrary act does not of itself destroy the acquired habit.

c) The fervent practice of the individual infused moral virtue, for example, of patience, brings about the increase of that virtue, of sanctifying grace, and the general betterment of the whole supernatural organism, since all the infused virtues are rooted in sanctifying grace.

The energetic practice of a natural virtue perfects that virtue only, without necessarily strengthening the other natural virtues. Thus the practice of natural patience does not necessarily make a man generous to the poor. It will readily be seen that attempted natural education has less cohesion than Christian education.

Therefore the infused and natural moral virtues are distinct virtues even though they may deal with the same material object; for example, acquired and infused temperance each deal with the regulation of pleasure related to the sense of touch.[118] It is obvious, however, that the two are closely co-ordinated and subordinated in actual operation, much more so than the correlative parts of a machine, or the color threads of a design, or man's two eyes. It is always the person, substantially one and undivided, who acts.

THE GIFTS OF THE HOLY GHOST are yet another array in man's supernatural equipment for the attaining of Christian perfection.

These gifts are supernatural, operative habits by which the faculties of the soul are disposed to obey the movements and inspirations of the Holy Spirit promptly and easily. These habits have a certain passivity about them whereby man's faculties are made sensitive to such inspirations. They differ from the infused virtues[119] and also from actual graces. They are enumerated as seven: wisdom, understanding, counsel, fortitude, knowledge, piety, and fear of the Lord. They are united in charity, nor can they be possessed without charity.[120] They are bestowed according to the measure of charity and grow with charity. By the progress of charity man can merit condignly the higher degrees of the gifts con-

---

natural virtues generate an acquired natural habit either *directly*, since a natural act is virtually contained in every supernatural act (cf. Molina, Ripalda, Billot, Merkelbach) ; or *dispositively*, since repeated acts of the infused moral virtues dispose the potency toward the development of a natural habit of the same virtue (John of St. Thomas, Billuart, Schiffini). Cf. Coerver, *op. cit.*, 1946, pp. 65–72.

[118] Cf. Donlan, *op. cit.*, p. 26.

[119] Cf. *Summa*, I–II, q. 68, a. 1.

[120] *Ibid.*, a. 5.

sidered as habits. He can merit congruously in the broad sense the
actual inspirations of the Holy Ghost corresponding to these higher
degrees of the gifts "for as a rule the Holy Ghost enlightens and inspires
souls according to the degree of their habitual docility, humility, and
love of God."[121]
These gifts are necessary for salvation.[122] St. Thomas clearly explains
their need. The activity of reason as elevated by the theological virtues
is not sufficient for the attaining of God in Himself, the supernatural
ultimate end, unless it be assisted by the special motions of the Holy
Spirit, the Sanctifier.[123] The reason is that the supernatural virtues,
although truly exalted in themselves, are not perfectly possessed by
man — since we know and love God imperfectly here on earth. So man
needs something more, namely, the special impulses of the Sanctifier
Himself — just as the apprentice surgeon whose knowledge is not yet
fully perfected needs the prompting of the master surgeon in his
operating.
But for the special motions and promptings of the Holy Ghost man
needs special powers whereby he is made receptive and sensitive to these
motions. Even in daily life, even in the mechanical order, we realize
that there should be a proportion between the mover and the thing
moved.[124] Nobody puts a B-47 engine into a motor scooter! A trans-
mitter needs a radio, not a washing machine, as its correlative. In this
case the nobility of the mover, the Holy Ghost, gives us a clue to the
perfection of the gifts that make us sensitive to His activity. They
excel the infused moral virtues whereby man's appetite is made obedient
to the dictates of reason; they do not, however, excel the theological
virtues in perfection.[125]
Therefore man needs these special powers and they are called the
gifts of the Holy Ghost. They excel the virtues in their manner of
working rather than in the kind of works they produce.[126]
Through the gifts, God works in us with a special directness. "Jesus
. . . was led by the spirit into the desert."[127] "For whosoever are led
by the spirit of God, they are the sons of God."[128] The spiritual man,
however, does not cease to act freely just because the gifts of the Holy
Ghost are highly developed in him. Rather it is the Holy Ghost who,
with omnipotent delicacy, causes these movements of his free will. "For
it is God who worketh in you, both to will and to accomplish."[129]
This illumination of the Holy Ghost through the gifts produces in us
acts that have no need of the deliberation and calculation required for

[121] Cf. Garrigou-Lagrange, *P. & C.*, p. 353.
[122] Cf. *Summa*, I–II, q. 68, a. 2.   [126] *Ibid.*, a. 2, ad 1.
[123] Cf. *ibid.*, a. 2.   [127] Lk. 4:1.
[124] *Ibid.*, a. 1.   [128] Rom. 8:14.
[125] *Ibid.*, a. 8.   [129] Phil. 2:13.

acts of the infused virtues.[130] Moreover, it produces acts which are above the capacity of the infused virtues. Yet these acts of the gifts do not cease to be meritorious, because we consent so to be moved; nor do they render the acts of the virtues unnecessary. These special acts produced by the inspiration of the Holy Spirit are called fruits of the Holy Ghost,[131] because they are the outcome of the gifts and are performed with deep, spiritual joy. This explains why the happiness and peace of a truly devout life is beyond "scientific" human understanding. The beatitudes are "fruits" which are perfect and excelling, bringing man the highest type of spiritual blessedness.[132]

The gifts of the Holy Ghost have been likened to the sails of a ship catching the sea winds and giving the vessel an impetus and a direction over and above the power of its engines, whose own power can be likened to the activity of the virtues.[133] A soul moved by the Holy Spirit may be illustrated as a modern air liner caught in the jet stream and swept toward its destination more rapidly than its own powerful engines could bring it. From the viewpoint of the special guidance that the gifts bring to man, they can be likened to the electronic equipment, sensitive to the "beam," which brings the plane unerringly to its destination — even amid fog — without navigational computations.

Garrigou-Lagrange insists that there is not a distinct twofold mode in the operation of the gifts, one common and the other extraordinary; rather there is continuity with only a difference of degree. At first they are exercised in a latent manner; in advanced perfection their exercise is more frequent and more manifest.[134]

The mean of the gifts is the Holy Ghost Himself, inspiring and directing. In human affairs we say the mean or measure of pianoforte playing is the pianist himself who will produce music that is delicate, robust, or wistful according to his taste, provided only that the piano be tuned and receptive of his skill.

The relationship between the gifts and the infused virtues can be seen by considering an infused virtue and its corresponding gift. The matter may be the same but the manner of operating and the mean will be different. For example, the infused virtue of faith adheres simply to the truths of revelation; the gift of understanding helps us penetrate their depths. The virtue of prudence, whether acquired or infused, directs

---

[130] Cf. Garrigou-Lagrange, *P. & C.*, p. 293.

[131] The fruits of the Holy Ghost are traditionally enumerated as: charity, joy, peace, patience, benignity, goodness, long-suffering, mildness, faith, modesty, continency, and chastity.

[132] Cf. *Summa*, I–II, q. 70, a. 2.

[133] This is Cardinal Billot's comparison, quoted in P. Parente, A. Piolanti, and S. Garofalo, *Dictionary of Dogmatic Theology*, trans. E. Doronzo (Milwaukee: The Bruce Publishing Co., 1951), p. 110.

[134] Garrigou-Lagrange, *P. & C.*, p. 353.

172 **The Proximate Aim of Education**

man to take counsel either of himself or another according to principles that reason can grasp,[135] deliberating, examining, re-examining; and man is obliged to take such care in a difficult situation. Yet, even so, our counsels are uncertain and can remain so despite great deliberation. Humble prayer is sometimes rewarded with a sudden clarification proceeding from the gift of counsel, and the final outcome indicates its heavenly wisdom. The life of every saint evidences such counsel.

The heavenly power and the significance for the world of these gifts can be gauged from just one example. At the present time in America approximately 200,000 Catholic men and women are consecrated to God in the priestly and religious life, consecrated to a life that is inexplicable by worldly standards. This is the effect of the gift of counsel, and the works of education and charity — to mention only two outcomes — made possible thereby are a witness to its efficacy.

The gifts of the Holy Ghost present a paradox expressed well in the words of Bishop Gay: "They confer at one and the same time pliability and energy, docility and strength, which render the soul more passive under the hand of God, and likewise more active in serving Him and doing His work."[136]

Their significance in the Christian life is incalculable. For example, John Blank has the faith; yet Holy Communion, the Real Presence, hell, etc., mean little to him. He needs the development of the gift of understanding whereby he penetrates the meaning of the truths of faith. Joseph Blow is wholly engrossed in his bank book and the luxuries it will buy him. He must have his Cadillac, his color television, his week ends at the shore — even at the price of a Christian family! He needs the gift of knowledge whereby he can judge created things according to their proper value. Who will deny that many, many people need to cultivate the gifts of the Holy Ghost?

Likewise who can fail to see the need and the opportunity in Christian education for understanding, emphasizing, and cultivating these gifts.[137] Education should instruct children solidly in the truths about these divine gifts, and in the sufficient understanding of each. It should foster the spiritual ambition to produce in life the fruits of the Holy Ghost culminating in the beatitudes as the only really worthwhile, yet satisfying outcomes of life in whatever sphere life is to be spent. This is within

---

[135] Cf. *Summa*, II–II, q. 52, a. 1, ad 1.

[136] Bishop Gay, *De la vie et des vertus chretiennes,* quoted in Garrigou-Lagrange, *P. & C.,* p. 275.

[137] James Poggi, "The Gifts of the Holy Ghost and Their Implications for Education" (unpublished M.A. dissertation, Department of Education, Catholic University of America, 1955). Cf. James A. Hannan, "An Investigation of the Applicability of St. Thomas Aquinas' Treatment of the Gifts of the Holy Ghost to High School Religion Courses" (unpublished M.A. dissertation, Catholic University of America, 1945).

reach of all. It should foster habits of prayer for the guidance of the Holy Ghost and prayer to Mary the Mother of God for an increase in charity and the gifts.

To sum up: the gifts of the Holy Ghost are supernatural habits distinct from the infused virtues and from actual graces. They make us susceptible to the impulses of the Holy Spirit, which we need for salvation. They tend to move us swiftly and unerringly toward our true end. They are given and measured and increased with charity. It behooves Christian education to be deeply cognizant of them and to cultivate them.

Man has been given astonishing equipment for his co-operation with God's plan of perfection in Christ; it functions on different levels, supernatural and natural; it concerns many specifically diverse objects and some of these objects are more important than others; it functions in different ways.

There is accordingly an ontological hierarchy of equipment between levels — the supernatural virtues transcend the natural; and also between virtues of the same level — charity excels mortification, the habit of natural wisdom concerned with metaphysics excels the habits of memory; yet all are needed in their different contributions.

It will be clear that the final perfection of all this equipment must preserve this hierarchy of excellence. Yet, since man grows gradually to his perfection, it will also be clear that there will be a functional order in the development of this perfection. What this functional order may be is a vast study in itself and beyond our scope here.[138]

We now review in diagrammatic form what has been said about man's natural and supernatural equipment (see next page). Diagrams tend to be subjective and therefore inadequate — sometimes perplexing. This one may help to summarize and depict the basic truths of the chapter.

Beginning from the left we see that man's objective, supernatural, ultimate end is the Triune God. We see that man has two levels of equipment, natural and supernatural, by which he attains this end. As the diagram indicates, God the Creator is infinitely above man the creature. Man finds the Triune God through Jesus Christ, the Second Person of the Blessed Trinity made man by a unique union of the divine and human natures. Christ, God and man, is man's way to God; but with Christ is inseparably associated His mother, Mary. She is a creature, but she is His mother.

Considering man's natural equipment, we see that he is substantial and one. It is the one person who acts — who studies, sings, prays, sleeps. The "box" indicates this substantial unity of man. His various

---

[138] Cf. St. Thomas Aquinas, *The Division and Methods of the Sciences*, trans. by Armand Maurer (Toronto: The Pontifical Institute of Mediaeval Studies, 1953), pp. 83–85.

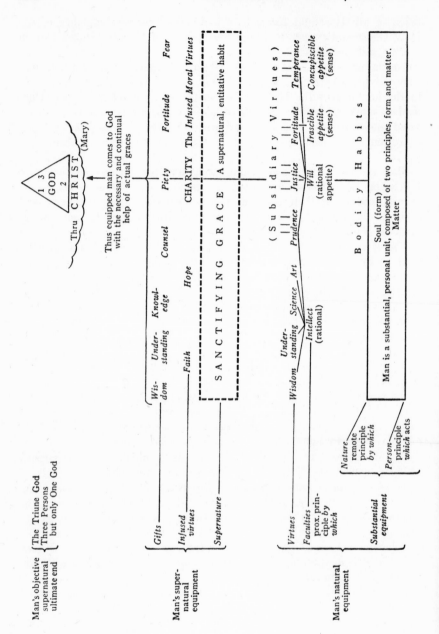

powers for action and the virtues which perfect them are also indicated. These faculties and virtues are accidental. They are real, but their reality does not destroy the substantial unity of man any more than the redness of a brick wall destroys the unity of the wall and somehow makes a second brick wall.

As well as his natural equipment, man has supernatural equipment. He has a quasi-nature, indicated by the broken "box." He has infused virtues of which the greatest is charity. He has the gifts of the Holy Ghost.

The vertical line indicates how man, through the activity of his perfected will, attains God, his supernatural ultimate end.

Place a sheet of paper over the top two-thirds of the diagram and see the inadequacy of even the best natural education. Such "education" ignores reality — and indeed the loftiest. It is an airplane that never flies; it never gets off the runway! Yet naturalistic education seldom reaches even its own best. In most cases it does not take cognizance of the whole natural endowment given to man, e.g., the varied virtues perfecting his rational nature.

A fitting scholion to this entire treatment of man's equipment is the following succinct paragraph from Pius XI. All that has been said gives us a clue to the fullness of the terse words.[139]

> It must *never be forgotten* that the *subject* of Christian education is *man whole* and *entire, soul* united to *body* in *unity* of nature, with *all* his *faculties, natural* and *supernatural,* such as *right reason* and *revelation* show him to be; man, therefore, *fallen* from his original estate but *redeemed by Christ* and *restored* to the *supernatural* condition of *adopted son of God,* though *without the preternatural* privileges of bodily immortality or perfect control of appetite. There *remain,* therefore, in human nature the *effects of original sin,* the chief of which are *weakness of will* and *disorderly inclinations.*

This completes our consideration of Christian perfection considered in itself. We have seen God's over-all plan for our perfection, culminating in our restoration in Christ; we have seen the elements involved in this restoration.

We have analyzed some aspects of the perfection. Its bond or core is charity. The call to perfection is given in varying degrees to all men.

We have considered each of the elements involved in this restoration — the elevation to the supernatural order through grace, the divine indwelling, the divine adoption, the imitation of Christ the Exemplar, the incorporation into His Mystical Body the Church, and finally our active co-operation, absolutely necessary yet wonderfully facilitated by

---

[139] Pius XI, *Christian Education of Youth,* p. 23 [italics added].

the superb natural and supernatural equipment given to man by God. We noted that these elements of our perfection in Christ are not mutually exclusive or independent or chronological or detachable; they are not like stamps on an envelope. Rather they are angle views of the "one pearl of great price"[140] which each man is meant to find in life and to hold fast.

Having seen the elements and connotations of Christian perfection, we are in a position to see its congruity as the proper and immediate end of education.

---

[140] Mt. 13:46.

CHAPTER VI

THE CONGRUITY OF CHRISTIAN PERFECTION AS THE PROPER AND IMMEDIATE END OF EDUCATION

WE HAVE examined the concept of perfection at some length in its various elements and connotations, passive and active. Now we are in a position to appreciate this concept in its general relation to education and to see that it contributes everything that education can rightly demand, despite objections that might be made. We shall also consider some philosophical aspects which will further clarify and integrate our notions and will enhance the congruity we are discussing. Finally, we shall give a definition of education; it will be terse, but the preceding chapters will be its commentary.

General Congruity

1. Christian perfection is a *self-perfection*.

The perfection of a person by education must be internal, inhering in the person — not something extrinsic, assumed, merely imputed.

But a man's perfection in Christ is something primarily internal and deeply personal, for it primarily concerns man's soul which is one of his essential principles, and indeed the formal principle.

Hence Christian perfection is a self-perfection of a kind and degree to satisfy the most rigorous educational requirements.

2. Christian perfection necessitates *self-activity*. Self-activity is a beloved cliché in modern education. Rightly understood, it is a valid one. Here we gather up the relevant points seen *passim* in the previous treatment.

Christian perfection necessitates self-activity. We have already seen that this is prescribed by Revelation as part of our restoration in Christ, is philosophically required by man's nature, and is a fulfillment

177

of man's psychological need. We have also seen that the penalty for neglect is hell.

Moreover, we have seen the dynamic natural and supernatural organism given to man in the array of virtues and gifts he possesses. But the perfection of virtues is found not in the habits themselves but in their acts; just as the perfection of an automobile consists in running well. A man is virtuous not because he *can* live virtuously but because he actually *does* so. Therefore the very bestowal of this varied dynamic organism on man makes its active use an exigency for his perfection.

Further, the full perfection of man's equipment demands that it be *fully activated* both as to degree and variety. This means that each power of the organism, whether transient or immanent, should normally be fully developed. Man's perfection in Christ therefore demands more energetic and varied self-activity than would merely natural perfection. Hence naturalistic education cannot reach the summit and the richness of self-activity possible to true Christian education. Dewey, in effect, amputated the child's supernatural leg; then told him to run!

3. Christian perfection involves *the whole man* — another plank of modern education. This follows from the previous point. For the perfection by self-activity of each and every power that man has, means his development in every respect. The diverse objects of his powers — natural and supernatural, speculative and practical, immanent and transient — assure his development and fruitful living in diverse ways, constituting the versatility and excellence that we all admire in a well-educated man.

4. Christian perfection necessarily involves *contact with and concern about reality*. This is implicit in what we have discussed in the previous and present chapter. Brameld, however, thinks otherwise:

> The perennialist is a reactionary because he would deal with contemporary issues by reacting against them in favor of solutions extraordinarily analogous to those of a culture long past — or even by escaping into an intellectual realm of timeless perfection.[1]

Philosophy, the handmaid of Revelation and theology, tells man that he is a contingent being, dependent, whether he likes to admit it or not, on a first cause which is also his last end, which cause exists quite independently of this thinking. Revelation tells him that God really exists and that only the fool says there is no God.[2] On both scores he is obliged to accept and face reality.

Philosophy reminds him that in the natural order his powers put

---

[1] Theodore Brameld, *op. cit.*, p. 82.   [2] Ps. 52:1.

him in contact with reality by knowing it in the particular and in the abstract, by tending appetitively toward its particular goods and toward transcendental good. All his natural powers produce acts that relate variously to reality, transiently and immanently. Philosophy tells him plainly that this reality around him is independent of his thinking. His supernatural powers put him in contact with the truths and goods of the supernatural order — immaterial, invisible, but very real. Things such as gamma rays help us to understand how something which is intangible and invisible can be real — real enough to kill a man.

The Revelation about Christian perfection goes further; it clearly and specifically obliges man to make good use of reality, and thus it reinforces the natural law. It tells him of his dominion over the material universe,[3] of his obligation to use it well,[4] and of the account he will have to render to God in judgment for the use of created things.[5] The virtue of temperance regulates his use of particular desirable goods, here and now; the virtue of fortitude strengthens him to face the rigorous ways of present reality; the virtue of justice constrains him to render their due to society and to his fellow man; the virtue of charity, in leading his love to God, diffuses it also to all men bidding him wish and even do good to *all* men, in the spiritual and corporal works of mercy, even to the extent of laying down his life for them. The Christian is told that he cannot be perfect unless he love his neighbor and help him in his needs. "If any man say I love God, and hateth his brother; he is a liar."[6]

He that hath the substance of this world, and shall see his brother in need, and shall shut up his bowels from him; how doth the charity of God abide in him.[7]

And Christian perfection demands all these things of man, with the highest motivation, God, and the heaviest sanction, hell; and it demands them of him each day, here and now, whenever opportunity or crisis presents itself, whether a person is sick or healthy, ten, sixteen, or sixty.

---

[3] *Supra,* p. 80.

[4] Mt. 22:21: "Render therefore to Caesar the things that are Caesar's; and to God, the things that are God's." Also 1 Cor. 10:31: "Whether you eat or drink, or whatsoever else you do, do all to the glory of God." The true perspective of the Christian toward reality, together with the delicate balance between self-activity and dependence on God is admirably expressed in the Collect for the Third Sunday after Pentecost: "O God, the protector of all who hope in Thee, without Whom nothing is strong, nothing holy, multiply Thy mercies upon us that with You as our ruler and leader, *we may so pass through the good things of the present as not to lose those of eternity.*"

[5] Lk. 16:2: "Give an account of thy stewardship: for now thou canst be steward no longer."

[6] 1 Jn. 4:20.

[7] 1 Jn. 3:17.

A priori, then, education ordained to a student's perfection in Christ is not going to make him a visionary, a sphinx, or a drone in a practical world — forgetting or being only half concerned with the present for the sake of the dim future. Despite Dewey's dichotomy,[8] there is no conflict between Christian education's wholehearted emphasis on a supernatural end not yet obtained and its wholehearted emphasis on the present; for the use of the present situation is the sole means to future perfection. Christian education, then, is wholly concerned with the proper use of the present realities for its progress to the future supernatural end.

A posteriori, Christian formation has not made lives sterile. True Christians have *de facto* always been concerned with the reality of this life, not merely as affecting themselves but as affecting others. In the case of contemplatives, however, their influence on social realities has been chiefly through spiritual means.[9]

These social fruits of Christian perfection are endless. No one can deny the civilizing influence of Christianity, seen, for example, in the Benedictine monasteries — Fulda, Bec, Corbie, Bobbio, Cluny, Jarrow, and thousands of others — and in the Jesuit reductions of Paraguay. No one can deny the social fruits of the work of Catholic missionaries who, having left their homes to practice the Christian counsels in their own lives, teach or nurse without the reward of personal pay and the solace of personal family life — all because of Christ's spiritual call, "Come, follow me."[10] The lifework of St. Peter Claver[11] — washing, feeding, consoling, baptizing the African Negroes in the slave-trade hell of Cartagena — is a case in point. We need social justice always; but we need personal charity too. A sick man needs care, not a parliamentary law. The antislave laws and the war between the American states of the mid-nineteenth century were two centuries late for the ill-treated, diseased, and befouled Negroes whom St. Peter tended for some forty

---

[8] John Dewey, *My Pedagogic Creed*, p. 7.

[9] Cf. the significant words of Pope Pius XI to the Carthusians. "It is easy to understand that they who assiduously fulfill the duty of prayer and penance contribute much more (*multo plus*) to the growth of the Church and the welfare of the human race than those who cultivate the Lord's field by their labours. For unless the former drew down from Heaven the showers of divine graces needed to water the field, the evangelical laborers would indeed reap only scanty fruits from their labor" (*Umbratilem*, AAS, XVI [1924], 389). This does not dispense with the need of active workers — including teachers — or lessen the heroicity of their zeal. But it underscores their need to join charity and prayer to their own labors, and points up the two-dimensional apostolate that awaits the thoroughly Christian teacher.

[10] Mt. 19:21.

[11] Cf. Butler's *Lives of the Saints*, ed. by H. Thurston and D. Attwater (12 vols., London: Burns, Oates & Washbourne, Ltd., 1934), IX, pp. 106–114. Cartagena, in what is now Colombia, was a central slave market.

years until 1664. This was surely a practical concern with contemporary
social issues. The social fruits of St. Vincent de Paul's personal holiness —
his varied and colossal charities — need no detailing here. Janssen, the
voluminous German historian, says that it was the overthrow of
Catholicism with its institutions and its influence that caused the ruin
of the working classes and the rise of the so-called proletariat of later
times.[12] When Florence Nightingale accepted the request from the
British War Office to gather nurses for the English soldiers in the Cri-
mean War, ten Catholic nuns, five Sisters of Mercy and five Irish Sisters
of Charity, offered themselves within twenty-four hours.[13] This was
practical concern with the reality of the moment. Some of these nuns
were Irish with vivid memories of the persecution, famine, and pro-
selytizing soup that the Irish had recently endured in the English
administration. In their case, personal generosity wore the crown of
Christian forgiveness.

Nano Nagle was a wealthy Irish girl who was introduced to society
life in Paris. Returning during the early hours of the morning from a
lavish ball, she saw from her carriage window the poor gathering for
early morning Mass. The sharp contrast between French devotion and
Irish ignorance stirred her deeply — so many of her native people were
in religious ignorance because of laws that proscribed Catholic schools.
She consecrated her life to God and founded the Presentation Sisters,
now spread in several countries and devoted to education.[14] This was
surely a practical concern with contemporary issues.

Catherine McAuley was an accomplished lady who, despite opposition and even persecution, devoted her time, home, and inheritance to
the assistance of others less fortunate. She was motivated by the love
of God. The very ardor of her charity led gradually to the establish-
ment of the Sisters of Mercy in order to bring the balm of Christian
mercy to every human need. This society is now world wide. How can
anyone doubt that Christian perfection has a practical impact on
contemporary affairs?

The hundreds of thousands of boys educated in several countries by
the Irish Christian Brothers owe their schooling ultimately to the piety
of Edmund Rice, a prosperous merchant of Waterford. He saw the
spiritual and human ignorance of neighboring boys resulting from a
penal law that for two centuries neglected, prevented, and punished
their education. Moved by charity, he relinquished his business and

---

[12] Johannes Janssen, *History of the German People at the Close of the Middle
Ages* (London: Kegan Paul, Trench, Trübner & Co., 1896), Vol. II, 103.

[13] J. J. Walsh, *The History of Nursing* (New York: P. J. Kenedy and Sons,
1929), p. 229.

[14] F. P. McGahan, "Presentation, Order of the — Nagle, Nano," *Catholic Encyclopedia*, Vol. XII (1912), 398.

gave himself personally to the work in a way that has now blossomed into an international educational institution of voluntary workers.[15]

Frederick Ozanam, a Christian gentleman and professor, was shocked and moved by the destitution he saw in Paris. People were suffering. He did not wait for the cumbersome machinery of law to remedy the situation; his personal charity went into action at once. Some other Christian young men joined him in procuring food and work. Sophisticated contemporaries scoffed at the ineptness of the approach; they advocated legal and civic measures. Ozanam's work grew, as Christian charity does, and soon a large minority of the total Paris poor were being personally assisted — and the law parchments were still blank as far as this civic emergency was concerned!

There are some four million Catholic children in the Catholic elementary and high schools in America this year, citizens of this country but being educated with only incidental costs to the public treasury. These children are by and large receiving their education from approximately one hundred thousand consecrated teachers who have left their family circles and receive no personal pay, their motive being the pursuit of Christian perfection. This, too, is surely practical concern with present reality — and socially significant.

These are just random samples of the social fruits that follow the development of that personal charity which is the core of Christian perfection.

Pope Pius XI lists four outstanding social fruits of Christian activity:

1. The true friendship between men of all social ranks.
2. An appreciation of the dignity of labor.
3. The great institutions of charity. (Even Karl Marx acknowledges this.[16])
4. The powerful guilds of every trade.[17]

Pope Leo XIII wrote a special encyclical, *Sapientiae Christianae,* telling Christians of their obligation as Christians to be good citizens.[18]

Pius XI stated authoritatively:

> The true Christian does not renounce the activities of this life, he does not stunt his natural faculties; but he develops and perfects them, by co-ordinating them with the supernatural. He thus ennobles what is merely natural in life and secures for it new strength in

[15] *Edmund Ignatius Rice and the Christian Brothers* (New York: Benziger Bros., n.d.).

[16] Karl Marx, *Capital* (New York: Carlton House, 1932), p. 187.

[17] Pope Pius XI, encyclical, *Divini Redemptoris;* cf. Lerhinan, *op. cit.,* pp. 100–101.

[18] Leo XIII, *Sapientiae Christianae:* "On the Chief Duties of Christians as Citizens," January 10, 1890, trans. John J. Wynne, *op. cit.,* pp. 180–207.

the material and temporal order, no less than in the spiritual and eternal.[19]

Catholic education is sometimes accused, more or less openly, of being "otherworldly" in its viewpoint to the neglect of this world and its daily realities, public and private. This accusation is ignorant, false, and unfair. We are primarily concerned with the next world and secondarily with this; we are directly concerned with both. The next hinges strictly on the present.

5. Christian perfection is truly *ennobling*. Education sets itself the task of making better men, not merely efficient men. It is obvious that Christian perfection contributes powerfully to man's betterment by giving him — over and above his natural powers — a Supreme Exemplar, the means of supernatural goodness, a temporal and eternal motivation.

Some Objections

Now we consider some objections that may be raised against the notion of Christian perfection as the proper and immediate end of education.

Objection 1. The end of education as outlined is anti-intellectual. It de-emphasizes the attention hitherto given to the acquisition of learning in all its forms. It says in effect that, if we suppress all academic instruction in all schools and concentrate on teaching children their prayers and how to be "good," we are giving them the essence of an education. It says in effect that an illiterate who can neither read nor write but is nevertheless baptized and devout is essentially an educated man.

Answer. The Christian view of education is not anti-intellectual. Pius X succinctly says:

> We do maintain that the will cannot be upright nor the conduct good when the mind is shrouded in the darkness of crass ignorance. A man who walks with open eyes may, indeed, turn aside from the right path, but a blind man is in much more imminent danger of wandering away.[20]

Hence Christian education is deeply concerned with intellectual formation. Correct thinking is necessary for correct acting.

To say that one thing, charity, is more important than another,

---

[19] Pius XI, *Christian Education of Youth*, p. 37. In the same context he quotes a vigorous passage from Tertullian explaining the same point to dispatch the same criticism over seventeen hundred years ago!

[20] Pius X, *Acerbo Nimis*, Yzermans, *op. cit.*, pp. 49–50.

knowledge, is not to say that the other is unimportant. To say that a man's heart is more important for him than his eye is not to say that his eye is unimportant. Christian education does not de-emphasize intellectual development; it does not regard academic instruction in the schools as unimportant and accessory. On the contrary, it positively emphasizes and fosters intellectual development and its correlative academic instruction. We have seen that the charity of the will, a blind faculty, absolutely requires for its act a knowledge of God in the intellect, and that the more we know a true good the more we love it;[21] we have likewise seen that Christian perfection demands of man the use and development of all his talents,[22] according to their dignity and measure — and one of the loftiest of his powers is his intellect. One cannot have too much of a virtue, and this is true for the virtues perfecting the intellect. A man with a keen intellect could not be holy unless he developed and used it to the full.[23] St. Thomas would not have become a saint had he neglected to write his *Summa*. Christian perfection does not de-emphasize intellectual development; it rather emphasizes charity more, because charity is more important. St. Thomas conceived and wrote a brilliant intellectual synthesis in his *Summa* — a work that takes even able students a lifetime to comprehend. Yet he himself spoke of that synthesis as only a little straw compared with the spiritual riches he had savored by the gift of God.

The case of the illiterate as adduced is largely hypothetic and sophistic, an argument *ad hominem;* because in America any sane person who really wishes it can attend school and at least become literate. However, a navvy who through no fault of his own is an illiterate but decent Christian is essentially educated in the strict sense of the word and is essentially realizing the purpose of his existence, just as a blind man is essentially a man despite his lamentable handicap. He has in his will charity, which is superior to all knowledge in this life.[24] He has in his intellect firm certitude about the essential truths of faith which are nobler, loftier, more important than any or all human knowledge.[25] He has knowledge of his true ends, natural and supernatural.

---

[21] *Supra,* p. 24.

[22] *Supra,* p. 105.

[23] It is nevertheless true that the best thing we can do with the best of things is to sacrifice it, *provided* we safeguard the hierarchy of the gifts of God and of the virtues and do not sacrifice something superior to what is inferior. Had Dr. Edith Stein, the German Jewess, relinquished her intellectual pursuits from sloth or discouragement or for what has been called cocktail living, she would have done wrong and would have placed an impediment to her growth in perfection; yet by relinquishing her brilliant philosophic studies and lectures to become a contemplative nun in Carmel, she sacrificed and sublimated her lesser activities to a greater one.

[24] *Supra,* p. 107.

[25] *Supra,* p. 165.

He has, through the virtue of prudence and its annexed virtues, knowledge of the right means to these ends. He will, by perseverance, attain his ultimate end and know eternal things that a lifetime of study could not have given him, and know them forever — things which a humanly learned scholar in hell will never know. Therefore this hypothetical navvy's development is such that he is now able to fulfill his true purpose in life — to know and attain his true ends. Thus he is essentially educated.

Literacy is not the ultimate criterion of education. What does the average literate person read? If newsstands are an indication, inability to read pulp press is no loss. There are also other sources of essential information besides reading where this is unavoidably excluded. Who can deny that the refined, modest, house-competent, enlightened but illiterate St. Maria Goretti was better educated than some of this country's college students whose dormitory raids and *similia* are reported from time to time in the national and international press!

In no sense can these comments be fairly interpreted as contempt for or indifference toward literacy, which is, indisputably, important in education. We are merely emphasizing what, according to Christian principles, is *indispensable*. Cultivate literature, pursue science to the *nth* degree; "but above all these things have charity" (Col. 3:14).

Objection 2. The concept of perfection in Christ as the proper and immediate end of education reduces the study of education to the study of theology.

Answer. In one respect, yes; in other respects, no.

In one respect the study of education must be the study of Revelation as this is elaborated in theology. No engineer can handle explosives safely unless he knows whether he is dealing with dynamite, gelignite, nitroglycerine, or whatever you will; the penalty is disaster. Nobody can properly and constructively educate the dynamic human person unless he knows as accurately as possible what he is educating; and the penalty of ignorance is disaster in one form or another — another Marx or Stalin perhaps. All this can be known in full only from what theology adds to philosophy about the educand's destiny, means thereto, and his present condition.

No teacher can guide the educand to his proper ends unless the teacher knows these ends. He can know the educand's objective, absolute ultimate end[26] in virtue of which all other proximate and intermediate ends are to be sought[27] only through theology, since it is a supernatural end.

No teacher can guide the educand adequately unless he knows all the means the latter has at hand to assist him along the way to his

---

[26] *Supra*, p. 38. [27] *Supra*, p. 39.

ultimate end. The means to the ultimate supernatural end are themselves supernatural,[28] even when the matter of the act involved, for
example, kindness to another, may be in itself no more than natural.
Therefore the educator can know these means only from theology.

No teacher can guide the educand adequately and safely unless he
knows accurately the latter's nature and condition, just as it is important
for the physician to know accurately the condition of the athlete's
cartilage, torn muscle, etc., if he wishes to make a safe decision about
training and taking the field. Only through theology can the educator
know fully the condition of the educand, for example, as affected by
original sin. Hence we say that in one respect the adequate study of
education must involve truths of theology.

But in another respect the study of education requires much more
than the study of theology even though this be basic and indispensable.
Man is natural before he is supernaturalized; and therefore whatever
in natural knowledge — philosophy, psychology, psychiatry, biology,
sociology, experimental procedures — contributes to educational theory
is not only valuable, but also necessary. Recall that the supernatural
order in no way dispenses with natural exigencies; it perfects nature
without vitiating it.[29] Hence we say that the concept of perfection in
Christ as the proper and immediate end of education does not equate
educational theory and theology.

Objection 3. This concept of education reduces the practice and
methods of education to the practical principles of ascetical theology.
The educator is to be essentially concerned with means of avoiding
sin, of practising virtue, of increasing charity; other practical courses
are merely accidental.

Answer. The answer to this objection follows from what has been
said previously. From all that has been said about man's objective
supernatural ultimate end and God's fundamental plan for our restoration in Christ through the imitation of Christ, it will be clear that any
so-called education which fails to orientate the student accordingly,
fails essentially, dismally, and irrevocably. How can a teacher plume
himself for giving the student information about Columbus, polygons,
and blastulae, if the deficiencies in the education have perhaps con-
tributed powerfully to the student's eternal ruin in hell?[30] Compared
with this, everything else is accidental. But accidental is by no means
to be understood as incidental, arbitrary, a matter of whim. We have
already seen that man cannot grow to perfection in Christ unless all
his powers are developed *according to their hierarchy* in the best way

---

[28] Namely grace, the infused virtues, the gifts of the Holy Ghost, treated earlier.
[29] *Supra*, p. 160 f.
[30] *Supra*, pp. 46 f, 49 f.

possible. He may not succeed in the case of each of his natural powers but he must try according to the providential circumstances in which he finds himself. The practices and detailed methods for developing his natural powers will be positively garnered from the natural sciences and experimental evidence according to what was said in the previous objection; yet subject to the extrinsic guidance of theology insofar as they involve morality.[31] Ascetical theology says nothing about the relative strength of hearing and seeing impressions or about the optimum association of ear and eye — precedence or concomitance — in the learning of Latin vocabulary; nothing about the distributing or massing of typing practice, about the length of time the brain remains fresh for study, about the effectiveness of the multiplicative over the divisive method in the teaching of arithmetical division. For all these and *similia*, Christian educational practice legitimately refers, not to ascetical theology, but to the pertinent natural science or experimentation.

Objection 4. The conception of Christian perfection as the proper and immediate end of education is idealistic. It might be desirable but it is utopian, chimerical.

Answer. Idealistic can be taken in two senses: first, as a line of action ordained to a high ideal; second, as a line of action ordained, or apparently ordained, to an impossible ideal, something fanciful. That this conception of education is ordained to a high ideal, as the preceding considerations show, we readily concede. That this ideal is fanciful, utopian, impossible, we deny. The ideal is unquestionably high, but it is attainable by all who earnestly wish it.

As we have seen, it is flatly unattainable by man's unaided natural powers; but it is attainable by all who will use *properly* and *consistently* the distant natural and the special supernatural means given them. Arbitrary or spasmodic effort is of no avail in this, as in anything else worthwhile. If people devoted to it one eighth of the time, energy, and consistency they give to their professional success, or to the winning of athletic pennants, they could grow rapidly "unto the measure of the age of the fullness of Christ"[32] destined for them by Providence.

There will undoubtedly be difficulties in this attainment; but God's ruling providence presides over all things and His promise is clear: He will not permit us to be tempted above that which we are able to overcome with the help of His grace.[33]

---

[31] Cf. *Summa*, I, q. 1, a. 6, ad. 2: "Whatsoever is found in other sciences contrary to any truth of this science (theology) is to be condemned as false." A teacher could not use a classroom method that was sinful or scandalous, even though its effect might be vividly instructional. It is hardly likely that any teacher would intoxicate or drug a student to show the evil effects of alcohol or narcotics but this, to illustrate the point, would be immoral. This consideration could easily apply in the matter of sex-education films, etc.

[32] Eph. 4:13.   [33] Cf. 1 Cor. 10:13.

Hence we deny that this ideal is chimerical.

Christian education alone has' the concept and realities that can give meaning to the fanciful language currently fashionable in educational writings. If writers mean what they say, Catholic education alone has what they seek — and has it in abundance.

Lueck wishes to elevate humanity:[34] we offer this elevation in the divine adoption through grace.

Lueck wants the teacher to believe in the "improvability of humanity";[35] Lee, in the "perfectibility."[36] We offer not only this ideal but also the efficacious means, viz., the Christian sacraments. In seeking an infinite perfectibility, Lee involves himself in philosophical self-contradiction. We do not claim to offer such a chimera, but through Revelation we offer man a perfection and glorification in heaven beyond the limits of Lee's imagination.

Lueck wishes the teacher to aid mankind in leading "more useful and exemplary lives."[37] We offer not only the efficacious means for this same ideal; we also offer to mankind its Supreme Exemplar.

Lueck seeks for enriched living.[38] We offer man the unsearchable riches of Christ for the enrichment of his living.

Lueck, quoting Stiles, wants man to be in contact with the beauties of the natural world and to transport himself, by reading, "into new and strange lands."[39] But why stop with the beauties of *this* world? We offer man rational contact now with a newer and stranger world, heaven. One day in actual habitation there — if he merits such a destiny by his "worthwhile activities" — man will not just read, but will *see,* face to face.

Lueck desires for the educand the development of friendship; we offer also the divine friendship.

Lueck, a materialist, fears that civilization can become too materialistic. (But if man is only matter, why should he not express his nature perfectly by pure materialism?) We can offer Lueck the antidote he seeks by preserving man's neat balance of matter and spirit, and so save Lueck's civilization from the consequences of his own philosophy.

DeYoung complains of the mere lip service to democracy[40] — the logical result of a philosophy of words divorced from objective truth. With a philosophy of values based on objective truth we can inject an unequivocal meaning and sincerity into the language that pledges fealty to democracy.

---

[34] William R. Lueck, *An Introduction to Teaching* (New York: Henry Holt and Co., 1953), p. 33.

[35] *Ibid.*

[36] Lee, *op. cit.,* p. 39.

[37] Lueck, *op. cit.,* p. 33.

[38] *Ibid.,* p. 72.

[39] *Ibid.*

[40] DeYoung, *op. cit.,* p. 456.

Various authors wish that children might attain "spiritual values,"[41] "high ideal and ethical standards,"[42] "the good life,"[43] "superior designs and philosophies of living."[44] To this end, we offer the requirements clearly detailed, the helps that human nature needs, the encouragement of the Perfect Exemplar.

Authors speak of "the team spirit" in the school,[45] "comradeship in the classroom,"[46] "fair play";[47] we synthesize and sublimate these in Christian charity.

Crow and Crow[48] note the immeasurable influence of the home and say that no teacher can underestimate its importance. We see in the home a sacramental dignity and we recognize and make available sacramental graces to help parents exert the best influence on their children.

Crow and Crow[49] call for "forward-looking goals." We present goals of education that look forward beyond the horizon of even the longest life.

Crow and Crow[50] say there is, in education, a need for wide vision and high ideals. We offer a vision of education that is far wider than merely American democracy and academic prowess, yet by no means inimical to them — a vision of education that is as universal as human nature and has ideals as high as heaven.

We make these startling claims, not figuratively, but in literal truth.

Philosophical Aspects of Christian Perfection as the Proper and Immediate End of Education

1. The true Christian is the product, the *finis effectus* or the *finis operis*[51] of the work of education conceived as a total process. It is the "work produced" by education, just as a cabinet is the work produced by the cabinetmaker.

Pius XI says:

> The true Christian, product of Christian education, is the supernatural man who thinks, judges and acts constantly and consistently in accordance with right reason illumined by the supernatural light of the example and teaching of Christ; in other words, to use the current term, the true and finished man of character.[52]

2. In the minds of educators, and indeed of the educand according to his progressive maturity, "the true Christian" should also be the

---

[41] Crow and Crow, *op. cit.*, p. 478.
[42] *Ibid.*
[43] *Ibid.*, p. 251; also Lueck, *op. cit.*, p. 33.
[44] Lueck, *op. cit.*, p. 19.
[45] Hughes and Hughes, *op. cit.*, p. 193.
[46] *Ibid.*, p. 253.
[47] Crow and Crow, *op. cit.*, p. 65.
[48] *Ibid.*, pp. 453–470.
[49] *Ibid.*, p. 59.
[50] *Ibid.*, p. 70.
[51] *Supra*, p. 36.
[52] Pius XI, *Christian Education of Youth*, p. 36.

finis cuius gratia.[53] This is so because man is a free agent and must move himself to his ends according to his nature, as we have seen. Therefore, perfection in Christ must be set before children as an ideal from the earliest dawning of reason, but always in a way proportionate to their condition. It will need tact and patience, but it is the fulfilling of a philosophical exigency and of a beautiful Gospel injunction: "Suffer the little children to come unto me."[54]

3. Christian perfection, the proper and immediate end of education as a total process, is to be conceived as a perfection in first proximate act (*in actu primo proximo*). When we speak of education as total process we mean the co-ordinated and consummated work of the three principal agencies of education — Church, home, and State.[55] We shall now explain the significance of "first proximate act."

"Act," as will be recalled from philosophy, may be divided in various ways, essentially and accidentally. One of the accidental divisions of act, considered as relating to another act, is first act and second act.[56]

First act is one that is the first in a series of acts so that second act proceeds from it or is capable of proceeding from it. First act does not presuppose another act of that series. Man's soul is called the first act of prime matter.

Second act presupposes a previous act *in that same series* and follows it. Every action of a faculty is a second act in relation to the faculty. The action of the faculty presupposes the faculty itself!

Grenier points out that act may be called first or second act in a relative sense.[57] The second act of one series may be the first act of another. Thus the intellect, considered absolutely, is second act in relation to man's soul; but it is first act in relation to its own operation of thinking.

First act is further divided into remote and proximate. Proximate first act is an act on which second act immediately follows; thus a faculty is said to be in proximate first act when it has all the requisites for its operation. Remote first act is act on which second act does not immediately follow. An example may help to materialize these distinctions. The New Yorker reading his Friday evening paper in the crowded subway can be called potentially a fisherman. Arrived in the Catskills the next day with tackle and flies and knee boots, and the gleam of trout in his eye, he can be called a fisherman in first act. At the water's edge with his line assembled and hooked, net ready and game bag handy, he can be called a fisherman in proximate first act. The operation of catching the trout makes him a fisherman in second act.

[53] *Supra*, p. 14.   [54] Mk. 10:14.
[55] Cf. Pius XI, *Christian Education of Youth*, pp. 6–22.
[56] Cf. Gredt, *op. cit.*, II, pp. 38–39; also Bittle, *Ontology, op. cit.*, p. 6C
[57] Grenier, *op. cit.*, 111, p. 69.

Consider education as a total process "preparing man [born a *tabula rasa*] for what he must be and for what he must do here below, in order to gain the sublime end for which he was created"[58] — preparing him by perfecting each of his natural and supernatural powers;[59] compare analogously the growth of these intellectual and moral powers to perfection, with man's natural growth to adulthood. An abstraction can be made for man's educational maturity as it is made for his physical maturity. It can be said: Now he has sufficient all-around development and maturity to be considered educationally an adult; he can launch a career, can make his way in the world as a Christian with that advanced degree of self-reliance and independence that differentiates the adult from the child and even from the adolescent. We do not consider that this maturity can be clocked, as being present today but absent yesterday. We do not consider that all further development ceases or that man is now entirely self-sufficient for himself.[60] But by an abstraction, made analogously with physical adulthood, we consider that he has now reached educational adulthood, that is, Christian perfection in a sufficiently mature degree. To continue this abstraction in terms of first and second act: the youth poised on the threshold of educational adulthood, ready to step off into a responsible, integral, Christian life, can be said to have reached educational adulthood — Christian perfection — in first proximate act. This is the intangible moment to which his educational preparation has pointed. Now he steps off into that life of spiritual adulthood in which his developed virtues and gifts operate integrally to show forth that degree of prudential, responsible, meritorious Christian living which characterizes Christian maturity and which is expected of all Christians.[61] This on the spiritual level is Christian perfection in second act.

There is no implication whatever that henceforth the Christian will make no further development. Giving a pilot his "wings" and sending him off in a sabre-jet squadron as a responsible, mature flier does not mean that he will not eventually progress to a B-52. The new fisherman in second act will, after many Saturdays, undoubtedly develop into a cannier fisherman.

---

[58] Pius XI, *Christian Education of Youth*, pp. 4–5.

[59] Recall what was said above of the natural moral virtues and prudence, and also of the interconnection of the theological and moral virtues in charity and their growth in charity with an equality of proportion.

[60] Always we presuppose man's social nature; also his utter dependence on God's natural concursus and, in the supernatural order, on grace.

[61] "You are the salt of the earth" (Mt. 5:13). "He that received the seed upon good ground is he that heareth the word and understandeth, and beareth fruit, and yieldeth the one an hundredfold, and another sixty, and another thirty" (Mt. 13:23). Recall the incident of the barren fig tree (Mt. 21:19); and the parable of the talents (Mt. 25:15–28).

There is no implication that up until now the educand has exercised no virtues, gained no merit — has remained in a sort of developmental trance. There have of course been myriad embryonic developmental acts and even perfected subordinate acts of a lesser series whereby he has become partially self-directive — just as the fisherman was first a buyer of his line in second act before he was a fisherman in first act — since he still lacked the boots, the flies, the hooks, etc. But up until now, the *total process,* including the combined influences of the educational agents and the self-activity of the subject, has not brought the educand to that state of integral spiritual maturity that can be called *simpliciter* — Christian perfection.

The word "integral" is important;[62] it signifies a whole having all its due parts and elements in proper proportion. Only a man who exhibits such integral spiritual maturity can be said simply and without qualification to exhibit Christian perfection; just as only a man who has the free use of all his limbs can be called *simpliciter* active. A man with only the right arm unparalyzed by polio cannot be called active without qualification, even though this right arm is quite strong and free. By treatment he recovers first the free use of his right leg, then the left arm, then the left leg. The time comes when all his limbs can operate efficiently and co-ordinately; then he is again an active man in first proximate act. He is discharged from convalescence to take over again the duties of a patrol officer; now he is active in second act.

It is here submitted that it is the over-all function, the proper and immediate end of education to bring the educand to the state of Christian perfection in first proximate act. Thus, essentially and integrally prepared, a man can proceed to the full, mature, meritorious, Christian life that is Christian perfection in second act.

This seems to be in accord with the words of Pius XI quoted above: "education consists essentially in *preparing* man for what he must be and what he must do"[63] [italics added]; and again "the proper and immediate end of education is *to cooperate* with divine grace *in forming* the true and perfect Christian"[64] [italics added]. These words italicized imply a gradual, preparatory process at which stage it can be said that the total educational process is not complete, even though individual virtues or accomplishments may be sufficiently developed. Yet the Pope is certainly well aware that meritorious acts of supernatural virtue will have been long since fostered in and performed by the student with the help of Christian teaching and the fruitful reception of the sacraments.[65]

---

[62] We use the word "integrally" here in its ordinary English usage, and not in the technical sense of an integral whole as distinguished from a potential whole according to St. Thomas' usage in the *Summa,* I, q. 76, a. 8; q. 77, a. 1, ad. 1.

[63] Pius XI, *Christian Education of Youth,* pp. 4–5.

[64] *Ibid.,* pp. 35–36.

[65] *Ibid.,* p. 29.

But the true Christian in second act, the fruit, the product of Christian education, "is the supernatural *man* who thinks, *judges* and acts *constantly* and *consistently* in accordance with *right reason* illumined by the supernatural light of the example and teaching of Christ."[66] This is Christian perfection in second act — energetic, fruitful, meritorious living characterized by maturity and breadth. Notice the words which connote maturity — "man," "judges," "constantly and consistently," "right reason."

St. Thomas says: "Nature intends not only the begetting of offspring, but also its education and development until it reach the perfect state of man as man, and that is the state of virtue";[67] this formation implies the preparation to be given by education as a total process until the state of mature, developmental adulthood is reached.

Definition of Education

Now, after all these considerations, we propose a definition of education as a total process. *Education as a total process is the passive and active development, in first proximate act, of the Christian perfection of man in all his powers, natural and supernatural, whereby he is constituted maturely self-directive toward his final end.* The brief elaboration of the terms used will serve as a recapitulation.

"Development." Education is necessarily gradual, by reason of man's gradual maturation and by reason of the repeated acts normally needed for the acquisition of acquired operative habits.

"Passive and Active Development." Education implies a passive process. Man is born a *tabula rasa*. His intellect is dependent on reality for knowledge. He needs the guidance and instruction of the agencies of education. Education also implies an active process. Man must perfect himself by his *own immanent activity*. This is the basis for pedagogical self-activity.

"Perfection." Man is born substantially complete, but accidentally is incomplete, e.g., he is without full stature, without knowledge, without supernatural virtues. Education leads him to this complete accidental perfection.

"Christian." This indicates the providential Source and Exemplar of man's perfection.

"In proximate first act" as just explained. It signifies that abstract stage in education when all man's powers have been integrally developed, making it possible for him to live an energetic, meritorious, integral, responsible Christian life.

"Man." Animals are not the subjects of true education. Moreover, man must be baptized for the benefits of Christianity.

---

[66] Pius XI, *Christian Education of Youth*, p. 36. The italics have been added.
[67] *Summa*, Supplem., q. 41, a. 1.

"In all his powers." This implies not merely essential but *integral* development. Someone lacking normal intellectual culture cannot be called integrally educated. It also implies an *harmonious* development. Since there is already an ontological hierarchy of powers and virtues (charity is the queen of the supernatural virtues, wisdom of the natural intellectual virtues, etc.), their development connotes this same hierarchical harmony.

"Maturely." This indicates the analogous adult stature of his developed perfection.

"Self-directive." Man as a free agent directs himself to his own end, saving always God's natural concursus and supernatural grace.

"Toward his final end." Man seeks every end in virtue of his final end. All his activity is to be directed ultimately toward his final end. And his final end is a supernatural one — God supernaturally known and loved. Any merely natural education is therefore incomplete and defective.

As a *state*, whereby we say "He is an educated man," education is the Christian perfection of man, essentially and integrally, in second act.

Since, however, grace, charity, etc., are not directly observable, whereas natural knowledge and natural external habits are, we tend in popular speech to identify education with its integral *observable* traits and to consider only those people educated who have discernible knowledge, accomplishments, etc. This is, in effect, a sort of metonomy describing the whole by the part. But an army officer is still such without his uniform, and a purloined uniform does not make a true officer. The essence must be considered before the accidents, even the proper accidents. The words of Pope Pius XI are clear: "There can be no true education which is not wholly directed to man's last end."[68] A man of human learning who does not know his true last end is guilty of ignorance more abysmal than any other ignorance.

We now present in schematic form a summary of our whole treatment of the proper and immediate end of education, that is, of Chapters IV, V, and VI.

Summary

I. Proof That the Proper and Immediate End of Education Is Christian Perfection From the Words of the Popes

II. The General Consideration of Christian Perfection

    1. *God's General Plan for Man's Perfection: Restoration in Christ*
    Preliminary. The Notion of the Supernatural Order
    a) Creation and man's original endowment
    b) His fall and helplessness re the supernatural order

---

[68] Pius XI, *Christian Education of Youth*, p. 5.

    c) His restoration — and its elements — through Christ
      1) Elevation to the supernatural order
      2) Sanctifying grace and its sequelae
      3) The divine indwelling
      4) The divine adoption
      5) Christ, the Perfect Exemplar
      6) Incorporation into the Mystical Body of Christ
      7) Our co-operation with God (treatment deferred for convenience)
      Scholion 1. Now we can say ". . . *mirabilius reformasti. . . .*"
              2. Christ, the center of the world

  2. *Analysis of Some Special Aspects of Christian Perfection*
    a) Charity is the core of perfection, proved from Sacred Scripture. Yet it is not an exclusive virtue.
    b) The degree of charity. Charity is a precept without limit.
    c) The variation of charity. It should increase; it does not diminish directly; it may be lost, and the loss is a supreme calamity.
    d) The call to Christian perfection. All are called, but in different senses.

  3. *Man's Co-operation With God for the Attainment of Perfection in Christ*
    a) Necessity of this co-operation, theologically, philosophically, psychologically
    b) Mode of this co-operation
      1) Objective aspect: fulfilling the objective divine plan, especially full membership in the one true Church
      2) Subjective aspect: firm, confident adhesion to the will of God
    c) Man's equipment for this co-operation
      1) Natural:
        a. Substantial
        b. Accidental: faculties, perfected by habits and indeed virtues
      2) Supernatural:
        a. Grace, sanctifying and actual
        b. Infused virtues, theological and moral
        c. Gifts of the Holy Ghost

III. CONGRUITY OF CHRISTIAN PERFECTION AS THE PROPER AND IMMEDIATE END OF EDUCATION

  1. It is a *self*-perfection.
  2. It involves self-*activity*, even of the highest order — immanent activity.

3. It involves the *whole* man.
4. It necessarily involves contact with *reality*, including contemporary and social realities.
5. It is truly *ennobling*.

IV. OBJECTIONS TO CHRISTIAN PERFECTION AS THE PROPER AND IMMEDIATE END OF EDUCATION, ANSWERED

1. Such an end is not anti-intellectual.
2. It does not reduce the study of education to theology.
3. It does not reduce practical pedagogy to the principles of ascetical theology.
4. It is not too idealistic, in the fanciful sense.

V. PHILOSOPHICAL ASPECTS OF CHRISTIAN PERFECTION AS THE END OF EDUCATION

1. The "true Christian" is the *finis effectus* of the work of education as a total process.
2. The "true Christian" should be the *finis cuius gratia* for educators and for educands.
3. Education as a total process is to bring man to Christian perfection in first proximate act. Education as a state is this perfection in second act.

VI. DEFINITION OF EDUCATION

CHAPTER VII

PARTICULAR IMPLICATIONS
FOR EDUCATION

MANY implications can be drawn from these considerations about the proper and immediate end of education.

Implications for Catholic Educational Theory

Charity, the core of Christian perfection, is based on truth.[1] It attains Him who is Truth itself and the inexhaustible Fountain of truth. Therefore, Christian educational theory must adhere firmly to the truth, develop the truth, and always present the truth.

Adhere firmly to the truth. A particular truth or prudential conclusion may be currently out of fashion; but eventually the pendulum will swing and approximate our position, at least for a time, as it passes by. This swing of the pendulum has already been seen between prescription and electivism in the curriculum, fear and license in discipline. One would not have to be prophetic to foresee in classroom practices a swing back to more methodical teaching.

The Church itself with its doctrine of "Christ, true God and true man, one person in two natures" was out of fashion for centuries as the pendulum of heresy swung from Apollinarianism to Nestorianism, back to Eutychianism and then to the attempted compromise of Monothelitism.

Develop the truth. Merely to adhere to principle in limpet style is good, but not good enough. Educational principles are dynamic, not static. We must investigate, develop, and apply them, persistently and courageously. We should not be frightened by the logical conclusions of our own principles. Yet, Robert Hutchins has said in accusation: "Catholic Education is not Catholic enough."[2] We owe it to God, to ourselves, and to others to bring forth out of our "treasure, new things and old."[3] It is not enough to wait for other educators laboriously and courageously to

---

[1] *Supra,* p. 104.
[2] Quoted in E. J. Baumeister, "Whither High School Latin," *Catholic Educational Review,* XLI (November, 1943), 524.
[3] Mt. 13:52.

modify educational attitudes and practice on the basis of some natural truth that all the while has been clear but dormant in our granary; then subsequently to claim that this modification is in accordance with our traditional principles and can be found in St. Thomas. It is not enough to find principles in St. Thomas; we must use them efficaciously. Self-activity as a notion was clearly and adequately elaborated in Scholasticism; yet we did not make it fully operative in later Catholic education.

God is the Author of all truth. When some non-Catholic scholar makes a genuine educational advance through the application or discovery of some natural truth, we can and should accept it gratefully and apply it to the lofty purposes of Christian education.

Present the truth. In all presentations and statements of our Catholic theory of education in public and private we must strictly respect the truth, natural and supernatural. Any attempt to compromise or dilute it under the guise of charity or of winning acceptance is un-Christian and fallacious. This compromise could easily show itself in whittling down the supernatural aspect of Christian education. Charity must be based on truth. Pius X expressly warns:

> You can plainly see, then, Venerable Brethren, how they err who think they are rendering service to the Church and reaping fruit in the salvation of souls when they, out of human prudence, try to be liberal in granting concessions to a science falsely so called. They are deceived in thinking they can win over those in error more easily. . . . Truth is one; it cannot be divided. It remains forever, free from the vicissitudes of time. "Jesus Christ is the same, yesterday and today, yes, and forever."[4]

Hence in this dissertation we have attempted to present the truth, such as we see it, about Christian education, even though chance readers may scoff at the unconcealed emphasis on the intangible supernatural realities. If they are not interested in an expression of what we at any rate seriously believe, the fault (may we say it without harshness!) is theirs, not ours. But strict adherence to the truth in no way necessitates or excuses malevolence toward those who genuinely hold a different view. Nor does it preclude a presentation in a way that is understandable to the recipient, provided the truth itself be not sacrificed.

Implications for Moral Formation

Man, as contingent, has an absolute, ontological dependence on God, his Creator; he is, in fact, most truly and realistically himself when he acknowledges this dependence. This dependence includes the tendency

---

[4] Pius X, *Iucunda Sane,* letter for the thirteenth centenary of St. Gregory, trans. by Yzermans, *op. cit.,* p. 39.

toward God as his ultimate end, which tendency is called his moral perfection. Therefore, man's moral perfection is ontologically expected of him.

Man's moral perfection demands the development of the moral virtues to perfect the working of his appetites in the natural and the supernatural order. Children need external guidance and vigilance in the formation of virtues;[5] adolescents need it in diminishing degree as they approach the stage of mature self-reliance;[6] and this external guidance and vigilance is called moral formation. Hence we say that, a priori, moral formation is a necessary part of man's over-all education. To sum up: moral perfection is ontologically expected of men and moral perfection needs moral formation. Hence moral formation is necessary.

Ordinary experience confirms this. Without moral formation schools can be places of depravity. Matthew Arnold[7] and C. S. Lewis[8] have written forcefully of school depravity in some of the hallowed English public schools, even before the so-called degeneracy of "modern times."

Moral formation is desirable even from the viewpoint of intellectual development. A sinful life intensifies the clouding of reason.[9]

> If two individuals should be exactly equal in intellectual capacity and opportunity, the one having greater moral perfection would be able to develop the intellectual virtues more perfectly.[10]

Moral formation is necessary in man's education; but it must be the right kind of moral formation, according to God's objective plan for our co-operation.[11] Pius XI fittingly warns: "It is not every kind of consistency and firmness of conduct based on subjective principles that makes true character, but only constancy in following the eternal principles of justice."[12] Any system of moral formation which negates or ignores any of the substantial elements of man's perfection in Christ — grace, charity, infused virtues, divine adoption, the Mystical Body — is abortive; it is the husk for the wheat.

One such system is a Deistic moral formation without "Dogma"! In the days of Luther and the Reformers the general theme was: "Deeds are inconsequential; dogma is vital." So the Diet of Worms, 1527, con-

---

[5] *Supra*, p. 143.

[6] Even after the moral virtues have been sufficiently developed all men need some encouragement and guidance in some form; but we are here considering the initial formation.

[7] Matthew Arnold. Cited in Robert Schwickerath, *Jesuit Education: Its History and Principles* (St. Louis: B. Herder Book Co., 1904), p. 552, n. 1.

[8] C. S. Lewis, *Surprised by Joy: The Pattern of My Early Life* (London: Geoffrey Bles, 1955), Chap. VI.

[9] Cf. *Summa,* I–II, q. 85, a. 3.

[10] Donlan, *op. cit.,* p. 36.

[11] *Supra*, p. 128 ff.

[12] Pius XI, *Christian Education of Youth, op. cit.,* p. 36.

demned the doctrine that good works were necessary for salvation; Luther's dictum urged: "Sin strongly but believe more strongly"; Calvin burned the Unitarian Servetus at the stake in 1553 for denying the Three Persons in the Blessed Trinity; death, exile, prison — fifty-eight death sentences and seventy-six exiles in five years[13] — were the fate of those Genevans who dared to reject or criticize the doctrine of Calvin's "Institutes."

But at present the successors of these reformers, while they still hail the "glories of the Reformation" in histories, official statements, and idealized movies, feel no embarrassment in saying that *dogma* is *inconsequential, deeds are vital!*[14] Yet Logic should blush at the anomaly!

Another such system is moral formation without God: doing good because it is the good thing to do, either for the sake of democracy, the old school tie, or of convention — since nearly everybody who is considered respectable does "good." In schools one sees plaques such as: "The good American is kind." Some writers speak of democracy in religious terminology — even to the extent of listing ten quasi commandments of democracy.[15] However earnest and laudable may be the intentions of their protagonists, all such systems are ultimately inept.

Pius XI speaks pertinently:

> So today we see, strange sight indeed, educators and philosophers who spend their lives in searching for a universal moral code of education, as if there existed no decalogue, no gospel law, no law even of nature stamped by God on the heart of man, promulgated by right reason, and codified in positive revelation by God Himself in the ten commandments. These innovators are wont to refer contemptuously to Christian education as "heteronomous," "passive," "obsolete," because founded upon the authority of God and His Holy Law.[16]

The moral formation given in Catholic schools must be worthy of perfection in Christ. Idealism must never be lowered despite *de facto* lack of co-operation. Those responsible for training the young can never be content with the mere aim of keeping them out of mortal sin. Training should foster in the students a humble desire of loving God much and of avoiding deliberate venial sin through His special help to be obtained by the powerful means of grace.

---

[13] William Barry, "Calvin," *Catholic Encyclopedia*, Vol. III (1912), 197. In noting these facts we do not wish to express or imply any opinion one way or the other in the matter of execution for conscience beliefs. We merely wish to underscore the radical change in attitudes toward dogma.

[14] Cf. the statements made by Billy Graham at Oxford University reported in *Time*, Vol. LXVI, No. 21, November 21, 1955, p. 54. This is only one example of an attitude that spots the pages of current religious reports.

[15] *Supra*, Chap. III, n. 27.

[16] Pius XI, *Christian Education of Youth*, pp. 24–25.

Now we consider the precise means of this moral formation. Can it be taught in the strict sense of the word? No: because moral formation is essentially a perfecting of the will, and the will is not a cognitive faculty. How can this moral formation be given the educand?

1. Give him an ideal, tactfully. He must never be nagged with ideals.
2. Give him an exemplar for the ideal, because the ideal will be most effective when it is objectified in some exemplar. Present this exemplar according to the principles of exemplary causality detailed above;[17] present it as something *able* to be imitated not just as something which should be imitated. This aspect of being imitable depends, first, on the parity of the situations and, second, on the sufficiency of the means to effect imitation. Educators should beware lest the pregnant phrase "imitation of Christ" become a mere cliché evoking not action but reaction in the form of boredom, nausea, or frustration.
3. Give him motivation to see this ideal as not merely imitable but *desirable for him*. In this, follow the ordinary educational principles of motivation, intrinsic and extrinsic. Supernatural virtue requires supernatural motivation. There are even grades of supernatural motivation; the lower grades, e.g., fear of hell, are not to be despised and excluded.[18]
4. Give him, by good teaching, sound and adequate knowledge about moral ends and means. He needs clear, well-understood, concrete principles. This is indispensable, because a man's will necessarily depends on his reason. One important aspect of this instruction will be his development of a rational scale of values for assessing true worth; another is an understanding of the virtues and their hierarchical role, for example of faith, humility, and mortification as the foundations of the Christian life.[19] He must be led to realize that the school athletes are not necessarily life's heroes.
5. Give him reasonable supervision. This will include:
   a) Law. True law is security and a kind of instruction. It is like the protective railing on a bridge restraining a man from a false step.
   b) Kindly vigilance.
   c) Tactful guidance according to valid philosophical and psychological principles. No educator should be ostrich enough to believe that his mere *telling* what should be done will always *effect* what should be done.
   d) Opportunities proportioned to his condition for the practice of the moral virtues.

---

[17] *Supra*, p. 86 ff.
[18] *Supra*, p. 119 f.
[19] Cf. Boylan, *op. cit.*, Chaps. 17 and 18.

e) Protection from unnecessary proximate occasions of sin, as far as possible. This is by no means a superfluous warning especially in coeducational schools.

6. The abundant opportunity for the use of the supernatural means of grace — the sacraments[20] and prayer. Teachers must regard the sacraments as indispensable means of moral formation and therefore of education.

7. The creation of an atmosphere both at home and at school that implements the ideals and the instruction. Good environment exerts a uniform, unnoticed, powerful stimulus toward personal goodness. A child is not likely to acquire a spirit of Christian self-denial in a home which lacks it; he is not likely to acquire a respect for authority, respect for patience in a classroom that lacks these virtues.

We return briefly to a consideration of the supernatural means, mentioned in No. 6.

Prayer has already been discussed.[21]

It is surely an anomaly to have Catholic high school children coming each day to school and seldom if ever making a voluntary visit to the Blessed Sacrament in the church nearby. The fostering of such a devotion means tact and skillful leadership, but it is worth the effort. The anomaly becomes a positive incongruity in at least one city where a beautiful church, whose walls are a few feet from the Catholic school, is kept locked all day!

It is unfortunate that even with the best of intentions many high school children cannot attend morning Mass. Distance to a large central school is so great that it becomes difficult to be present at morning Mass and especially Holy Communion without traveling or breakfast complications. The school cannot very well serve a full breakfast; even so, breakfast should be a home meal; so in the name of Catholic education, many students are being deprived of the opportunity to accept Pius X's invitation to frequent, even daily Communion with its grace *ex opere operato!* Yet who will deny that at this age they need special grace?

Here, it seems, is a case where we should not merely accept a less desirable situation for want of some initiative, courage, and some personal sacrifice. We must energetically and zealously seek ways and means, even with some inconvenience, to make our basic truths operative.

In view of the recent facilities for the Eucharistic fast before evening Mass, could not one legitimately hope for the day when, similarly, a late Mass could be said at 11:30 a.m. or midday for the students, so that those fasting from solids for three hours and otherwise prepared could receive Holy Communion? Thus their diet would be unaffected, home life

---

[20] Cf. Pope Pius XI, *Christian Education of Youth*, p. 29. The Holy Father here speaks of the educational value of the sacraments.

[21] *Supra*, p. 163 f. Cf. also Donlan, *op. cit.*, p. 30.

undisturbed, school not seriously disrupted; yet a great gain for personal and school life could accrue. If it is felt that compulsory attendance at Mass every day is undesirable, attendance could be optional on three or four days, the time to be otherwise devoted to class preparation or reading. There seems no a priori reason why such a plan enthusiastically implemented would not produce personal and general fruits that would more than compensate for whatever inconvenience might be entailed by the rearrangement.

Mere daily presence at morning Mass by the school student body is not enough. Undoubtedly it does good. A Catholic educator cannot rest until such presence achieves its maximum good; and that needs a multiform effort. Children on the threshold of life and not yet matured cannot be expected to pray the Mass with full profit each day if unassisted in some way. Sometimes a Low Mass in a large church becomes for them a half hour of complete silence disturbed only by the bells. A daily sung Mass, poorly sung, nauseates the singers and bores the nonsingers. Yet the Mass is the Supreme Sacrifice, the focal point of Christian worship, a source of unlimited blessings in personal and social Christian living. It is our responsibility as educators to use all the potentiality of the Liturgy, all the motivation and ingenuity of good teaching to gear our students to the immeasurable power of the Mass. The following suggestions are tentatively made.

Could not the school Mass follow some varied schedule such as this for the five days of the school week?

1. Dialogue Mass.
2. Sung Mass, Gregorian Chant.
3. Low Mass with some *few* group prayers in English that are brief, in the spirit of the Mass. Over and above the dialogue Mass it is important to teach children in the language they understand to pray the principal parts of the Mass — for example, to pray the Offertory in the spirit of the Mass and in reference to their own needs.[22]
4. Low Mass, silently followed as at Sunday Mass.
5. Sung Mass, Gregorian chant or an approved unison Mass — *not* polyphonic — in modern music according to the norms of Pius X's *Motu proprio*.[23] If desired, a polyphonic motet could be sung at the Offertory and Communion, *servatis rubricis*.

It is essential that the students participate as actively as possible leading the singing and prayers audibly and confidently, with the teachers and choir director as much as possible in the background.

A dogmatic, moral, liturgical, ascetical, or apostolic discourse related

---

[22] Cf. Pius XII, in reference to the place of private devotional prayer at Mass. *Mediator Dei,* Vatican Library translation (Washington, D. C.: N.C.W.C., 1948), nn. 24–32, 172–184.

[23] Pius X, *Motu Proprio, ASS,* XXXVI (November 22, 1903), pp. 329–339.

to the Mass and given by the priest just before the Mass could be a stimulus to enlightened devotion and a bridge between studying the Mass in the classroom and praying it in the Church. This brief discourse — it need not exceed two minutes — could be given every day or at least frequently. In this way monotony would be avoided and the students would be functionally instructed in the Mass; they would be more apt to receive its *ex opere operantis* benefits in their daily lives and their development of sound devotional habits would be guided and encouraged.

Confession is another major means of moral formation. Much could be said on this subject but most of it is irrelevant for the educator. But somebody, usually the school principal, has serious decisions to make.

If the Catholic school is going to assume responsibility for seeing that its students go to Confession each month, and as a fact this is usual, then the whole matter must be handled *well* and with a supernatural perspective, even at the price of considerable personal and administrational inconvenience; and all under penalty of the gravest spiritual disorders.

It is no excuse to say that a large school makes this virtually impossible. This is equivalent to saying that in a large high school we inevitably produce one situation which could tear down for some individuals all that the other school influences seek to build up. If this be true, then it is one strong argument against the large, little-city high school.

But is it true? That is a question to be examined honestly, courageously, and supernaturally by those concerned. Since the spiritual health of the present high school population is at the very heart of Catholic education and has incalculable personal and parochial consequences for public devotion, lay co-operation, happy marriages, etc., time spent constructively now will save time and frustration later. Time "saved" now (for what? What is more important than the soul's medicinal reception of a sacrament?) will later be spent doubly trying to repair the indifference and the ravages that undue haste can cause.

Perhaps the most pertinent questions facing the educator are these: (1) Is it necessary to send all the students to confession on one day? (2) Must older students — even seniors — be *sent* to confession during class hours? If students can remain after school for athletic or concert practice, could not one of the upper-class students likewise linger in order to go to confession in his own time? For each student the time taken would be negligible. Such an arrangement need not lessen or disorganize the time given to cocurriculars, certainly need not lose the school a trophy! But if there were some schedule conflict between this sacramental opportunity and the athletic program, then it would be time to remember St. Paul's words as a criterion for gauging effort and emphasis: "Everyone . . . striveth for the mastery . . . they indeed that they may receive a corruptible crown, but we an incorruptible one."[24] With proper orienta-

---

[24] 1 Cor. 9:25.

tion according to guidance principles and techniques, older students can be trained to assume the personal responsibility of going to confession regularly and thereby be helped to make the transition from school to adult life. (3) How prudent and farsighted is it for teachers simply to assign even upper-elementary students to confessionals without giving them that easy freedom of conscience which is everyone's right?

Nothing clear-cut can be laid down for all situations. Each needs a prudential judgment.

We have seen that moral formation is necessary in education, that it must be of the right kind according to the "eternal principles of justice," that it cannot strictly be taught, but can be strongly fostered. Suggestions and possibilities for the school use of Mass and the sacraments have been mentioned.

[Happily the wish about the possibility of midday Communion is now obsolete. Further changes (1957) in the Eucharistic fast make midday Mass and Communion quite feasible for school children. Before the changes were announced an experienced and highly qualified educator expressed the view that such a midday Mass was unworkable. Already the practice of some schools refutes his verdict — an interesting sidelight on what was said earlier about the things which "can't be done" in schools!]

Implications for the School

PRECISE FUNCTION OF THE SCHOOL

What is the role of the school in fostering Christian perfection? Man's education necessarily includes moral formation. Moral formation cannot be taught. The school is the institution where, traditionally, teaching is given. Is the school then accountable for the student's positive moral formation as a primary objective? We are not here concerned with those non-Catholic writers who would make social adjustment in one form or another the function of the school and education.[25] We are concerned with those Catholic educators who accept the general Catholic position yet are in disagreement about the school's precise function.

This question has been much discussed recently. It is too big to be handled adequately here in all its pros and cons. It could well be a special dissertation in itself; yet, since the school is a means of education, its role is naturally related to the proper and immediate end of education. Hence we consider it briefly here — with some diffidence. Renowned

---

[25] This is the well-known emphasis of Dewey and his followers. Cf. also the Harvard Report, *General Education in a Free Society* (Cambridge, Mass.: Harvard University Press, 1945). Also the report of the President's Commission on Higher Education, *Higher Education for American Democracy* (New York, 1946).

names well accoutered with philosophy, theology, and pedagogy have entered the lists in this dispute and have broken a lance for one side or the other.

The background for the disagreement is the prevailing pattern of school programs currently offered in this country. Apart from the technical courses that have moved from the factories, shops, and technical schools into the regular high school, some schools offer credits for working in the school shop or the school bank, for courses in automobile driving, general etiquette, the cooking and serving of meals, interior furnishing and decorating, social relations and "dating" — this "course" including the conversation of two students, boy and girl, at separate tables.[26]

Many of these things were formerly done at home; many are best done at home *if* they are done there. Others were formerly done in technical schools.

But because children need these things in some degree, because broken, incompetent, or shrunken homes or cramped housing fails to provide them, because the age requirements preclude regular work and prevailing social pressure requires a person to go to school and get a diploma — even if it actually means little more than proof of sufficient attendance, the school has enlarged its scope and staff to perform these functions. The result has been a partial decline in academic requirement, a state of alarm among some educators and parents expressed in the phrase: "The school is doing too little because it is trying to do too much," and a demand for the clarification of the school's precise function. It will be readily realized that the issue has sociological, economic, industrial causes and repercussions.

Opinions. Many opinions have been expressed, reducible in general to two main camps. One group holds that the Catholic school should not have the moral formation of students as an essential and primary function. They by no means deny the importance of such moral formation; but that, they say, is the essential role of home and Church. The school's essential function is intellectual, which will include giving the student that instruction which is necessary for moral perfection. The school will contribute in some way — variously formulated — toward moral perfection by its atmosphere, etc., but the Church and the home have the essential function of providing this moral formation. Thus, according to these educators, the work of education is divided between several agents, each having its special and distinct function; yet there is to be a close co-ordination between them. This general attitude we here term the Intellectualist view.

Cardinal Newman held that knowledge was the specific and proximate

---

[26] Cf. A. Lynd, *Quackery in our Public Schools* (Boston: Little, Brown and Co., 1953); also M. Smith, *The Diminished Mind* (Chicago: Henry Regnery Co., 1954).

aim of a Catholic college and university. Knowledge is a good in its own right, not a pure means to some other good.[27] It is however a subordinate end ordained to man's true ultimate end. It must be itself acquired thoroughly if it is to become an intermediate end.[28] Newman certainly does not deny the greater need for virtue. But he emphasizes also the lesser need for sound knowledge and this he says is the primary function of the college.

Dr. Vincent Smith,[29] in the inaugural and keynote lecture for the N.C.E.A. convention at Atlantic City, Easter Week, 1955, supports the view that the essential function of the school is to teach the teachable subjects. Education includes many things — intellectual virtue, moral teaching, physical development, craftsmanship, even how to walk and feed oneself and safeguard health. Among all these needs the function of the school is by tradition and by right to teach. But one can only teach what is teachable. Only knowledge, and in the last analysis only scientific knowledge, is truly teachable. There are six teachable subject areas: logic (understood in its broadest sense to include the language arts), mathematics, study of nature, moral studies, metaphysics, theology. "The proper end of the school is not democracy, not adjustment, not citizenship, not economic gain, not even moral virtue, though all of these aspects of the human person can claim immeasurable benefits as by-products of a school that does the school's work."[30] The school's primary aim is to communicate knowledge and truth. "Where the school surrenders the primacy of knowledge, it will finally lose its own priceless premise — the truth that makes its teaching free."[31] The intellectual formation which we give and the principles of the objective moral code which we teach will, as a by-product, bear fruits of good citizenship and of patriotism and will bring forth many other things commonly listed as desirable outcomes. The school as a moral substitute for the parents must attend in varying degrees to the child's health, his doing of things in the practical order — prudence — and his making of things in the productive order — art. But these things are not strictly teachable, therefore not the unique mission of the school. They are concomitant.

This, then, is Dr. Smith's conclusion. The school is a part of Catholic education; its part — and primary function — is to communicate knowledge and truth by teaching. Its work will be and necessarily must be in co-ordination with the work of the Church, the home, and the State. If

[27] John H. Newman, *The Idea of a University* (London: Longmans, Green and Co., 1902), pp. 102–103, *et passim*.
[28] Cf. Edmond O. Benard, "Theology as Pivotal: Newman's View," *Integration in Catholic Colleges and Universities*, ed. by Roy J. Deferrari (Washington, D. C.: The Catholic University of America Press, 1950).
[29] Vincent E. Smith, "The Catholic School: A Re-examination," *Bulletin* (Washington, D. C.: N.C.E.A.), LII (August, 1955), pp. 37–48.
[30] *Ibid.*, pp. 41–42.   [31] *Ibid.*, p. 42.

it adheres to and fulfills its special function it will also produce valuable educational by-products. Its primary function is intellectual.

The faculty and consultants of St. Xavier's College, Chicago, have inaugurated an energetic study of education with special reference to the elementary, secondary, and college departments that constitute St. Xavier's. The zeal shown in this study could well be a stimulus and a model for other educational institutions.

An unpublished, private, and anonymous study on the school and moral training states their position with admirable clarity and brevity:

A. The specific and therefore primary work of the school is to train youth in intellectual virtue which *in se* does not include the task of the cultivation of the moral virtues.

B. Though the essential role of the school does not include cultivation of moral virtue, its integral role does involve training in moral virtue on two general grounds:

(1) The nature of intellectual training of youth.

(2) The atmosphere which is absolutely necessary for a Catholic school.

The nature of intellectual training requires the contribution of moral dispositions, and includes instruction in moral science, on which moral formation is founded. The Catholic atmosphere of the school involves student conformity with school ordinances, lofty teacher qualification, and the permeation of teaching, syllabus, textbooks, class instruction with the Catholic spirit.

In another private, unpublished study this definition of the school is proposed: "The school is a social institution initiated by the Church and the family where teachers instruct the young in the arts and sciences for the advance and prosperity of civil society." The school is a social institution of Catholic education "which means that it is in perfect moral union with family and Church and an instrument of them. This in turn means that the ultimate end of the school will be the same as that of the family and of the Church." Thus, for the St. Xavier's group, the primary function of the school is intellectual.

Monsignor John Tracy Ellis, a Catholic University historian, complains, in a recent article, of Catholic education's failure to produce proportionate national leaders and to exercise a decisive intellectual influence in America. He criticizes "the overemphasis which some authorities of the Church's educational system in the United States have given to the school as an agency for moral development, with an insufficient stress on the role of the school as an instrument for fostering intellectual excellence."[32] He does not, however, say explicitly that the essential func-

---

[32] John Tracy Ellis, "American Catholics and the Intellectual Life," *Thought*, XXX (1955), 377–378.

tion of the school is intellectual rather than moral, nor does he define the proper relation of intellectual and moral formation in the school.

Father Donlan[33] laments the tendency to regard the school as a total cause of education as though the school alone were responsible for all education. It does not have to be the ideal instrument for every kind of human perfection. Christian perfection, he says, is the proper and immediate end of education, but not of the school; each part cannot have the same proper and immediate end as the whole, and the school is only a part of the whole educational process. The school has as its proximate or immediate end the perfection of man's mind through the intellectual virtues. This is its distinct contribution to man's whole education. By a subordination of ends this intellectual perfection is ordained to man's total perfection in Christ and to the ultimate end of life. Thus, for Donlan, the primary specific function of the school is intellectual.

Many others espouse the same general viewpoint.

This viewpoint is clear, and it is convenient. The school's proximate end is intellectual formation. Its remote end, to which intellectual perfection, a good in itself, is directly ordained, is man's Christian perfection. Its ultimate end is man's possession of God in heaven.[34] The school says in effect to the other influences in the educational process: We will concentrate on our intellectual part as perfectly as we can; you do your parts perfectly. They will fit together perfectly and man will run perfectly like a well-made car along the road to his ultimate end — good tires doing the work of tires, a good engine doing the work of the engine reliably.

It is convenient because, in the event of moral breakdown along the road, the school could justifiably call for water and wash its hands of responsibility.

Statements of the Popes. It is hard to see how this general Intellectualist view can be reconciled with the statements of the Holy See.

1. Pius XII says: "According to the Catholic concept the object of the school and of education is the formation of the perfect Christian. . . . Your entire school and educational system would be useless were this object not the central point of your labor."[35]

---

[33] Donlan, *op. cit.,* pp. 54–65.

[34] Cf. *supra,* p. 35, for the meaning of these categories of end.

[35] Pius XII, *Counsels to Teaching Sisters,* September 13, 1951, AAS, XLIII (1951), 742–743. "A questo riguardo non abbiamo bisogno di ripetervi . . . che secondo il senso cattolico lo scopo della scuola e dell'educazione è di formare il perfetto cristiano, ovvero, per applicare questo principio alla vostra condizione, di esercitare un tale influsso spirituale e morale e di ottenere una tale assuefazione della fanciulla e della giovane, che essa, quando sarà fasciata poi a se stessa rimanga salda nella fede cattolica e la metta in atto fin nelle quotidine conseguenze pratiche, o almeno si abbia fondata speranza che l'alunna vivrà più tardi secondo i principî e le norme della sua fede.

The implication and, we think, the obvious implication of the Pope's words is that the formation of the perfect Christian is the proper and the primary work of the school. He does not distinguish between "education" and the "school" in regard to Christian perfection. (A consideration of how both can be immediately concerned with perfection in Christ will be made later.)

Christian perfection as a remote or mediate end of the school's work does not fulfill the implication of the strong words "central point" used by the Pope. Recall what has been said in Chapter II about a remote end, which is an end attained mediately through some prior end. This prior end is an end in its own right and may be suitably, but is not necessarily, ordained by a free agent to a further end, i.e., the remote end. If that which is immediately attained by an agent were only a pure means leading of its nature to the real good, just as medicine is a means to health and is taken only for the sake of health, then this good and not the pure means could literally be called the object, the central point of the activity. If, however, that which is immediately sought is a good in its own right — as intellectual perfection certainly is — "central point" is literally applied to the agent's immediate end rather than to its remote end. Hence, the proximate good, intellectual perfection, and not the remote good *should* more fittingly be called the "central point" of the school's labor, if the Pope's words are to favor the general Intellectualist view; but in point of fact the Pope calls the formation of the perfect Christian the central point of the school's labor, implying that moral formation in Christ is the immediate and not the remote end of the school's work. If the school is meant to attain the formation of the perfect Christian only remotely through some prior good, why would the Pope emphasize the *mediate* or remote good as the *central point?* Would he not normally speak of the prior or immediate good as the central point?

In other words, if A's work is to attain B and if A attains C through B, why would someone tell A that C is the central point of his work? Would he not normally speak of B as the central point of A's work? If B were simply and solely a pure means to C, C could then be called the central point. In our case, however, B (intellectual perfection) is certainly not a pure means; it is itself a good, even though it is capable of being ordained to a higher good.

Hence we say that the general Intellectualist view of the function of the school is not easily reconciled with the obvious implication of the Pope's words.

"Tutto il vostro sistema di scuola e di educazione sarebbe vano, se questo scopo non fosse al centro dell'opera vostra. Lavorare a tal fine con tutte le vostre forze, è ciò che il Signore vuole da voi. Egli vi ha chiamate alla missione di educare la gioventù femminile per farne perfette cristiane." This statement of the Holy Father *"per applicare questo . . ."* bears on the distinction of Christian perfection in proximate first act and in second act. *Supra,* p. 190 ff.

Moreover, Christian perfection as the remote or mediate end of the school's work does not verify the strong word "useless" used by the Pope in the same passage. Failure to attain a remote end still leaves the agent in possession of the proximate end; therefore, his entire efforts, though without additional fruition, cannot be called useless. For example, a college graduate's failure to be hired by General Motors does not render his college degree and his entire efforts thereby useless. Presumably, failure in the formation of the perfect Christian — the remote end — could take place through somebody else's neglect even after the school had perfectly attained its own proximate end of intellectual perfection. How then could the Pope imply that the labor of the entire school system would be useless since it would have attained its own proximate end — all that could reasonably be expected of it?

Further, the Pope's words seem to imply that failure to attain moral perfection in Christ would be a failure in the central point of school effort. For some writers such failure would only be in the school's integral, not its essential, role! But failure in integrity does not render *essential success* "useless." The loss of a limb does not by any means render the rest of man's life useless.

An example may help; but it must be accepted with the limitations of an illustration. It is meant as an illustration, not a proof.

An artisan cuts diamonds by trade. We can say that the proximate end of his labor is to produce the cut and polished diamond, a thing of beauty and value in itself. That diamond could be set in a bracelet, a ring, a pendant, but actually it is set in a crown for Queen Elizabeth — the finished crown being the product of several master artisans.

According to the Intellectualist opinion the school is the artisan, intellectual perfection the diamond, the Church, home, and state the master artisans fashioning the crown of Christian perfection into which the diamond fits perfectly and where it glitters most brightly. Undoubtedly, intellectual perfection — and the diamond — are noblest when set in the crown. Yet in themselves they remain as "good" and can be possessed as valuable apart from the crown. A man can have some intellectual perfection apart from moral perfection: he can have the virtue of science and lack charity. It could not be said of the diamond cutter that the "central point" of all his labor was to fashion a crown and, because of the incompetence of one of the master goldsmiths, that his whole labor in cutting and polishing a perfect diamond was "useless." Similarly in the Intellectualist view it could not be aptly said that the "central point" of the school effort is the remote end of perfection in Christ; nor, because of the incompetence of some other educational influence, could the school's entire labor in producing perfect intellectual development — its own proximate end (*sic*) — be fairly called "useless."

Hence we say that the Intellectualist opinion cannot be reasonably reconciled with the words of the Pope.

2. Pius XII, speaking to the Union of Italian Teachers said:
You, the teachers of today, who draw your sure directives from the past, what ideal of man must you prepare for the future? You will find that ideal fundamentally designed in the perfect Christian. By the perfect Christian we mean the Christian of today, child of his own era, knowing and cultivating all the advances made by science and technical skill, a citizen and not something apart from the life led in his own country today.[36]

The normal presumption is that in these words addressed to a group of teachers, gathered as teachers, he speaks of the proximate, essential end of their activity, not of the remote end and not of something pertaining merely to the integrity of their work.

These words cannot reasonably be reconciled with the Intellectualist idea of the teacher's role in the school. Rather they imply that the teacher in the school is to be immediately and essentially concerned with the pupil's moral formation in Christ, the perfect Christian.

The implication that Christian education must be concerned with contemporary life, social life, and with keen intellectual life[37] should be noticed in passing — "the Christian of today," "a citizen," "cultivating all the advances made by science. . . ."

The Pope in this same address urges the teachers to direct the minds of the children "to discover the inexhaustible strength of Christianity for the improvement and renewal of peoples," to awaken their moral conscience early, to train them to Christian charity, to form them as men of science and technology on the foundation of this moral conscience, to form them as strong men capable of diffusing justice around them, to train their minds to sound criticism but at the same time to a sense of Christian humility. "What is at stake in the school is the salvation or ruin of every single soul,"[38] he says.

"Conscience," formation in justice and in "charity" pertain to moral formation; and the Pope enumerates these side by side with intellectual formation in speaking to *teachers*.

It seems that the Intellectualist view of the school cannot be aptly and easily reconciled with these words and their spirit.

The reasonable interpretation is that the Pope views the teacher in the school as someone essentially and immediately concerned with moral as well as intellectual formation.

[36] Pius XII, *Address to the Union of Italian Teachers*, September 4, 1949, quoted in *Catholic Action*, XXXI (October, 1949), p. 18.
[37] *Supra*, p. 178 ff.
[38] Pius XII, *Address to the Union of Italian Teachers*, September 4, 1949, *loc. cit.*

3. Pope Pius XI in speaking of the De La Salle Christian Brothers said:

Each Brother in the Christian Schools is a missioner in his class.[39]

It is true that every Christian by his prayers and sacrifices should be a missioner in intention whether he be baking bread, tending the sick, teaching school, or sweeping the house — a missioner *ex fine operantis*. But the Pope, in speaking of the teacher in the classroom as a missioner, clearly implies that missionary work is done by teachers in the school from the very nature of their work — *ex fine operis*, as well. And missionary work *ex fine operis* is work essentially and immediately ordained to moral formation in Christ.

The Intellectualist view, which would make the school a place of intellectual perfection with moral perfection a remote and/or integral concern, does not aptly verify these strong words of the Pope.

Again their reasonable and obvious meaning is that the teacher in the school is essentially and immediately concerned with the student's moral formation.

4. At Ars in the lifetime of the Curé, two girls under his guidance founded a little *Providence*,[40] where fifty or sixty girls between the ages of twelve and eighteen were taught the elements of knowledge and simple housecrafts — sewing, laundry, knitting, etc.

There can be no doubt that the emphasis of the school was on formation in true piety. (With the holy Curé as chaplain, could it be otherwise?) While contemporary witnesses assert that the *Providence* gave an adequate elementary education, the standard of intellectual formation given these girls of twelve to eighteen would shock the intellectuals — Catherine Lassagne, one of the mistresses, was somewhat erratic in her spelling. The "plant" would have shocked school administrators; they would never have "approved" it. It was overcrowded to double capacity. There was only one classroom, measuring eleven by six by two and a half meters, where all the lessons went on simultaneously for the resident and the additional day scholars. But pilgrims to Ars who crowded the doors to hear the Curé teach Christian doctrine marveled at the peace, the contentment, the delightful spontaneity of the students; girls "graduated" at nineteen and twenty as truly Christian women; and St. Pius X in an official decree called it a *"model* of popular education."[41]

While no Catholic would belittle the religious atmosphere of the

---

[39] Pius XI, quoted in the *Catholic Standard* (Washington, D. C.), Friday, March 18, 1955. These are the words spoken by Pope Pius XI to Frère Adrien, Superior-General of the Brothers of the Christian Schools. They are quoted by Frère Athanard-Emile, Superior-General of the same institute in the *Circulaires Instructives et Administratives*, No. 329, "Apostolat Missionaire," 1949, p. 120.

[40] F. Trochu, *The Curé D'Ars*, trans. by Ernest Graf (Westminster, Md.: The Newman Press, 1949), pp. 195–211.

[41] Pius X, decree, February 21, 1904, *Acta Sanctae Sedis*, XXXVI (1904), 622.

Providence, the Intellectualists could only regard this institution as a confused, partial failure, since it positively emphasized moral training even for the day scholars and it attained the school's proximate end, intellectual formation, in a very limited degree. How then justify its praise by the Pope as a "model"? Only if the Christian schools have moral formation as an immediate and essential end could this school, despite its very ordinary intellectual standard, be called a "model."

5. In speaking of the homes (*domicilia*) and schools (*collegia*) founded for boys by St. John Bosco, Pius XI praises the true Christian education given therein — the training in the human studies and moreover, *"quod est praecipuum,"* Christian formation. He praises that education as being wholly imbued and nourished in every fiber with the evangelical precepts and the shining example of Jesus Christ.[42]

These strong words could hardly be true of the educative work of the school if this was only integrally or remotely concerned with positive Christian formation.

6. Pius XII in his radio message to the Fifth Inter-American Congress on Catholic Education at Havana said among other things:

> Good teachers finally are careful to educate rather than merely to instruct; capable *above all* of forming and of moulding souls. . . . You will interest yourselves *more* in education than in mere instruction[43] [italics added].

The Pope is here speaking to teachers about their immediate work in the schools. It is hard to see how the notions "above all," "more," could aptly apply to what, according to the Intellectualist viewpoint, would only be integral and/or a remote end.

It is true, as St. Thomas points out, that the will tends toward an end in a twofold way: immediately; and mediately, that is through something else. In both cases the will can be properly said to tend to the end.[44] But the cumulative force of the papal words indicates a propinquity between the school and religious formation and an urgency of attention that is more aptly verified only in the case of an immediate

---

[42] Pius XI, *Homily* for the canonization of St. John Bosco, April 1, 1934, *AAS,* XXVI (May, 1934), 220–221: "illam (educationem) nimirum quae evangelicis praeceptis praeclarisque Jesu Christi exemplis imbuitur tota per omnesque venas alitur; illam, qua, christiana religione virtuteque duce . . . iuveniles rediguntur ac componuntur mores. . . . Illam denique . . . quaeque, si humanas omnes disciplinas, ad praesentem vitam excolendam ornandamque opportunas, discipulis impertit, at quod est praecipuum non neglegit, Creatoris nempe ac Remuneratoris Dei doctrinam atque Ecclesiae praecepta."

[43] Pius XII, "El Especialísimo Amor," *AAS,* XLVI (1954), pp. 60, 61. "Buenos maestros, en fin, cuidadosos de educar antes que de enseñar; capaces, sobre todo, de formar y de plasmar almas . . . preocupándoos siempre más de la educación que de la instrucción. . . ." This address has been translated in *The Pope Speaks,* I (First Quarter, 1954), under the title "The Secret of Good Schools."

[44] St. Thomas, *2 Sent.,* Dist. 38, q. 1, a. 5.

end. Why would the Popes speak so emphatically to teachers of the second, remote good, passing over the *immediate* good which, hypothetically, it would be their proximate business to attain?

It should be noticed, too, that some Intellectualists would regard the Catholic school as unproportioned to this mediate end, viz., religious formation. For them, the school is a partial cause fulfilling its own part of education, leaving other aspects to other partial causes, the whole work of education being the perfect co-ordination and subordination of perfect partial ends.

To represent this diagrammatically, it is not, they say, a case of:

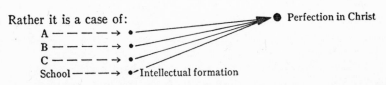

                       (*Immediate end*)   (*Mediate end*)

    School — — → • Intellectual Formation — — → • Perfection in Christ

Rather it is a case of: • Perfection in Christ

A — — — — → •

B — — — — → •

C — — — — → •

School — — — → •⁻Intellectual formation

But if this view were correct the Popes in the previously quoted statements would be repeatedly urging the school to attain a remote end not proportioned to it, usually passing over the immediate good for which it is properly proportioned and competent.

Hence we say that in the mind of the Popes the school is to be essentially and immediately concerned with religious formation. This conclusion seems to be further confirmed by a passage in Pius XI's encyclical. It is not as clear as the preceding statements, but we discuss it here.

In the Intellectualist view the school would provide the flawless intellectual formation; the home and the Church would make this dynamic by moral formation. Logically, the school need not be concerned with moral formation except incidentally and correlatively and negatively, that is, chiefly by excluding whatever would be opposed to perfection in Christ. The school merely does its part; then hands the student over to the others for their proper contribution, making sure only that he suffers no harm in the school's atmosphere. Likewise, an oculist need not be concerned with every patient's heart except incidentally, correlatively, and negatively. Yet Pius XI and Leo XIII stress that the Christian spirit and piety must regulate and permeate teachers, syllabus, and textbooks, *"in every branch"* and in *"every . . . subject,"* to produce a sacred atmosphere.[45] This special permeation, piety, and sacred atmosphere pervading even mathematics would be essentially

---

[45] Pius XI, *Christian Education of Youth*, pp. 30–31.

irrelevant for the development of the intellectual virtue of science in sufficient degree to satisfy the exigencies of mere intellectual formation; that is, in order to fulfill what the Intellectualists would regard as the school's own proximate and immediate end. One can be trained well in mathematics without being formed to Christian piety. This permeation of mathematics would be as irrelevant as the oculist's or the dentist's cardiograph of every patient's heart out of concern for his health. This thorough permeation, piety, and positive sacred atmosphere expected of the school by the Popes becomes logical and relevant only if the essential and immediate end of the school be the pupil's moral formation.

Donlan explains that this positive permeation is fulfilled in two ways: (1) negatively by the exclusion from the school of whatever is in any way prejudicial to perfection in Christ — Naturalism, Scientism, etc.; (2) positively by the proper, hierarchical ordering of the arts and sciences according to the norms of metaphysics and theology.[46] We readily concede that this degree of permeation is altogether necessary; but it seems incomplete and insufficient if left just there. Such a hierarchical ordering as Donlan envisages may fulfill the papal injunction of positive permeation regarding the syllabus and curriculum, but it hardly verifies the injunction of "piety," of the Christian spirit in the teaching, and of a "sacred atmosphere." It is not enough to relegate the fulfillment of these characteristics to the general school environment as Donlan does.[47] That, in the Intellectualist theory, would be tantamount to saying that the Catholic school can fulfill its essential and immediate function of teaching the intellect and yet, according to the words of the Pope, not be a "fit place for Catholic students"[48] until something incidental or at most integral, namely, environment, was present; and concomitants cannot be the condition justifying the essence. It is true that elsewhere the Pope speaks of "the utmost importance" of the child's environment;[49] but it is clear from the context that he uses the word in a sense different from Donlan. The Pope uses "environment" here to signify the total educational influence exerted by the principal agencies of education — family, Church, State — and the school. He is not using it in the sense of the general tone of a *school* supplementing the teaching given in the school, as Donlan does in this reference.

Hence we say that this thorough Christian permeation, the piety, and sacred atmosphere expected of the school by the Popes, is logically and fully warranted only if the child's moral formation in Christ be considered as the school's essential and immediate end.

As a conclusion from all these considerations it is here submitted that,

46 Donlan, *op. cit.*, pp. 62–63.
47 *Ibid.*, p. 64.
48 Pius XI, *Christian Education of Youth*, p. 30. The Pope regards this complete permeation as necessary in order to make a school a fit place for Catholic students.
49 *Ibid.*, p. 27.

in the clear mind of the Holy See, the Catholic school must be essentially and immediately concerned with the student's formation in Christ (yet without in any way relenting in its academic efforts, as we shall see). In no sense does this mean that the school tries to dispense with the home and Church.

Only such a concept of the Catholic school makes the marvelous school efforts of Catholics in this country justifiable. In 1954 the Catholics of America spent approximately $500,000,000 on Catholic school construction. In the same year by conducting their own Catholic schools, they saved the United States public treasuries, to which they had already contributed as citizens, $620,692,000 in operating expenses. So that year the government of America was in pocket $1,120,692,000 because Catholics believe firmly in the *necessity* of Catholic schools. And this figure does not include the additional financial loss in California coming from real-estate taxes on parochial schools, "in spite of a law to the contrary" says Archbishop O'Hara. Nor does it even touch the nonmonetary cost, the work hours and afterwork hours, the administrational headaches, the committee efforts of thousands of organizers, supervisors, leaders — time and energy that could be so well used elsewhere.[50]

Why do we make such a colossal effort? Is it just an egoistic, do-it-yourself intellectual effort? Is it, asks Dr. Odenwald,[51] so that our first graders may be pushed to read a few more books than other first graders and our eighth graders may be pressured to win a national spelling bee or an oratorical contest? Is it to secure nothing *essentially* different from the intellectual formation given in the public schools — apart from religious instruction which, as such, we could append somehow to the child's school day without a billion dollar expense each year? Is all this to secure something merely integral but not essential to the Catholic school?

The answer is no. We make this effort to secure, essentially and immediately, children's moral and intellectual formation in the Catholic school. And as moral formation is *indispensable* for the Christian, the colossal effort to equip Catholic schools is justifiable.

Pius XI speaks of the Church's "full right" in "founding and maintaining schools and institutions adapted to every branch of learning and degree of culture."[52] Later he says: "Since however the younger generations must be trained in the arts and sciences for the advantage and prosperity of civil society, and since the family itself is unequal to this task, it was necessary to create that social institution, the school."[53]

---

[50] The information in this paragraph is taken from the N.C.W.C. Domestic News Service, 8-1-55-S, pp. 6–7.

[51] Robert P. Odenwald, "Personality Development Versus Academic Achievement," *Catholic Educational Review,* LIII (April, 1955), 231.

[52] Pius XI, *Christian Education of Youth,* p. 9.

[53] *Ibid.,* p. 29.

It is clear, then, that the Christian school has to do with intellectual formation as its very function; and that this is brought about by teaching. It is not only a place essentially and immediately concerned with moral formation; it is vitally concerned with the intellectual formation needed for the full development of the Christian's personal and social life. Thus a retreat house for the students is a different place from their Catholic school; the retreat house is wholly concerned with their moral formation.

Hence the Catholic school has the immediate and primary task of contributing to the student's religious formation in Christ and of giving him intellectual formation.

It seems to the writer that there is no conflict between the attaining of these two ends, especially when one remembers the substantial, personal unity of the child. It is Tom who studies, Tom who is morally formed. He is the subject of both developments. They are not mutually exclusive as contrary ends so that attention to one necessarily excludes or lessens competence in the other. In fact, Father Donlan points out well that high moral perfection makes easier the development of the intellectual virtues.[54]

The Thomistic view generally accepted and mentioned earlier is that in practice there are no morally indifferent acts. All the human acts of a man, whatever the matter of the act, are good or bad in some degree. All those human acts concerned with intellectual formation can, by positive ordination to God, become morally good acts pertaining to the exercise and formation of the moral virtues, can be informed by charity, and therefore can contribute directly to the person's moral perfection. Thus, what in its own order is formally an intellectual act becomes in another order the matter for the exercise of moral virtue and the love of God.

Since all man's acts *de facto* will be morally good — in varying degrees — or morally bad, it is clear that in every act of the most academic program an Intellectualist could devise, man can ardently advance his moral perfection in Christ. There can be no doubt that the writing of the *Summa* not only clarified St. Thomas' knowledge of God but intensified his love of God. Christ says, "If any man will come after me, let him deny himself, and take up his cross daily, and follow me."[55] There must be no postscript "except at school" added to this daily process of following Christ. "Whether you eat or drink, or *whatsoever else you do*, do all to the glory of God"[56] [italics added]. Theorems, problems, assignments can be done not for the class prize, the "A" mark, but immediately for the glory of God, with all the thoroughness and academic excellence of which the student is capable.

---

[54] Donlan, *op. cit.*, p. 36.   [55] Lk. 9:23.   [56] 1 Cor. 10:31.

Indeed the teacher must remember efficaciously that it is more important for the student to exercise fortitude, patience, humility under the aegis of supernatural charity in this schoolwork than to produce and remember the right answer: yet there is of course no dichotomy between charity and mathematical rectitude. Holiness of the will is no justification for shoddy intellectual habits.

Schwickerath, writing of Jesuit education, says:

> It is one of the most important duties of the Society [the Jesuits] to teach all the sciences which according to our institute may be taught, in such a manner as to lead men to the knowledge and love of our Creator and Redeemer Jesus Christ.[57]

It is a vital lesson for each student to learn well at school — but few do — that we can make the ordinary things of ordinary daily life into one long chain of love for God. Holiness does not consist in initiating a special series of religious acts distinct from routine daily acts — as though moral life and daily life were parallel railway lines meeting somehow only at Sunday stops! We are not required to relinquish our academic curriculum and devote the time to courses in moral formation instead.

It is beyond our purpose here to show how this ordination and sublimation of humdrum daily life can be made.

For all these reasons this study deferentially disagrees that the stated failure of American Catholic education to produce adequate intellectual leadership would be due to overemphasis on moral training. If that failure be proven — the question is not considered here — the cause is not the emphasis on moral training. There is no opposition between high intellectual and sound moral perfection: the two perfections concern different faculties, different objects, and have different developmental conditions — intellectual perfection requires a keen intellect and extensive study, absorbing much time; moral perfection in Christ is dependent on a sincere will and the *intensity* of charity, requiring relatively a modicum time for the acts of religion. Hence they can coexist. Emphasis on one need not cause hindrance to the other.

The care for moral perfection expected of the Catholic school by the Popes will necessarily include positive training in the moral virtues and in the acts of religion according to the condition of a school and the rights of home and Church. How this training in the moral virtues can be accomplished by the school has been indicated briefly above. Some suggestions and comments regarding the acts of religion have also been noted earlier.[58] We do not pretend here to treat the "how" of this question adequately; we are concerned with the fact that it is needed and belongs by right in the school.

[57] Robert Schwickerath, *op. cit.*, p. 528.   [58] *Supra*, p. 201 ff.

We do not say that whatever can be the matter of a moral act must be dealt with directly and explicitly by the school as a part of moral training. This would be to say that the school must do everything — which is both unworkable and unnecessary.

What then is to be the norm for deciding with which moral acts the Catholic school must be concerned directly and positively? The norm is prudence. The whole matter needs a strictly prudential judgment, as will be discussed later.[59]

THE TEACHING FUNCTION OF THE SCHOOL

How is the teaching function of the Catholic school to be explained precisely? What is its relationship with home and Church? The school is a "social institution," owing its existence historically "to the initiative of the family and of the Church"; it is by its very nature "subsidiary and complementary" to the family and Church; it is united with them in a "perfect moral union" so as to form "one sanctuary of education."[60]

The teaching function of the Catholic school in relation to the Church and the home can, it seems, be explained as a quasi-instrumental relationship. We say "quasi" because here we are dealing with moral, not physical, units; therefore ironclad applicability must not be expected. This quasi-instrumental notion could well be developed at length in all its ramifications; we touch it briefly here.

An instrumental cause pertains to efficient causality.[61] An instrument, e.g., a pencil, a knife, has its own proper effect; for example, a pencil makes a line. Without this proper effect it would cease to be an instrument and would become instead a mere medium for the power of the principal cause. The instrument is moved transiently and intrinsically by a principal cause of a higher order to produce an effect surpassing its own unaided power, in such a way that the instrument is subordinated to — not merely co-ordinated with — the principal agent and *dependent* on it. If a man and a horse together push and pull a car out of a country bog, no one would say that the man, even though he does less than the horse, is an instrument of the horse, since he himself acts entirely by his own strength and receives only extrinsic aid from the horse. Man and horse are co-ordinated, not subordinated instrumentally. The proper action of the instrument, however, modifies the activity of the principal agent: thus, my hand, making the same motions, will produce ink marks or scratches on the paper according as I use pen or pin.

Hence for best effect instruments are to be used according to their

59 *Infra*, p. 236.
60 Pius XI, *Christian Education of Youth*, p. 29.
61 Cf. Phillips, *op. cit.*, II, pp. 242–244.

nature, and the better the instrument the better the effect — that is why a man calls for a good pen.

The action of the instrument is all one with the action of the principal cause since it depends on it intrinsically; hence a single effect is produced. Both the principal cause and the instrument are responsible for the whole of the effect, *totus sed non totaliter.* This Latin phrase may be rendered here as "wholly but not exclusively." Thus the pen produces every ink mark of my writing; without the pen nothing would be written on the paper. But without the writer the pen would be folded in its place, and again nothing would be written on the paper. Yet, neither the pen nor the writer produces the whole page of writing *exclusively;* this is the force of saying that the instrument produces the *whole* effect *sed non totaliter.* Notice that the two effects, ink marks and the writing, are attained *per modum unius,* that is, after the manner of a single effect. They are inseparably associated. Take away the ink mark and the written truth vanishes. These are some notions on physical instrumental causality seen in the use of a pen, chisel, hammer, or knife. These considerations cannot be applied rigorously to the relationship of school, home, Church, and State in the education of the child. But by similitude there is a certain moral instrumentality about the functioning of the Catholic school.

Human teaching is an academic human act in the natural order; it produces knowledge in another person. This is its own proper effect. Left to itself, this is all that human teaching, properly speaking, does, whatever the age of the learner or whatever the circumstances; yet, this is itself a wholly desirable end.

The Catholic school is a subsidiary of the Christian home and the Christian Church, subject to the prior rights of the family and to the permission and control of the Church;[62] it is moved, as it were, by family and Church. Its teaching, as well as operating in its own natural academic way, is accordingly elevated as a quasi-instrument in the "hands" of the movers, Church and Christian home. Thoroughly permeated with the Christian spirit, this teaching not only produces knowledge but at the same time advances the pupil toward perfection in Christ, since the academic striving can and should become the matter for acts of the infused moral and theological virtues,[63] especially of charity. Therefore, the very teaching in a Catholic school has a formality about it distinct from the teaching of a public school, no matter how academically excellent the latter may be in itself. In this way the student's academic advancement and his religious formation are fostered *per modum unius.* Thus we have the perfect moral union between Church, home, and school about which the Pope speaks.

---

[62] *Codex Juris Canonici* (Westminster, Md.: Newman Press, 1952), Canons 497, 1379, 1382.   [63] *Supra,* p. 218.

Usually the school does all the academic work, oftentimes raising the child to an achievement level far above that of this own home. (The case is on private record of a Boston gentleman, who said proudly: "My son has written a book, and I can't understand a word of it.") Yet without proper authorization, negative and positive, the Catholic school as a teaching institution could neither exist nor operate. This quality of dependence about the school's functioning is a similitude of the production of the effect in true instrumental causality, *totus sed non totaliter*. Even though the Catholic school seems to produce the whole academic effect, it does not produce that effect independently and exclusively.

Clumsy and defective instruments are of little use anywhere; hence, we want our teaching in Catholic schools to be good, the best possible in fact — just as a writer wants a good pen, and a surgeon, the best instruments.

Yet the whole function of the Catholic school in man's moral formation is not restricted to this instrumental teaching. In other respects the school serves, and legitimately so, as a direct medium for the passage of the power of the quasi-principal cause[64] — home and Church. Thus the Catholic school will give positive training in the practice of virtue, the acts of religion — prayer, the sacraments, the hearing of Mass, as already discussed. This direct moral and religious training and worship cannot strictly be called teaching. In this case the school serves as an admirable medium through which the spiritual power proper to the Church reaches the children with a special impetus.

The Catholic school, then, is not conceived as something operating apart from the home and the Church. It is "in positive accord with [these] . . . two elements" forming with them "a perfect moral union, constituting one sanctuary of education."[65]

Clearly, the Catholic school has a definite role to play in education; it must adhere to this role unswervingly. A high school, for example, must not be regarded as a convenient way of keeping students off the street, a place for occupying them pleasurably with a curriculum suitably diluted — until such time as labor laws permit them to fly out into the world of work. If students cannot or will not learn, they do not belong in a high school. If labor laws needlessly raise the age for beginning work, then it is not enough to lament the difficulty; courageous agitation must be made to modify and perfect the law. It is far less damaging for the student to begin controlled work at fourteen and a half or fifteen as his recent ancestors did and other people still do, than to waste his energy in rationalized idleness doing something

---

[64] Cf. Phillips, *op. cit.*, II, p. 244.

[65] Pius XI, *Christian Education of Youth*, p. 29. Cf. Benedict XV, *AAS*, XIV (1922), 8,

he hates, frustrating a teacher, and disrupting a class. The whole matter is a complex difficulty; but it is neither solved nor excused by inept lamenting. Educationalists, sociologists, economists need to face it energetically and systematically.

OBJECTIONS AND QUESTIONS

It may be objected that the proper and immediate end of the whole is not the proper and immediate end of each of its parts. But the school is a part of education; therefore it cannot have the same immediate end as the whole of education, namely, perfection in Christ.

There are some natural dispositions and habitudes very remotely and accidentally related to perfection in Christ whose development cannot be considered as the immediate end of the school, such as the habit of washing, shaving, etc. But these do not affect the essence of perfection with which the school is immediately concerned.

Moreover, the school is not to be conceived as a distinct part of education, not even as an integral part according to St. Thomas' usage of the term "integral."[66] The true parts of the educational process are found in the operations of the principal agencies — the Church, the home, the State. The school is a subsidiary and complementary institution in perfect moral union with the home and Church. Of itself, it is not a co-ordinate part of man's education to perfection in Christ; it is almost as inept for *Christian* formation as a pen lying on the desk for want of a principal agent to move it.

It may be asked or objected: How, then, does the Catholic school differ from a novitiate or a seminary?

Candidates in a novitiate are pursuing perfection in Christ according to a particular state of perfection, namely, the observance of the counsels — which means a special way of life and corresponding preparation for it. Hence a novitiate has its characteristic atmosphere distinct from a school, not precisely because of the essence of Christian perfection since pupil and novice are each required to seek holiness, but because of the observance of the counsels through which it is being sought.

It may be further inquired or objected: Does this concept of the school imply that all purely professional schools in the scheme of Catholic education — barbers' schools, engineering, architectural schools, etc. — be immediately concerned with Christian perfection and have moral training of the students as an immediate and principal function?

Everybody must be more concerned with being a good Christian than

---

66 Cf. *Summa,* I, q. 76, a. 8; q. 77, a. 1, ad. 1; III, q. 90, a. 3; also II-II, q. 48, a. 1.

a good barber, etc., but there is no reason why one cannot be both, as we have seen.

Nobody, nothing should waive God's plan for man's restoration in Christ. Nothing should ever interfere with its fulfillment, not even the acquisition of such technical or executive competence as would master the commerce of the whole world.[67] Therefore, nothing in such schools should be in any way inimical to the attaining of perfection in Christ.

But are such schools required to give *positive* moral training to all their students? *Per se,* no. Christian education is ordered to the perfection of man in proximate first act — to the attaining of what can analogically be called spiritual adulthood. The normal Catholic adult can be presumed to have had the spiritual training needed by and given to children,[68] can be presumed to have attained that spiritual adulthood which becomes his natural adulthood. Each professional school designed to foster in man specialized, natural skills immediately concerned with his adult livelihood is not bound to recapitulate *ab ovo* the moral training in the development of the virtues and the acts of religion normally given to children and adolescents. But the obligation is certainly on any individual among the student body who lacks such training to seek it himself, since as an adult, he is mentally mature and is self-directive toward his ends.[69]

Since, however, all the acts of man should lead him toward his perfection, directly or indirectly, such schools, as well as excluding whatever might be inimical to perfection in Christ, should in their whole tone be conducive to this end. Therefore, it is altogether desirable that the recognized images of religion be found on their walls, that the members join in corporate prayer and be mutually encouraged by good example.

Per accidens: If, pertaining to the avocation, there be some particular branch of sacred knowledge or some particular mode of Christian conduct not ordinarily developed in general Christian education, these Catholic professional schools should give this training *ex professo.* Such could be knowledge of particular moral principles affecting a profession — law, medicine, nursing, etc. — and also the virtuous conduct required in certain situations of the profession. Such training given now — and it can be given without too much difficulty — can have an extensive and immeasurable effect in later professional conduct.

Per accidens, too, it could happen in a particular specialized school that remedial religious formation may be necessary for all because of some general or regional disorder in early schooling.

Since, however, there is an endless need in Catholic action for excellent

---

[67] Cf. Mt. 16:26: "What doth it profit a man if he gain the whole world and suffer the loss of his own soul." Cf. also Mk. 8:36, 37.

[68] *Supra,* p. 143.

[69] Cf. *supra,* p. 30.

Catholics — a need partially catered for by study clubs, adult education, etc., such adult, professional schools provide an excellent opportunity for postgraduate Christian instruction and guidance. This can be given without thwarting the professional purpose of the school. In our use of such opportunities we Catholics should not be outdone in zeal and ingenuity by the Communists!

It may be asked: What does a Catholic educator think of a public school or any nonreligious school? Does he regard it as something evil of its nature, something to be despised?

No. Good teaching in public schools can foster a high level of knowledge. Good teachers and administrators can and should foster moral goodness, at least according to the natural law. The Catholic Church has been given by Christ the mandate to guard and teach the whole truth of Revelation. However, "the Church does not say that morality belongs purely, in the sense of exclusively, to her; but that it belongs wholly to her. She has never maintained that outside her fold and apart from her teaching, man cannot arrive at moral truth."[70]

We esteem and appreciate the sincerity of good teachers and administrators in the public schools, the value of the academic formation they give, the formation in the natural virtues they give. All this is thus far good, laudable, and necessary. But their very sincerity will make them appreciate our candor in saying that we regard this, though good and necessary in itself, as truncated and insufficient.

An example already mentioned will make the viewpoint clear. A certain public school carries the plaque: "The good American is kind" — with which we thoroughly agree. But a Catholic school explicitly offers its children a perfect *Exemplar,* Christ, who was infinitely kind to all and whose stimulating image can be seen on the walls. It offers more powerful *motivation* — kindness done to others is done also to Christ and merits His eternal reward as well as special peace in this life. It offers powerful *aids* to kindness — it teaches the children about the grace of God, shows them how to attain this powerful help by prayer and the sacraments, especially when an act of kindness might, naturally speaking, be very difficult to perform.

This is why we regard all natural moral training in nonreligious schools as good in itself, laudable, and necessary, but truncated. It rises no higher than man's feet of clay.

SUMMARY

We have seen that there is an issue between Catholics about the precise and essential function of the Catholic school. Some, whom for convenience we have called the Intellectualists, consider that the

---

[70] Pius XI, *Christian Education of Youth,* p. 8.

school's proximate and immediate end is to provide intellectual formation, which end, however, would be regarded as subordinate to moral perfection; in this view, cultivation of moral virtue belongs only to the integral role of the school.

It was pointed out that this interpretation of the function of the Catholic school cannot be reasonably aligned with the insistent words of Popes Pius XII, Pius XI, Pius X, and Leo XIII.

It was submitted as the clear mind of the Popes that the school has as its immediate and essential end the religious formation of the child.

The school is to seek the attainment of this moral perfection in its students by encouraging them to make their typically academic acts the matter for the exercise of the moral virtues and the love of God. It is also to give positive training in the development of the moral virtues and in the performance of the acts of religion. The norm for the extent of such moral training by the school was said to be a prudential judgment which would consider especially the school's material facilities, the staff, the needs of the child, the right of the Church, home, and State.

It was suggested briefly that the teaching function of the school, in relation to Church and home, could be developed after an analogy with instrumental causality. The answer to the objections showed that the school is more than an integral part of the education process, and differentiated the Catholic school from a novitiate and from a specialized professional school.

Implications for the Curriculum of the School

A full consideration of the curriculum of the Catholic school would be an entire study in itself. Such studies have already been made.[71] Here we can only note some of the curriculum implications that arise from the proper and immediate end of education and the role of the school.

Immediately we are faced with a semantic problem. What does "curriculum" mean? Does it designate the academic program or does it refer to all that goes on in the school in an organized or semiorganized way, from biology to working in the school bank? Writers disagree over the right terms. We bypass the disagreement: it is the concepts signified and not the labels that really matter. For convenience we speak of the instructional curriculum and the noninstructional curriculum.

---

[71] George Johnson, *The Curriculum of the Catholic Elementary School* (Washington, D. C.: The Catholic University of America, 1919). Also: James T. Cronin, *A Basic Plan for Catholic Curriculum Construction* (Washington, D. C.: The Catholic University of America, 1927).

We are concerned here only with the total content required for the fullness of education, not with the distribution of that content among elementary school, secondary school, college, and university curricula.

CURRICULUM AND TRUTH

Since Christian perfection is necessarily founded on reality and truth, the instruction program of the Catholic school must be concerned with reality and truth, independently of racial, physical, and local factors. This truth, obviously, is twofold. "Now truth, which should be the only subject-matter of those who teach, is of two kinds, natural and supernatural."[72] Obviously, every Catholic school will teach Christian doctrine with maximum emphasis. But it will also be really concerned with natural knowledge since man is lord of the universe and must live this life well so as to merit the reward of the next.

It follows that we are primarily concerned, not with mere disciplines and methods of attaining the truth, but with the truth itself. The so-called disjunction between how to think and what to think as a goal of education is unwarranted. Thinking about the best things is the best way to develop the best thinking habits. The penetration of the deepest and richest truths affords the best training in intellectual habits. Method is valid only when ordained to content. We truly need both, but the content is more important. The food is more important than the fork.

It may seem platitudinous and superfluous to say that the curriculum, the course of study, the textbooks and teaching which materialize the curriculum should be concerned with the truth about reality.

Yet schools, under pressure of an un-Christian patriotism, can garble or even warp the truth, especially in social studies.

Who won the Battle of Waterloo, 1815?

Every British schoolboy studies the Battle of Waterloo and expands an inch or two with national pride. But who was responsible for winning the Battle of Waterloo? History teachers of various countries gave this answer.

English:	Wellington
American:	Wellington
Italian:	Wellington
German:	Blücher, also Wellington
French:	Chiefly Blücher, also Wellington
Danish:	Chiefly Wellington, also Blücher
Austrian:	Wellington and Blücher equally
Norwegian:	Wellington and Blücher equally

---

[72] Leo XIII, *Libertas Praestantissimum*, 1888, trans. John J. Wynne, *The Great Encyclical Letters of Pope Leo XIII* (New York: Benziger Bros., 1903), p. 153.

Belgian: Wellington was indeed Commander-in-Chief, but he
would have lost the battle had not a Belgian general
disobeyed Wellington's order to retreat.[73]

It does not matter very much which name is credited with winning the
mighty battle, but the national emphases given by teachers are significant.
A piece of Russian garbling will come as no surprise.

Shakespeare (1564–1616) — English poet, one of the most important dramatists in world literature. Wrote his works in the age of the
rise of manufacture, of the change from feudal landownership to
wealthy bourgeoisie, the time of the beginners of English commercial
supremacy. Very highly approved by Marx and Engels.[74]

Who can deny these specific items? But who outside Russia would
call it an accurate word picture of Shakespeare!

An Italian textbook in Mussolini's time gave the impression that only
Italian explorers made the extensive geographical discoveries of the
fifteenth and sixteenth centuries. It did this by mentioning only Italian
explorers. The list included, of course, the great Italian, Cristoforo
Colombo — without mentioning the fact that he was commissioned and
financed by Spain![75]

Let us not think that such things don't happen in our democracies.

British school histories tend to garble the Hundred Years' War. Students learn about the victories at Sluys, Crécy, Poitiers, Agincourt, and
thrill to the bravery of the Black Prince and Henry V. They are not told
so clearly that England lost the whole war in flat defeat and spitefully
executed Joan of Arc in a travesty of justice! The Spanish Succession War
tends to be conveniently garbled to bolster national prestige. Textbooks
spotlight Marlborough's victories, they detail England's colonial acquisi-
tions in the Treaty of Utrecht, but they seldom make it clear that England failed to gain the central issue of the war — the Spanish succession.
Needless to say, the French histories make the point quite clear!

In a Catholic school recently a class discussion waxed warm with
indignation and patriotism about the dastardly British act in burning
Washington during the War of 1812–1814. Neither the Catholic textbook nor the teacher told the class that this was a reprisal for the
previous American burning of Newark on the Canadian Niagara and
especially of York (Toronto). Here we make no attempt to justify either
vandalism. We comment only on the selective emphasis.

Students cannot nor need be given all the details of events, but they
should not have to wait for graduate study to find out the central truth

---

[73] E. H. Dance, "Who Won the Battle of Waterloo?" *The Educational Magazine,*
The Education Department of Victoria, X (March, 1953), p. 58.
[74] *Ibid.,* p. 59.   [75] *Ibid.,* p. 58.

of events. Pope Pius XII urged Catholic teachers to foster true patriotism. True patriotism must be founded on the *truth,* including curricular truth.

CURRICULUM AND CONTENT

Because of the way man acquires his knowledge and because of the providential place given him in the universe — to be lord of the universe and to render formal glory to God, the curriculum given the educand must put him in sufficient contact with the gamut of reality and must therefore develop the skills needed for this contact. Maximum insight into reality on the part of educators will tend to produce maximum insight on the part of the student. To deplore the teaching of content or subject matter to students[76] makes as little sense as to deplore the food they are served. Such an attitude is founded on a false philosophy of reality. Their education must not exclude the study of nature in the sciences; nor should it exclude all knowledge of philosophy, even metaphysics. All the intellectual virtues should be developed. The students should have a general appreciation of the whole of reality in its higher and lower causes. The gamut of teachable truth and its hierarchical order are discussed by Vincent Smith.[77] This contact is needed in the ideal order by every man as man, independent of racial, physical, local, and environmental factors. All need it not in the same degree; nor will they have it in the same degree because of the range of individual differences. But all, whether mediocre or brilliant, should be given a curriculum of the *kind* that offers them the contact with reality that man as man should have for the integrity of his perfection in Christ. For example all high school students — according to their ability and with all the adroitness of good teaching — should be given some curricular opportunity for the study of nature through one or other of the sciences. Even the very mediocre student can grasp something of scientific reality and see in it the footprints of God. It is educationally unsound to say that those with an I.Q. of 100+ or thereabouts can take physics, and those below that level can take a course in making fudge!

It is here submitted as lamentable that students leave high school with no notion of philosophy. Their knowledge of reality has no ceiling on it. A formal program in philosophy is not necessarily required; but in those countries where a high school student is given an intensive course of four or five years in mathematics, physics, or chemistry, etc., it is hard to find a reason why Catholic students should not be given a groundwork in philosophy. They leave school exuding history or chemistry; yet have

---

[76] Cf. H. Alberty, *Reorganizing the High School Curriculum* (New York: The Macmillan Co., 1947), p. 229.
[77] Cf. Vincent Smith, *op. cit.,* pp. 42–45.

no refined notion of being, finality, causality, the ontological and logical orders, act and potency, origin of ideas, etc.

Even where this most elementary introduction to basic notions cannot formally be given in high school, the basic principles of philosophy can and should be consciously interwoven through the matter already taught so as to give the students some orientation in sound philosophy — at least to make them proof against the slick Pragmatism, Relativism, Scientism, Positivism, and Nominalism which they are already reading and hearing in radio, television, daily papers, magazines, "cultural" talks, and with which they will be imperceptibly deluged later, even though they never go to college.

Let no one say that Christian doctrine can dispense with such philosophical notions. The supernatural order does not excuse the mutilation and truncation of the natural order.

This contact with the gamut of reality must not be interpreted as justification for teaching certain details about the dregs of life. Man must submit the activity of his intellect to the extrinsic guidance of moral norms, since moral norms are the road to his true end and happiness. Nor is he thereby deprived of anything worthwhile. It is the innocent, not those bogged in the mud of life, who have the air-borne view of reality and its distant horizons.

Since man has to live his life and seek Christian perfection in a particular nation and locale, the curriculum necessarily should introduce the student to the knowledge needed for such localized life. Thus, a curriculum for the American Catholic student fittingly should include content about America not found in a curriculum for an Austrian student.

THE INSTRUCTIONAL LEVEL OF THE CURRICULUM

We have seen a general principle governing the kind of knowledge to be covered in the total curriculum of Catholic education. Desirably, all should be given a sufficient contact with the gamut of reality. What are the criteria governing the degree of curricular instruction?

The maturity of the perfection in Christ that befits the educated man requires, correspondingly, a certain mature degree in his instructional level. An eight-year-old's knowledge of the catechism may be sufficient for his salvation, but it is just that — it is minimal. This level of knowledge in a man would not entitle him to be considered an educated man, even though all the other elements of education were present in greater degree. Just as there is a certain calory, vitamin, and protein standard for normal nourishment and bodily development, there can and should be a certain instructional composition and standard for normal intellectual development and for the fullness of human life.

This does not mean that we force the subject matter on the student willy-nilly, any more than a mother throws food anyhow on the table. The food, after being chosen on dietetic standards, needs to be skillfully and tastefully prepared according to the health or sickness of the child. Likewise, intellectual pabulum needs to be skillfully adapted to the child by well-planned courses of study and tactful teaching. In teaching, as in dietetics, it is the child's welfare with which we are primarily concerned. But his intellectual welfare needs the teaching of subject matter — truth about reality — according to his personal capabilities.

The precise degree of academic instruction which becomes the well-educated Christian and which should be provided by the school curriculum is a difficult question. Its solution rests on a professional, prudential judgment considering all phases of the question — the personal and social needs of the individual now and later, the social welfare, the educational facilities, and the like.

This may seem a vague response, but human actions cannot be registered in thermometer degrees; they are regulated by prudence.

An extrinsic guide to a sound prudential judgment in this matter of the curriculum standard can be had from the judgment and success of others. If students of one country or one section of a country can ordinarily reach a higher standard in more subjects without harm to health and happiness than students of another, then it is time for the second to do some clear, basic thinking and conscience-searching. Children have a right to the best education in all its aspects — and therefore to the best curriculum content that we can give and they can absorb.

To impair the health and adjustment of children in the name of "learning" is wrong. To stunt or dilute their "learning" in the name of health and adjustment is equally wrong.

The two thousand and more students of Boston Latin School have — and can manage — six years of English, six of Latin, five of mathematics, four of history, three of French, two of German or Greek, two of general science, one of physics, and an elective for one year; all this is in a five-hour class day with up to three hours of homework. They have some twenty-eight extracurricular clubs, such as aviation, dramatics, model crafts, chess, sailing, camera, etc. They are periodic winners in tennis, golf, track, etc. It is hard to see how and why unnumbered thousands of boys and girls with equal ability in other places in the country should be denied equal curricular opportunity for cultural and vocational development, and moreover be required to do little or no private home study for the curriculum they do have. It is here submitted that the restrictions created by home study are less damaging to the physical, emotional, and certainly the spiritual health of the student than idle hours from 2:30 or 3:00 p.m. to 11:00 p.m. spent at a movie house or in front of a television set or around the town.

If Catholic high school students in some countries can carry seven or eight subjects concurrently for the first two or three years of high school and after that six or seven, with classes each day in each subject, with homework each night and Saturday morning school in one or other year — all without harm to health, it is hard to see why students in other countries cannot do likewise. Such a curriculum has diversified benefits. Students do high school work while in high school, they have less time for the idleness that leads to mischief, less money for superfluous spending, and their formal schooling is not needlessly protracted.

It is generally accepted that instruction in elementary and secondary schools is at a higher academic level in Europe than in America.[78] This means that millions of brighter children here are being deprived of the cultural formation of which they are capable at that age.

It is not enough to say that we are concerned with mental adjustment. The high ratio of mental disorders and marriage breakdowns is not a convincing proof that we are achieving notable emotional adjustment.

Nor can health be alleged. A recent study shows that American youth is markedly inferior in health to continental youth despite the best food, airiest schools, and most plentiful civilization adjuncts in the world.[79]

It will be said perhaps that we advance all or nearly all our youth to a high school level, whereas the continental countries advance only the elite. This, indeed, is an admirable feature of American education. It is most laudable to give all the opportunity of instruction; but it is not laudable to force a child to an instructional level for which he is not by natural endowment fitted. Why try to force two talents from the child whose best is only one? If he can master the initial high school work, why not let him work hard at it according to his own capacity, secure a terminal diploma — for example, an "intermediate" high school diploma after two years,[80] then leave for his world of work with some objective, academic stature, and a legitimate pride of accomplishment? From this, both the student and the school would benefit. Far better to do this than to extenuate for him one or two years of real study to four years, just to

---

[78] Cf. "Are European Children Smarter than American?" *U. S. News and World Report* (October 21, 1955), pp. 45–50.

[79] Only 8.5 per cent of the European children, but 78.3 per cent of the American children given the Kraus-Weber test for physical fitness failed the test. The percentage of American children failing two steps of the test was more than fifty times the European percentage. This was reported in the *New York State Journal of Medicine*, as quoted in the New York *Times*, Sunday Supplement, November 6, 1955, p. 17.

[80] In the state of Victoria, Australia, a certificate may be earned according to uniform state conditions and public examination at the end of second year, third year, and fourth year of high school, giving the student entry to proportionate occupations. The student may take a longer time than here mentioned to gain these certificates, but when acquired, they represent an accomplishment of objective and accepted value. The fourth-year examination passed under certain conditions entitles the student to apply for college work leading to the B.A. Such an external examination system, however, creates its own special problems.

fill out the four years — robbing the earnest, above-average students who are delayed thereby of their instructional due. By what right do we feed these latter academic popcorn instead of protein?

It is false to allege democracy as justification. If other educators think that variation of academic instruction according to native endowment is undemocratic, we know better and should act differently. Here again we should have the courage to draw conclusions from our principles and act on them. If a person's condition requires that he should reasonably receive some special or different treatment, it is not an undemocratic respect of persons to give it to him.[81] We vary penicillin, diet, or physiotherapy according to the person's condition. Why not also vary mental instruction according to natural condition? We, as Christian educators, are committed in the truest and fullest sense to reality; and the reality is that students differ in ability. To insist on feeding all the same instruction is as unrealistic as serving everybody spaghetti despite different digestive conditions. Children should be helped even at school to adjust to their individual differences and deficiencies; some day they have to meet them face to face, perhaps sharply. Christ demanded five talents of one, two of the second, one of the third. We Christian educators have no excuse for demanding two of everybody — of the student who can give more and the other who can only give less. This is why we suggest the intensified curriculum and the intermediate diploma.

VOCATIONAL TRAINING

What of vocational formation in the Catholic school curriculum? Does it belong properly in the ordinary Catholic high school? This, in its ramifications, is a big and controversial question. Here we can only propose some general norms.

1. Every Catholic high school should give its students what can be considered as the remote vocational instruction and skills. The reason is that the students are to be Catholics of today, seeking their Christian perfection in the daily world around them.[82] The school must prepare them according to its nature for that daily life. This remote preparation will include:

   a) Instruction in the natural and supernatural meaning of vocation and the states of life.

   b) A definite orientation of the content instruction to contemporary life, at least in the applications of this instruction. Even speculative truth can be shown to have daily consequences. This by no means is the equivalent of saying that we ought to teach only "practical" subjects. The manner of this orientation will vary with particular subjects. In mathematics, there seems no

81 Cf. *Summa*, I–II, q. 97, a. 4, ad 3.   82 *Supra*, p. 178 ff.

reason why even the most brilliant student would not profit
from a brief treatment somewhere in his schooling of what is
called "Consumer Mathematics."

c) The perfection of the practical intellect.

d) The general communication skills such as reading, writing, discussion, public speaking, etc. — we want our students to be able
to acquit themselves well in all situations for the service of God's
truth.

e) The development of physical co-ordination and agility, chiefly
through a judicious program of general physical education. This
program means much more than a champion football team.

f) Instruction related to general home management.

g) General safety instruction and training.

This listing is meant only as indicative, not as exhaustive.

2. It is ordinarily not the role of the Catholic high school to give
proximate, specialized avocational formation — to seek to graduate
finished machinists, radio technicians, salesmen, cooks, etc., except
where this proximate formation is little more than an advanced
degree of educational content and skill needed by all. Most industries and businesses prefer to receive a student with a sound, adequate intellectual preparation; they can soon teach him the specific
vocational skills for their own work. If the school curriculum be
intensified as suggested earlier and the intermediate diploma be
introduced, there need be little conflict between cultural and vocational learning. The best specialized training the school can give
for most occupations is maximum cultural development. Clubs, a
private hobby, and perhaps one elective can do much to prepare a
student for specialized vocational work without diluting or fore-
shortening his general cultural development in school — an opportunity that will never return.

There is no question of giving in high school the proximate training
for the professions, since these require more intellectual development than
the high school can offer.

What is to be done for the very mediocre child who also has a right
to the fullest cultural development of which he is capable?

As was pointed out, his contact with truth and reality should differ
only in degree, not in kind, from that of the others. For him the advantage of an intermediate diploma with an objective standard is perhaps
best seen. He could work to this level according to his own capacity and
speed, terminate his academic instruction there with a legitimate sense
of accomplishment and of stature, and then turn to that particularized
vocational training he has selected.

What of the subnormal or handicapped child? Here is a case for the charity of Christ that is all things to all men. Many of these require special schools, unfortunately all too few.[83] The facilities needed for physically handicapped children in a large high school are usually more administrational and architectural than curricular. There is surely no reason why the outlay of some three million dollars for a high school and the corresponding operational budget should not include a special room and at least one teacher for those children of the locality who need special education. This is no more a hindrance to sound Catholic education than a hospital is a hindrance to a housing project.

The noninstructional curriculum includes those services in the school designed to develop man in ways that are not strictly academic. It embraces religious and moral training, personality adjustment, social relations, general health — all of which have a relationship to the educand's perfection in Christ.

Of the many things which can contribute to this general development in these ways, which are to be selected for inclusion in the school?

It would be convenient to have some sort of educational litmus paper for making this decision; but it seems that no absolute, universal decision can be made. The criterion must be a prudential judgment[84] taking into account the student's objective and subjective needs, the school purpose and facilities, the rights and duties of home and Church.

From the school's purpose some norms follow. The school is primarily concerned with the spiritual formation of the students. Its special instrumentality is teaching. Both of these elements are necessary for a Catholic school, and the best Catholic school will be that which is most effective in both. The best teaching in the world without the primary concern for spiritual formation does not make a Catholic school; neither does care for moral formation without teaching — this would make a retreat house or a Catholic hostel or the like, each excellent in its own way, but not a Catholic school. At times there have been administrators who judged their teachers almost exclusively by the success of their classes in examinations. Let us hope that this species of official is now extinct. If, however, such a Cyclops still roams a campus he would do well to review his attitudes.

Whatever, then, is prejudicial to the all-important religious formation and/or to the instrumentality of teaching has no rightful place in a Catholic school. But certain additional functions judged important, relevant, and yet unprejudicial to the school's teaching role can be admitted. A chip carver, for example, may use his knife as he works to

---

[83] W. Jenks, *Directory of Catholic Facilities for Exceptional Children in the United States* (Washington, D. C.: N.C.E.A., 1955).

[84] Cf. Sister Mary Vianney, "Activities Make or Break Your School," *The Catholic Educator*, XXV (March, 1955), pp. 425–428, for a vivid description of activities run riot.

flick the chips off the tray and for other uses outside the special instrumentality of a knife — yet judiciously, making sure not to impair the knife as a knife. In this way convenience is served without deordination.

The traditional religious exercises of the Catholic school, even though they shorten the minutes that could be given to study, are not, as we have seen,[85] prejudicial to teaching.

The precautions and ordinary care for personality and social adjustment are not at all prejudicial; they too facilitate effective teaching.

But the popular movie shown in the auditorium for the football fund, the visit of the class-ring agent, the measuring for the prom tuxedos, the sale of Christmas wrappers and of tickets, the drives, the recruiting for this and that and the other — all these activities interrupt, for the sake of money-raising or of a "successful" dance or club, the quiet order needed for effective teaching and learning. They have no place *per se* during class hours, and no place *per accidens* every day!

The allocation of those activities that are legitimately associated with the school also needs a prudent judgment. Why should they not be dispatched or transacted before or after class hours? The school-bus schedule, the janitor's convenience, or overtime pay is not a proportionate reason for blunting the teaching instrumentality of the school. And if the very large central Catholic school makes this wise allocation truly impossible, then it is clearly one argument against the advisability of such schools.

The best criterion for judging the relative importance of all the things admitted into the school by this prudential judgment is their propinquity to the end, namely, perfection in Christ. For example, it is more important that Catholic children be trained to self-denial, to the love of God, to a sense of sin, to enlightened devotion at Mass, to fervent and frequent Communion than that they be trained how to make home-budgeting. With full justification, then, would a Catholic school provide the opportunity for daily Mass, frequent Communion, daily Rosary, an annual retreat — and a real retreat, not just a few talks squeezed between strenuous athletic practice.[86] With full justification, too, would a Catholic

---

[85] *Supra*, p. 199.

[86] Boarding schools of course have special opportunities, and some make excellent use of them. At Sacred Heart Convent, Ballarat East, a renowned Australian high school conducted by the Sisters of Mercy, there are currently 160 boarders and 250 day scholars. During the three-day annual retreat, as many day scholars as possible are temporarily boarded; the remainder arrive in time for the 8 a.m. Mass and leave for home at approximately 8 p.m. Naturally, a day school has limited facilities; but if some day schools can suspend class for three days, devoting the whole day from 9 a.m. to 4 p.m. to the retreat with the silence remarkably well kept, why cannot others? Experience often shows that students rise to the challenge of a retreat better than their teachers expect of them.

school require the learning and understanding of Sacred Scripture rather than of merely profane literature. With far more profit for culture and daily living would students study and memorize "I am the true Vine,"[87] St. Paul on charity and on marriage, the parable of the Prodigal, passages from the Sermon on the Mount and from the sixth chapter of St. John's Gospel, etc., rather than T. S. Eliot's *Cooking Egg* and *The Love Song of J. Alfred Prufrock.* It is hard to see how the intelligent memorization of these and similar portions of the Scripture could be psychologically unsound and educationally detrimental, especially when one considers some of the inane modern songs that teen-agers memorize. These Christian texts are the purest wellsprings of whatever is just and beautiful in human documents and associations.

Christian perfection is the essential thing to be attained; yet, "these things you ought to have done and not to leave those undone."[88] So the Curé of Ars gave the children lessons in deportment and even in table manners.[89] But a Catholic school which would underemphasize religious formation under the plea of academic or vocational needs would be neglecting its primary and essential service to youth. It would be painting cultural frescoes on walls that would collapse in eternal ruin. It is hard to see, then, by what Catholic principles a Catholic college would have the works of Anatole France on the prescribed reading list, even though all his works were condemned *nominatim* in 1922.[90] This is a warped emphasis.

If the school curriculum and services be planned prudentially according to the proper end and instrumentality of the school and emphasized according to their propinquity to that end, the desirable objectives that educators list like loose grapes in a basket will take hierarchical order and gather in bunches around the strong stems on which they depend; many of them will be seen as corollaries which will flow connaturally from attainment of the principal ends. For example, the one virtue of Christian self-denial, as well as facilitating the individual's personal development, will radically amputate the egotism and selfishness that mar social and family relations in so many diverse ways. How many particular domestic problems, present and future, would be sweetened if not solved through the cultivation of this one virtue! The same is true pre-eminently of charity in all personal relations. The virtue of charity, the queen and core of perfection in Christ, will find a thousand "desirable outcomes" not found on even the longest current list. The Catholic school, then, by seeking energetically to fulfill its essential and immediate function can simplify, co-ordinate, and subordinate the services it admits into its nonacademic curriculum.

---

[87] Jn. 15:1 *et seq.*
[88] Mt. 23:23.
[89] Trochu, *op. cit.*, p. 208.
[90] *AAS*, XIV (1922), p. 379.

SUMMARY

We have seen some implications of the proper and immediate end of education regarding the content of man's intellectual formation. For the intellectual formation that the educated man needs as man — independently of racial, national, and local circumstances — there should be, through the instruction curriculum, contact in sufficient degree with the whole gamut of reality, natural and supernatural, according to the hierarchical order of truth.

The academic curriculum of education should also give the student particular knowledge pertaining to his country and locale since he has to live his life and earn heaven as a patriotic Christian citizen.

The maturity of the perfection in Christ that becomes the educated man implies, correspondingly, a certain maturity in his intellectual formation and therefore in the instructional curriculum through which this formation is achieved. Because truth is objective, no student who lacks this maturity can be called intellectually educated; yet, always and absolutely, the capacity and condition of the individual student is the determinant of the level of intellectual attainment expected of him.

Since the student has the right to the full development of his own talent, the suggestion was made that the instructional curriculum can and should be intensified without fear of maladjustment and weakened health. The giving of a worthwhile intermediate diploma after the second year was suggested as a possible help in solving some problems associated with differences of ability and taste. It is not undemocratic to recognize real differences in ability among people and provide for them, any more than it is undemocratic to make large and small shoes.

In regard to vocational instruction in the Catholic high school, we said that the Catholic high school should give all normal students that vocational instruction and those skills that can be called remote, as well as the simpler proximate skills, since man has to come to Christian perfection in his daily life. It must never be forgotten, however, that the first, indispensable, and essential vocational preparation is that cultural development which the whole high school curriculum, geared to the gamut of reality, offers to its students.

Proximate specialized vocational skills are best and willingly given by the respective industries and businesses, or can be secured through specialized programs following the general cultural development of the intensified high school curriculum.

The nonacademic program in the Catholic school includes the student's religious and moral training, personality, adjustment, general health, etc. These pertain in varying degrees to man's perfection in Christ. The selection of activities furthering these things is to be made according to a prudential judgment. The emphasis each selected activity receives is to be gauged according to the propinquity of each to the immediate end and the teaching instrumentality of the school.

Implications for the Teacher

We have already seen many implications for the teacher, directly and indirectly. Indeed, nearly everything said concerns the teacher more or less proximately. With academic decisions to make, class problems to solve, human relationships to assess, the teacher needs to be both Solomon and Daniel; sometimes, under pressure of class, parents, principal, educational theorists, and school board, he is merely Job. We cannot here repeat whatever has been said previously and has particular relevance for the teacher; rather we specify here certain focal points on which all that has been said can and should focus for the illumination and encouragement of the teacher.

THE TEACHER'S ATTITUDE TOWARD THE CHILD

From all that has been said it is clear that the Christian teacher should have a deep, sincere respect for the child whom he teaches. He, the teacher, may be lord of the classroom if he pleases — but he should never forget the example of Christ who used His Lordship to serve, and to wash the feet of His disciples. The children before him are not merely substantial personal units; they have, or are called to, a supernature; they have a supernatural destiny. They are actual or potential members of Christ's Mystical Body. A deep conviction of this and of the related Christian truths already seen will give the teacher a basic, two-dimensional respect for the child that will remain unshaken even amid the turmoils and frustrations of daily teaching.

GENERAL ROLE OF THE TEACHER

From all that has been said it can be clearly seen that the role of the Christian teacher is many-sided.

He is a teacher of truth. He is a guide to goodness, insofar as this falls within opportunity. He is an exemplar of this goodness, one of the living ideals materializing the notion of goodness for the child and presenting a pattern of conduct for imitation. He is a symbol of authority from whom the child, consciously or unconsciously, will draw deep-seated attitudes toward all holders of authority. He is a mature friend from whom in some degree the child can gain a notion of the warmth of human relations; apart from parents, the child sees more of the teacher than of any other adult. He is a co-operator with God and the principal agencies of education in the Christian formation of this child; it is his destiny to assist in forming fit members for the Mystical Body of Christ. He is an impetrator before the throne of God, praying the Giver of all gifts to shower His grace on the souls of these students; he should pray for them because these students represent his own apostolate for the kingdom of God. The teacher, however, is powerless to *cause* goodness or grace physically, as we have seen. The weakness of human nature and the possible failure of some teachers to realize these attributes sufficiently should not prevent us from recognizing and stating the ideal of the Christian teacher.

Necessarily, the teacher must fulfill well the school's instrumentality of teaching. But always he is doing much more than teaching, and the students are learning more than mere geography or mathematics. They are developing attitudes toward the subject, the teacher, the school, life, perhaps society as such. The teacher's enthusiasm — or his boredom; his kindness and patience — or lack of it; his respect for others in legitimate differences of opinion; his thoroughness; his adherence to Christian ideals; the manner in which he blesses himself and says the opening and closing class prayers; his attitude toward God and religion — all these things are imperceptibly noticed by the student even though they remain in his mind like photographic negatives to be developed only later on, and be admired and copied. These services the teacher renders the child over and above formal teaching, which however is never to be discounted or considered casually. For the business of the teacher is to teach; this is why he has entry into the classroom and why he belongs there, according to norms discussed in treating of the work of the school. Every teacher, therefore, must prepare himself conscientiously for his work of teaching, remotely and proximately. It would be an anomaly for him to have graduated to every educational accomplishment except that of being a *teacher*. Whatever his natural gifts he needs some professional skills; otherwise, he will shamble through his class time until he learns gradually from his own needless mistakes. He also needs that proximate preparation which suits his teaching to this particular class. A negligent teacher can always "get by" the class of the moment with impunity; he will usually command silence, even if he does not receive inward respect. But that is about as far as his success extends — and survives.

All this may seem highly idealistic; in the best sense of the word, as explained earlier, it is. And if it seems platitudinous, all that has been said earlier about objective reality and truth, man's supernatural privileges and destiny, the nobility of charity, the need of grace and the power of prayer, the reward of heaven and the ruin of hell — all these notions previously developed indicate the role that awaits the truly Christian teacher.

History and hagiography provide the example of such truly great teachers. Whatever Gerson's mistakes, everyone will admire his Christian zeal in the last years of his life, when, despite liberal ridicule, he, the great man of the Paris university, assembled the children of the poor in the collegiate church of St. Paul, Lyons, and taught them for ten long years.

All that has been said points to the dignity and importance of the teacher's vocation; and the words of Pius X confirm it. Teaching is a higher charity than relieving the wants of the poor, he says.[91]

QUALIFICATIONS OF THE CHRISTIAN TEACHER

All this indicates the qualifications that should be found in every member of the staff of the Catholic school — qualifications that are intellectual and moral, natural and supernatural, emotional and professional. None of these aspects can be overlooked. Again we say that the business of the teacher is to teach in the highest sense of that term; but he does much more than teach. Hence it is important that he be truly qualified and formed as a mature Christian, if he is to be entrusted with the Christian formation of the young.

THE TEACHER AND DISCIPLINE

The matter of discipline and "authoritarianism" is much discussed; it is too long for full consideration here.

Fearful things have been done in the classroom in the name of discipline and sometimes have been protected with the prestige of religion. Nor have these things been confined to the old Calvinist dominies. Temporary excesses are always lamentable; they serve at least to illustrate the frailties of human nature — even in an educated adult! But *habitual* thrashing with metal-knobbed walking sticks, brutal caning punctuated with ironic comments, severe facial blows, boastful displays of mass punishment, and all such incredible devices and aberrations of sadistic, egoistic, distorted personalities that were somehow installed behind a desk and *were left there* — these things do not belong in a Christian school or in sane human relations. This is not a loving extension of the guiding arm of the Great Teacher and Good Shepherd!

Yet we say unhesitatingly that the teacher must create and preserve discipline and adherence to valid norms. This follows basically from what has been said of the objective mode of our co-operation with Christ, of obedience as a prime law of life, and of the need for man to prune the rank outgrowths of his fallen nature. But, obviously, it will be a Christian discipline with a quality of the Sacred Heart in it.

In regard to this discipline, teachers and counselors should remember well the words of Holy Scripture:

---

[91] Pius X, *Acerbo Nimis,* Yzermans, *op. cit.,* p. 50.

If, when I say to the wicked, Thou shalt surely die: thou declare it not to him, that he may be converted from his wicked way, and live: the same wicked man shall die in his iniquity, but I will require his blood at thy hand. But if thou give warning to the wicked, and he be not converted from his wickedness, and from his evil way: he indeed shall die in his iniquity, but thou hast delivered thy soul.[92]

Since students are rational beings, self-directive toward their proper ends through good habits, future responsible citizens with the privileges and the obligations of freedom, we must indeed train them to self-responsibility, self-direction, and to the reasonableness of law, order, and right. It is better for them to make their mistakes and partially misuse their freedom in the corrective atmosphere of the school than to make more serious mistakes later. No one need be deceived by the ironclad "order" and pulverized "obedience" of the martinet's school or classroom.

Yet, at the same time, the young must be trained to respect for proper authority as such, even where they have no voice in its mandates and no understanding of all the reasons involved. The unperceived reasonableness is to be presumed in the proper authority, because all legitimate authority is from God. Since obedience to God is a prime law of life as we have noted, students, and indeed all must submit to the iron of obedience. Therefore, we must be careful lest we camouflage all obedience and discipline in school or home with psychological or democratic paint. Students must learn the reasonableness of obeying proper, but easily approached, authority as such. Here, as in so many issues, educators must navigate between Scylla and Charybdis.

THE TEACHER AND TRUTH

From all that has been said, it follows that the teacher's emphasis should be placed on the students' attainment of the truth, rather than on their search for it. Searching about for the right train only has value insofar as it leads one to find the right train in time. Only the finding of the truth gives research its raison d'être. No one denies the need of research attitudes and skills; but always it must be remembered that these are only means to an end, namely, the discovery of more truth. Hence, a Catholic teacher must be more concerned to have his pupils possess the truth than to be running around looking for it.

One has the impression that some educators think otherwise. Relativists of course do not believe in any real truth to be found. Some of those who do believe seem to think, perhaps unwittingly, that to teach the whole truth as they see it will somehow exhaust the truth too soon for the student! Others, forgetting the mind's invisible but dynamic, immanent

---

92 Ezech. 3:18, 19.

activity, seem to think that it would be an incentive to sloth to unveil the whole truth, as they see it, for their pupils. They forget what philosophy has to say about the mind's immanent activity. They forget that St. Thomas himself could not have written the *Summa Theologica* had he not been able to climb the pedestals of Aristotle, Augustine, Peter Lombard, Albert, and others, and from their eminence leap even higher into the transcendental realm. They forget, too, the proverb which says that the larger the circle of light, the bigger the fringe of darkness.

The Christian teacher will not, then, regard good teaching as somehow ignoble, unprofessional, and prejudicial to the best interests of the students. He will not make his students search and flounder as though they had no teacher — this is unsound pedagogy, built on a false philosophy of reality. Whatever teaching techniques he uses — lecture, demonstration lecture, problem method, case study, socialized methods, he will be more concerned with having his students understand and apply the truth than merely search for it. He will lead them to its possession as rapidly and solidly as possible. He will make that possession *dynamic*.

It would be false to interpret all this as a plea for sterile lengthy dictation — a practice still not extinct, unhappily — or for mere spoon-feeding in any of its forms. But it certainly is a criticism of that teacher who would do little more than hand his class a bibliography.

SUMMARY

Clearly, the teacher has a vital place in education. Everything said so far concerns him directly or indirectly, proximately or remotely.

The teacher must have a deep Christian respect for the child he teaches.

His role is many-sided; principally, he must be concerned with the child's religious development, and he must fulfill ably and conscientiously the school's teaching instrumentality. May our youth be spared from teachers who cannot teach!

The teacher must create and maintain Christian discipline, by which the student's character will be pruned and made fruitful in supernaturalized living.

The Christian teacher should be more concerned about having his pupils attain the truth than merely search for it.

Implications for Parents

All that has been said about the child's perfection in Christ — its details, its ramifications, its attainment — concerns the parents directly since nature itself gives them a mandate to rear and educate their offspring. Parents should show an active, unceasing, constructive interest in the child's Christian education. Hence, to consider the implications for parents adequately would be to reconsider the whole treatment. Here we merely note some points of prime importance.

The family has the right and duty of education. By nature the child is something of the father and mother;[93] by nature it is dependent on them before and during the development of its reason; by nature a child looks to its parents for all the care it needs and, conversely, good parents naturally desire the fullest and best care for the child they have begotten. This is a truism. They who gave the child existence have the natural duty and right of perfecting that existence; and this includes education.

The family's right is "anterior to any right whatever of civil society and of the State."[94] This follows from the above. The child enters this world through the family.

This right of the family is inalienable[95] because the fact of parenthood is indestructible and ineffaceable. Parents may delegate their right but never relinquish it. Where this right of education is partially delegated — as it usually is in modern society, parents still have the duty and right of such supervision as is prudentially necessary. The degree of this supervision will of course vary according to the circumstances of the particular school the child is attending. Generally speaking, the parents act prudently in leaving professional pedagogical matters to the trained staff. But the principle is clear. With full right, then, do parents choose a school for their child. With full right do parents step actively into some school issue when they honestly feel that the good of the child demands it; and school administrators can never rightfully resent such active interest, at least in principle. The parental visit is never something to be merely tolerated. In a large school this could become an administrative problem; it is never an encroachment. Nor is this active interest merely to be confined to the raising of money. Its primary aim is nothing else than the end of education itself; since the parent has from nature the anterior, inalienable right and duty of educating the child to perfection in Christ.

A postscript about the parental choice of school is in place. Parents should make this choice according to Christian standards. These will flow from all that has been said earlier and will be reducible to this general norm: Parents should, according to their circumstances, select that school where their children can best attain the proper and immediate end of education — perfection in Christ. No number of accidental gains could balance an essential loss. It would be an un-Christian, materialistic parent who would jeopardize the child's faith or morals for the sake of an "old school tie" and its open-sesame to society doors. If, because of some true necessity, a less desirable choice must be made, proportionate effort must

---

93 *Summa*, II–II, q. 10, a. 12.
94 Pius XI, *Christian Education of Youth*, p. 12.
95 *Ibid.*

also be made to counterbalance any deficiency; and this effort is binding in conscience. St. John Chrysostom's words were written more than fifteen centuries ago but their truth is timely because thoroughly Christian.

> We ought not to send children to schools where they will learn vice before they learn science, and where in acquiring learning of relatively small value, they will lose what is far more precious, their integrity of soul. . . . Are we then to give up literature? . . . I do not say that; but I do say that we must not kill souls. . . . When the foundations of a building are sapped we should seek rather for architects to reconstruct the whole edifice, than for artists to adorn the walls. In fact, the choice lies between two alternatives; a liberal education which you may get by sending your children to the public schools, or the salvation of their souls which you secure by sending them to the monks. Which is to gain the day, science or the soul? If you can unite both advantages, do so by all means; but if not, choose the most precious.[96]

The typical Catholic school unites both advantages admirably.

Since the end is the guide and measure of the means, the whole educational process will be affected by the proper and immediate end, namely, perfection in Christ.

We have considered some of the implications of this end for educational theory, moral formation, the school, the curriculum, the teacher, and parents. These ideas are necessarily general; they are nevertheless dynamic, and their practical consequences are innumerable. The practical power of an idea, however, is proportioned to the power of the mind it inhabits. The same idea can rot or flower in different minds.

---

[96] From A. T. Drane, *Christian Schools and Scholars* (London: Burns, Oates & Washbourne, Ltd., 1924), p. 20.

CHAPTER VIII

SUMMARY AND CONCLUSIONS

WE CANNOT summarize all the notions and applications introduced into this study; rather, we shall indicate briefly the general line of treatment.

The purpose of this book was to examine closely the proper and immediate end of education, considered in itself and in its principal ramifications.

We considered the notion and validity of finality, and saw that educational motivation is basically the operation of finality. We saw that man, as a free agent and self-directive toward his end, should be brought gradually to the recognition of the proper ends of activity as such if he is to be educated according to his nature; we saw that mere knowledge of the end, although a condition *sine qua non*, is not enough to stimulate man's activity toward his proper ends. He must be stimulated to see the end as something good and *befitting him* in some way. From all these points made in analyzing the end, we saw clearly the paramount importance in education of an end clearly perceived and efficaciously desired, becoming thereby the guide, measure, and norm of the educational means thereto.

We considered the ultimate end which every man in every human action seeks, at least virtually. We saw that the true, objective ultimate end is the same for all men and can only be one, even though individuals seek various false ultimate ends — external goods, goods of the body, created goods inhering in the soul. This one, objective, absolute ultimate end is the Uncreated Good, namely God; and, indeed, by a wholly gratuitous gift, God as the Author and End of the supernatural order. There is, *de facto*, no other ultimate end. ALL MEN must attain this end, or fail eternally and irreparably. Hence, the paramount importance of true Christian education, which is intimately and necessarily connected with the pursuance of this end.

"Proper and immediate" was seen to be a consideration of the end from two viewpoints: "proper" indicating that this is an end *per se* and not *per accidens* — not merely accidental or accessory; "immediate" indicating the proximity between the agent and the end. The "proper and immediate end of education" was said to be that end which education, conceived as a total process, should attain *per se* and *proximately* without the mediation of another end in the same series.

Various opinions about the proper and immediate end of education, insofar as they approximate to this delimited notion of end, show considerable variety, yet a certain over-all unity — if naturalism in its many forms can be considered as "unity." All purely naturalistic ends are clearly unacceptable. Evolutionary self-development, natural social efficiency, the "essentials" of culture garnered as the working conclusions of social experience, the mastery of "scientific" reality, so-called ethical formation even where perhaps it culls some of the truths of objective Revelation — all such aims are inadequate as the proper and immediate end of education.

From the words of the Popes, it was seen that the formation of the true and perfect Christian constitutes this proper and immediate end of education.

We examined the elements, historical and analytic, of God's plan for our perfection in Christ. In analyzing some aspects of perfection in Christ, we found that its bond and core is charity — the supernatural love of God and neighbor. We saw that the precept of charity is without limit, yet is sufficiently fulfilled — so as to avoid a transgression — if nothing else is loved more than God or equally with God. The precept requires, however, that we at least desire what is best. Charity above all is to be fostered in the educand if he is to attain perfection in Christ. We considered the motive, the source, the mode, the measure, the means of the increase of charity — and the penalty of its loss. We also saw that every child — Catholic, non-Catholic, pagan — is called to this perfection in Christ, but in different senses of "call." The accurate understanding of these points underscores the dignity and increases the fruits of education.

Man's active co-operation with God's plan for the attainment of perfection in Christ was seen and considered closely, though briefly, as one of the elements in our restoration in Christ. We saw that this co-operation was absolutely required, that it had an objective and subjective mode. We detailed man's equipment, natural and supernatural, for this co-operation. Only when one examines at some detail this natural and supernatural equipment does one really appreciate the richness and variety of man's potential for the self-activity required in his co-operation with God.

We noted also the congruity of Christian perfection as the proper and immediate end of education: it is a self-perfection; it involves self-activity, even of the highest order, namely, immanent activity; it involves the development of the whole man in all his powers, especially his intellect;

it necessarily involves contact with reality, including contemporary realities; it is truly ennobling. In considering the objections, we saw further
that such a notion of the end of education is not anti-intellectual, does
not reduce education to a study of theology, nor pedagogy to the principles of ascetical theology; neither is this concept of education too
idealistic.

We then considered some philosophical aspects of Christian perfection
as the proper and immediate end of education. The true Christian is
the *finis effectus* of the work of education conceived as a total process;
but in the minds of educators, and of students according to their maturity,
this should be clearly and definitely sought as a *finis cuius gratia*. The
definition was proposed and explained: Education as a total process
is the passive and active development, in first proximate act, of the
Christian perfection of man in all his powers, natural and supernatural,
whereby he is constituted maturely self-directive toward his final end.
As a state, whereby we say that someone is an educated man, education
is the Christian perfection of man, essentially and integrally, in second act.

Various implications of the proper and immediate end were elaborated,
chiefly in regard to educational theory, moral formation of the child,
the school, the curriculum, the teacher, the parents. In regard to the
school, we considered the precise function of the school in the scheme
of education; we also proposed a norm for deciding which things are to
be admitted into the curriculum of the school and which excluded.

Magna est veritas et praevalebit.

Man with his burning soul
Has but an hour of breath
To build a ship of Truth
In which his soul may sail,
Sail on a sea of death,
For death takes toll
Of beauty, courage, youth,
Of all but Truth.[1]

With truth will survive supernatural charity, which is the bond of perfection in Christ, who is Himself the Truth.

---

[1] John Masefield, "Truth," *Poems* (London: William Heinemann, Ltd., 1946),
p. 277.

BIBLIOGRAPHY

Books

Aertnys-Damen, *Theologia Moralis*, 2 vols. (Rome: Marietti, 1950).
Alberty, H., *Reorganizing the High School Curriculum* (New York: The Macmillan Co., 1947).
Alexander, Anthony F., *College Apologetics* (Chicago: Henry Regnery Co., 1954).
Ambrose, St., *De Virginitate.*
—— *Expositio Evangelii Secundum Lucam.*
Aquinas, St. Thomas, *Commentary on the Sentences.*
—— *Contra Gentiles.*
—— *De Perfectione Vitae Spiritualis.*
—— *De Veritate.*
—— *The Division and Methods of the Sciences*, trans. Armand Maurer (Toronto: The Pontifical Institute of Medieval Studies, 1953).
—— *Expositio in Librum Aristotelis de Somno et Vigilia.*
—— *Expositio in 10 Libros Ethicorum Aristotelis ad Nichomachum.*
—— *Expositio in 12 Libros Metaphysicorum Aristotelis.*
—— *In Epistolam ad Romanos.*
—— *Quaestiones Disputatae.*
—— *Summa Theologica.*
Aristotle, *De Anima.*
Augustine, St., *In Epistolam ad Parthos.*

Bagley, W. C., *Educational Values* (New York: The Macmillan Co., 1915).
—— *Education and the Emergent Man* (New York: Thomas Nelson and Sons, 1934).
Belloc, Hilaire, *Europe and the Faith* (New York: The Paulist Press, 1920).
Billot, Louis, *De Virtutibus Infusis* (Rome: Gregorian University, 1921).
Bittle, Celestine N., *The Domain of Being* (Milwaukee: The Bruce Publishing Co., 1939).
Bobbitt, F., *How to Make a Curriculum* (Boston: Houghton Mifflin Co., 1924).
Boyer, C., *Cursus Philosophiae*, 2 vols. (Bruges: Desclée Co., 1939).
Boylan, E., *This Tremendous Lover* (Westminster, Md.: The Newman Bookshop, 1947).
Brameld, Theodore, *Patterns of Educational Philosophy* (Yonkers on Hudson, N. Y.: World Book Co., 1950).
Breed, F. S., *Education and the New Realism* (New York: The Macmillan Co., 1939).
Butler, *Lives of the Saints*, ed. H. Thurston and D. Attwater, 12 vols. (London: Burns, Oates & Washbourne, Ltd., 1934).

The Catechism of the Council of Trent.
Cayre, F., *Manual of Patrology* (Paris: Desclée & Co., 1936).

Cicognani, Amleto G., *Canon Law* (2nd. ed. rev., Westminster, Md.: The Newman Bookshop, 1934).
Clark, H., and McKillop, A., *An Introduction to Education* (New York: Chartwell House, Inc., 1951).
Codex Iuris Canonici (Westminster, Md.: Newman Press, 1952).
Coerver, R. F., *The Quality of Facility in the Moral Virtues* (Washington, D. C.: The Catholic University of America Press, 1946).
Cole, Luella, *Psychology of Adolescence* (New York: Rinehart and Co., Inc., 1954).
Cronin, James T., *A Basic Plan for Catholic Curriculum Construction* (Washington, D. C.: The Catholic University of America Press, 1927).
Cronin, John F., *Catholic Social Principles* (Milwaukee: The Bruce Publishing Co., 1950).
Crow, L. D., and Crow, A., *Introduction to Education* (New York: American Book Co., 1950).
Cubberly, E. P., *Syllabus of Lectures on the History of Education* (New York: The Macmillan Co., 1904).

Deferrari, Roy J. (ed.), *Integration in Catholic Colleges and Universities* (Washington, D. C.: The Catholic University of America Press, 1950).
Deferrari, Roy J., Barry, Sister M. Inviolata, and McGuiness, Ignatius, *A Lexicon of St. Thomas* (Washington, D. C.: The Catholic University of America Press, 1949).
De Guibert, J., *The Theology of the Spiritual Life*, trans. P. Barrett (London: Sheed & Ward, 1954).
De Liguori, St. Alphonsus, *Opera Dogmatica*, 2 vols. (Rome: Philippi Cuggiani, 1903).
Denzinger, Henry, *et al.*, *Enchiridion Symbolorum Definitionum et Declarationum* (29th ed., Friburgi: Herder & Co., 1953).
Dewey, J., *Democracy and Education* (New York: The Macmillan Co., 1916).
─────── *My Pedagogic Creed* (New York: Kellogg & Co., 1897).
─────── *Reconstruction in Philosophy* (New York: Henry Holt and Co., 1920).
DeYoung, Chris. A., *Introduction to American Public Education* (New York: McGraw-Hill Book Co., 1950).
Donlan, Thomas C., *Theology and Education* (Dubuque, Iowa: Wm. C. Brown Co., 1952).
Drane, A. T., *Christian Schools and Scholars* (London: Burns, Oates & Washbourne, Ltd., 1924).

Falanga, A. J., *Charity the Form of the Virtues According to St. Thomas* (Washington, D. C.: The Catholic University of America Press, 1948).
Farrell, Walter, *A Companion to the Summa*, 3 vols. (New York: Sheed & Ward, 1939).
Farrell, W., and Healy, M., *My Way of Life* (Brooklyn, N. Y.: Confraternity of the Precious Blood, 1952).
Felder, H., *Christ and the Critics*, trans. J. L. Stoddard (London: Burns, Oates & Washbourne, Ltd., 1924).
Francis de Sales, St., *Introduction to the Devout Life*, trans. J. K. Ryan (Garden City, N. Y.: Image Books, 1955).

Gabriel, Fr., *St. John of the Cross* (Cork: The Mercier Press, 1946).
Garrigou-Lagrange, R., *Christian Perfection and Contemplation According to St. Thomas Aquinas and St. John of the Cross*, trans. Sister Timothea Doyle (St. Louis: B. Herder Book Co., 1937).
Gilleman, Gerard, *Le Primat de la Charité en Théologie Morale* (Paris: Desclée de Brouwer et Cie, 1952).
Gredt, J., *Elementa Philosophiae*, 2 vols. (Friburgi: Herder & Co., 1937).
Grenier, Henry, *Thomistic Philosophy*, trans. J. P. O'Hanlon, 4 vols. (Charlottetown, Canada: St. Dunstan's University, 1950).

Harvey, R. J., *The Metaphysical Relation Between Person and Liberty* (Washington, D. C.: The Catholic University of America Press, 1942).
Hoban, J. H., *The Thomistic Concept of Person and Some of Its Social Implications* (Washington, D. C.: The Catholic University of America Press, 1939).
Hughes, A. G., and Hughes, E. H., *Learning and Teaching* (London: Longmans, Green and Co., 1948).
Hugon, E., *Cursus Philosophiae Thomisticae*, 3 vols. (Paris: P. Lethielleux, 1936).

Janssen, Johannes, *History of the German People at the Close of the Middle Ages*, 16 vols. (London: Kegan Paul, Trench, Trübner and Co., 1896).
Jenks, W., *Directory of Catholic Facilities for Exceptional Children in the United States* (Washington, D. C.: National Catholic Educational Association, 1955).
John of St. Thomas, *Cursus Philosophicus Thomisticus*, 3 vols. (Turin, Italy: Marietti, 1933).
Johnson, George, *The Curriculum of the Catholic Elementary School* (Washington, D. C.: The Catholic University of America Press, 1919).

Kennedy, David, *Towards a University* (Belfast: The Catholic Dean of Residences, 1946).
Kilpatrick, William H., *Philosophy of Education* (New York: The Macmillan Co., 1951).

Lebreton, J., and Zeiller, J., *L'Eglise Primitive*, Vol. I of *Histoire de l'Eglise*, ed. A. Fliche & V. Martin, 24 vols. (Paris: Bloud & Gay, 1946).
Le Buffe, Francis P., *Let's Look at Sanctifying Grace* (St. Louis: The Queen's Work Publication, 1944).
Lee, Gordon C., *An Introduction to Education in America* (New York: Henry Holt & Co., 1952).
Lerhinan, John P., *A Sociological Commentary on "Divini Redemptoris"* (Washington, D. C.: The Catholic University of America Press, 1946).
Lewis, C. S., *De Descriptione Temporum* (Cambridge, England: Cambridge University Press, n.d.).
——— *Surprised by Joy: The Pattern of My Early Life* (London: Geoffrey Bles, 1955).
Lueck, William R., *An Introduction to Teaching* (New York: Henry Holt and Co., 1953).
Lynd, A., *Quackery in our Public Schools* (Boston: Little, Brown and Co., 1953).

Maquart, F. X., *Elementa Philosophiae*, 3 vols. (Paris: Andreas Blot, 1938).
Marique, Pierre J., *History of Christian Education*, 3 vols. (New York: Fordham University Press, 1926).
Maritain, J., *A Preface to Metaphysics* (New York: Sheed & Ward, 1948).
────── *The Rights of Man and the Natural Law* (New York: C. Scribner's Sons, 1943).
Marx, Karl, *Capital* (New York: Carlton House, 1932).
Masefield, John, *Poems* (London: William Heinemann, Ltd., 1940).
McCormick, Patrick, and Cassidy, Francis P., *History of Education* (3rd ed. rev., Washington, D. C.: The Catholic Education Press, 1953).
McKeon, Richard (ed.), *The Basic Works of Aristotle* (New York: Random House, 1941).
Migne, J. P., *Patrologiae, Cursus Completus* (Parisiis, 1844, seq.).
Moore, T. V., *Cognitive Psychology* (Chicago: J. B. Lippincott Co., 1939).

Newman, John H., *The Idea of a University* (London: Longmans, Green and Co., 1902).

O'Brien, John, *Around the Boree Log* (Sydney: Angus and Robertson, 1921).
O'Hara, James, *Limitations of the Educational Theory of John Dewey* (Washington, D. C.: The Catholic University of America Press, 1929).

Parente, P., Piolanti, A., and Garofalo, S., *Dictionary of Dogmatic Theology*, trans. E. Doronzo (Milwaukee: The Bruce Publishing Co., 1951).
Phillips, R. P., *Modern Thomistic Philosophy*, 2 vols. (Westminster, Md.: Newman Bookshop, 1935).
Prat, Fernand, *The Theology of St. Paul*, trans. John L. Stoddard, 2 vols. (London: Burns, Oates & Washbourne, Ltd., 1927).

Redden, J., and Ryan, F., *A Catholic Philosophy of Education* (Milwaukee: The Bruce Publishing Co., 1951).
Reid, John Patrick, *St. Thomas Aquinas on the Virtues* (Providence, R. I.: Providence College Press, 1951).
Renard, H., *The Philosophy of Being* (Milwaukee: The Bruce Publishing Co., 1943).
────── *The Philosophy of Man* (Milwaukee: The Bruce Publishing Co., 1951).
Rogers, Carl, *Client-Centered Therapy* (Boston: Houghton Mifflin Co., 1951).

Sacrae Theologiae Summa, 4 vols. (Madrid: B.A.C. 1952).
Sandifer, Sister Mary Ruth, *American Lay Opinion of the Progressive School* (Washington, D. C.: The Catholic University of America Press, 1943).
Scheeben, Matthias, *The Glories of Divine Grace*, trans. Patrick Shaughnessy (St. Meinrad, Ind.: Grail Press, 1952).
Schwickerath, Robert, *Jesuit Education: Its History and Principles* (St. Louis: B. Herder Book Co., 1904).
Sheehan, M., *Apologetics and Catholic Doctrine* (rev. ed., Dublin: M. H. Gill and Son, Ltd., 1924).
Sheen, Fulton J., *Philosophy of Science* (Milwaukee: The Bruce Publishing Co., 1934).

Smith, M., *The Diminished Mind* (Chicago: Henry Regnery Co., 1954).
Smith, W., and Hall, T., *English-Latin Dictionary* (New York: American Book Co., 1871).
Spencer, H., *Education: Intellectual, Moral, and Physical* (New York: D. Appleton and Co., 1886).
Stevenson, B. E., *Home Book of Verse*, 2 vols. (New York: Henry Holt and Co., 1940).
Stoddard, J. L., *Rebuilding a Lost Faith* (New York: P. J. Kenedy & Sons, 1923).

Tanquerey, Ad., *Brevior Synopsis Theologiae Dogmaticae* (9th ed. Paris: Desclée & Co., 1949).

VanderVeldt, James H., and Odenwald, Robert P., *Psychiatry and Catholicism* (New York: McGraw-Hill Book Co., Inc., 1952).

Walsh, J. J., *The History of Nursing* (New York: P. J. Kenedy & Sons, 1929).
────── *The Thirteenth, The Greatest of Centuries* (2nd ed., New York: Catholic Summer School Press, 1909).
Webster's New Collegiate Dictionary, 2nd ed., 1953.
Wynne, John J., *The Great Encyclical Letters of Pope Leo XIII* (New York: Benziger Brothers, 1903).

Yzermans, Vincent A., *All Things in Christ* (Westminster, Md.: Newman Press, 1954).

Public Documents

Benedict XV, *Letter to Fr. Bernadot*, O.P., *AAS*, XIII (1921).
Leo XIII, *Libertas Praestantissimum*, June 20, 1888, *Acta Sanctae Sedis*.
────── *Providentissimus Deus*, November 18, 1893, *Acta Sanctae Sedis*.
────── *Sapientiae Christianae:* "On the Chief Duties of Christians as Citizens," January 10, 1890, *Acta Sanctae Sedis*.
Pius X, *Acerbo Nimis*, April 15, 1905, *Acta Sanctae Sedis*.
────── *Ad Diem Illum*, February 2, 1904, *Acta Sanctae Sedis*.
────── encyclical, *Editae Saepe* for tercentenary of St. Charles Borromeo, May 26, 1910, *AAS*.
────── *Iucunda Sane*, letter for the thirteenth centenary of St. Gregory, March, 1904, *Acta Sanctae Sedis*.
Pius XI, *Christian Education of Youth* (Washington, D. C.: N.C.W.C., 1936; encyclical, *Divini Illius Magistri*, December 31, 1929.
────── *Christian Marriage*, December 31, 1930, *AAS*, XXII (1930).
────── *Divini Redemptoris*, *AAS*, XXIX (1937); translated in *The Ecclesiastical Review*, XCVI (1937).
────── *Mit Brennender Sorge*, *AAS*, XXIX (1937).
────── *Rerum Omnium Perturbationem*, *AAS*, XV (1923).
────── *Ubi Arcano Dei*, December 23, 1922, *AAS*, XIV (1922).
────── *Umbratilem*, *AAS*, XVI (1924).

Pius XII, letter declaring St. John Baptist De La Salle Patron of Schoolmasters, *AAS,* XLII (May, 1950).

————— address to the Union of Italian Teachers, September 4, 1949, translated in *Catholic Action,* XXXI (October, 1949).

————— "Counsels to Teaching Sisters," September 13, 1951, *AAS,* XLIII (1951).

————— "El Especialisimo Amor," *AAS,* XLVI (1954), translated in *The Pope Speaks,* I (First Quarter, 1954).

————— *Mediator Dei,* Vatican Library translation (Washington, D. C.: N.C.W.C., 1948).

————— encyclical, *Mystici Corporis,* translation (Washington, D. C.: N.C.W.C.).

————— *Nuntius Radiophonicus,* March 23, 1952, "The Right Formation of Christian Conscience in Youth," *AAS,* XLIV (1952).

Unpublished Material

Collins, Russel J., "The Metaphysical Basis of Finality in St. Thomas," unpublished Ph.D. dissertation, School of Philosophy, The Catholic University of America, 1947.

Endres, Sister Agnes, "The Educational Philosophy of Herman Harrell Horne," unpublished M.A. thesis, Department of Education, The Catholic University of America, Washington, D. C., 1934.

Everett, L. P., "The Primacy of the Virtue of Wisdom," unpublished M.A. thesis, The Catholic University of America, 1942.

Hannan, James A., "An Investigation of the Applicability of St. Thomas Aquinas' Treatment of the Gifts of the Holy Ghost to High School Religion Courses," unpublished M.A. thesis, The Catholic University of America, 1945.

Poggi, James, "The Gifts of the Holy Ghost and Their Implications for Education," unpublished M.A. thesis, Department of Education, The Catholic University of America, 1955.

Sheehan, Sister M. F., "Cultural Content of the High School French Curriculum," unpublished M.A. thesis, Department of Education, The Catholic University of America, 1937.

Solari, Frank J., "An Analysis of the Aims of Catholic Colleges for Men As Expressed in Their Catalogues," unpublished M.A. thesis, Department of Education, The Catholic University of America, 1953.

Tos, Aldo J., "Finality and Its Implications for Education," unpublished M.A. thesis, Department of Education, The Catholic University of America, 1955.

Reports

Harvard Report, *General Education in a Free Society* (Cambridge, Mass.: Harvard University Press, 1945).

Report of the President's Commission on Higher Education, *Higher Education for American Democracy* (New York, 1946).

Articles

Anderson, G. Lester, "Unsolved Problems in Teacher Education," *The American Association of Colleges for Teacher Education; Third Yearbook,* (1950).

Barry, William, "Calvin," *Catholic Encyclopedia,* Vol. III (1912).

Baumeister, E. J., "Whither High School Latin," *Catholic Educational Review,* XLI (1943).

Benard, Edmond O., "Theology as Pivotal: Newman's View," *Integration in Catholic Colleges and Universities,* ed. Roy J. Deferrari (Washington, D. C.: The Catholic University of America Press, 1950).

Dance, E. H., "Who Won the Battle of Waterloo?" *The Educational Magazine,* The Education Department of Victoria, X (March, 1953).

Ellis, John Tracy, "American Catholics and the Intellectual Life," *Thought,* XXX (1955).

Fenton, Joseph C., "The Doctrinal Authority of Papal Encyclicals," *American Ecclesiastical Review,* CXXI (1949).

Garrigou-Lagrange, R., "Subordination of the State to the Perfection of Man According to St. Thomas," *The Philosophy of Communism* (New York: Fordham University Press, 1949).

McGahan, F. P., "Presentation, Order of the — Nagle, Nano," *Catholic Encyclopedia,* Vol. XII (1912).

Motte, A., "The Obligation to Follow a Vocation," *Vocation* (London: Blackfriars Publications, 1952).

Odenwald, Robert P., "Personality Development Versus Academic Achievement," *Catholic Educational Review,* LIII (April, 1955).

O'Leary, T. F., "Philosophical Concepts of the Moral Virtues as Means to an End in Education," *American Catholic Philosophical Association: Proceedings* (1949).

Smith, Vincent E., "The Catholic School: A Re-examination," *Bulletin,* LII (August, 1955) (Washington, D. C.: N.C.E.A.).

Time, Vol. LXVI, No. 21, November 21, 1955.

Times, New York, "The Muscular State of the Union," Sunday Supplement (November 6, 1955).

U. S. News and World Report, "Are European Children Smarter Than American?" (October 21, 1955).

Valentine, P. F., "Progressive Education — A Defence," *The Educational Forum,* V (1941).

Vianney, Sister Mary, "Activities Make or Break Your School," *The Catholic Educator* (March, 1955).

Whitman, Howard, "The Struggle for Our Children's Minds: Our Schools — Afraid to Teach," *Colliers* (March 19, 1954).

INDEX

DISCIPLINE
  fear and license, 197
  graded, 143
  need for Christian, 41
  pupil motivation, 131
  and self-purification, 112
DIVINE ADOPTION
  differs from human adoption, 85
  formal effect of grace, 159
  proof of, 84
DIVINE CONCURSUS, 161
DIVINE INDWELLING, 84
DIVISION
  need for, 33
DOGMA, 199 f
DONLAN, T.
  on role of the school, 209

ECLECTICISM, 41
EDISON, 165
EDUCAND
  "born worker," 142
  dignity, 86, 91, 161
  diversity of gifts, 92
  endowment, 175 ff
  formation of, 212
  health, 231
  and hell, 120
  individual differences, 233
  knowledge of ends, 31
  learning Scripture, 237
  and moral formation, 201 ff
  and Mystical Body, 91
  not expendable, 135
  not to be pressurized, 100
  original sin, 82
  potential image of Christ, 86
  respect for, 135,
  rudimentary habits, 144
  and self-responsibility, 242
  social being, 38 f
  subnormal, 234 f
  substantial unity, 218
EINSTEIN, 165
ELEMENTARY SCHOOLS
  and hell, 120
ELLIS, MSGR. TRACY
  on intellectual leadership, 208 f
ELIOT, T. S., 237
END
  best, 28
  as cause, 22 f
  divisions, 34 ff
  first in intention, 28

love of, 26
more important than means, 28
as object, 13
proper and immediate, 37 f, 48
as purpose, 14
as terminus, 13
END-CAUSE
  cause in first act, 25
  cause in second act, 1, 26
  effects, 23
  first of causes, 27
  formal ratio, 24
  and knowledge, 24 f
  by metaphorical movement, 26
  a real cause, 26
ENDS OF EDUCATION
  must be clear, 28 f
  subordination, advantages, 237
  subordination, need for, 33 f
ENVIRONMENT, 202, 216
EQUIPMENT OF EDUCAND, 134 ff
  supernatural, 157 ff
ESSENTIALISM, 65
ETHICAL CULTURE
  aims, 68 f
  evaluation, 68 ff
  notion, 68
EUBULIA, 151
EX OPERE OPERANTIS, 117
EX OPERE OPERATO, 117
EXEMPLAR, 201

FACILITY OF OPERATION, 168 f
FACULTIES, 137 ff
FAITH
  Breed on, 66 ff
  dignity of, 165
  gratuity of, 165
  and Nominalism, 67 *n*
  not insult to intelligence, 165
  object of, 97
  theological virtue, 97
FAMILY
  rights in education, 244 ff
FARRELL, FR. W.
  on pleasure, 43
FENELON, 142 *n*
FINALITY
  importance for education, 2, 12, 23, 38
  not fixity, 57, 63
  principle of, 29 ff, 246
  see also End, End-Cause
FIRST ACT, 25, 190 ff, 224
FIRST PRINCIPLES
  habit of, 146, 149